Minority Memory, Identity, and Reconciliation

ETHNIC CONFLICT: STUDIES IN NATIONALITY, RACE, AND CULTURE

Series Editors: Daniel Rothbart and Karina V. Korostelina

TITLES IN THE SERIES

Minority Memory, Identity, and Reconciliation: The Turkish Muslim Minority of Greece and the Greek Orthodox Minority of Türkiye
Gül M. Gür

Book of the Disappeared: The Quest for Transnational Justice
Jennifer Heath and Ashraf Zahedi, Editors

First Nationalism Then Identity: On Bosnian Muslims and Their Bosniak Identity
Mirsad Kriještorac

Torture, Humiliate, Kill: Inside the Bosnian Serb Camp System
Hikmet Karčić

MINORITY MEMORY, IDENTITY, AND RECONCILIATION

The Turkish Muslim Minority of Greece and the Greek Orthodox Minority of Türkiye

Gül M. Gür

University of Michigan Press
Ann Arbor

Published in the United States of America by the
University of Michigan Press
First published July 2025

A CIP catalog record for this book is available from the British Library.

Library of Congress Control Number: 2024060633
LC record available at https://lccn.loc.gov/2024060633

ISBN 978-0-472-07745-8 (hardcover : alk. paper)
ISBN 978-0-472-05745-0 (paper : alk. paper)
ISBN 978-0-472-90504-1 (open access ebook)

DOI: https://doi.org/10.3998/mpub.12060196

The University of Michigan Press's open access publishing program is made possible thanks to additional funding from the University of Michigan Office of the Provost and the generous support of contributing libraries.

Cover photograph courtesy Steve Johnson / Unsplash

Authorized Representative: Easy Access System Europe, Mustamäe tee 50, 10621 Tallinn, Estonia, gpsr.requests@easproject.com

To my beautiful children, Atlas and Derin. You have made me stronger, more patient, and more fulfilled than I could have ever imagined. With you, this challenging task turned into an adventure. I love you to the moon and back.

Contents

Tables

Preface

My first in-depth encounter with minority issues occurred in Türkiye* during my undergraduate studies at Marmara University's Political Science and International Relations Department. It was there, during the fourth-year seminar course taught by Professor Ayhan Aktar in 2000, that I read his book *Varlık Vergisi* (Capital tax). I vividly recall presenting the book in class and even have a picture of that presentation, which I still cherish today. The book delved into the socioeconomic and political conditions in Türkiye leading up to the implementation of a discriminatory wealth tax on minorities, which was introduced in 1942 during World War II to finance Türkiye's defense expenditures. This wealth tax particularly affected the Jewish and Greek Orthodox communities throughout Türkiye. Exploring the rationale behind this policy, the legislative process, and its enforcement deepened my understanding of minority issues in Türkiye. I also remember the topic being highly controversial and sensitive in Turkish political history and the collective memory of Turks, which left me with a bitter taste over the injustices that minorities had experienced.

Subsequently, I pursued my academic journey in the US at the Carter School of Peace and Conflict Resolution at George Mason University. My desire to study more about minorities in Türkiye persisted and I began questioning why certain communities demanding their rights in con-

*In this book, both *Turkey* and *Türkiye* are used to refer to the country officially known as the Republic of Türkiye. While *Turkey* has been historically used in English, the name *Türkiye* has been adopted more recently as part of the country's official international representation.

temporary society are entrenched in historical narratives, which form a key part of their identity. This inquiry led me to focus on researching the intersections between history, memory, and identity, under the guidance of Professor Karina Korostelina. As I continued my research on the Greek Orthodox and Turkish Muslim minorities in Türkiye and Greece, I discovered convergences and divergences in their histories that have shaped the identities of both countries. What was particularly intriguing was the lack of research on communities excluded from the 1923 Population Exchange between Greece and Türkiye after the 1919–22 war. These new minority communities on either side of the Aegean Sea became the focus of my dissertation. I began examining how they interpreted their experiences over time, memorialized the past, and how they and these experiences shaped their identities. I realized that these communities, in both Greece and Türkiye, continue to grapple with past injustices inflicted by these states and their institutional practices, resulting in unhealed wounds. I concluded that the path to healing lies in rehumanizing and uplifting these minority communities without ignoring the historical context. Although both Greek Orthodox and Turkish Muslim minorities face distinct challenges, they both share a sense of injustice. As I argue in the book, constructive Greek-Turkish relations will always be partially contingent upon addressing past injustices and meeting the needs of these communities.

The stories of the minorities in Greece and Türkiye are not only about their respective nations but also reflects broader narratives of minority experiences within nation-states worldwide. As a firm believer in the power of human stories, I chose to begin this book with narratives of minorities from Istanbul (Türkiye) and Western Thrace (Greece). Prior to delving into each chapter, readers will encounter vignettes reminiscent of those in Jennie E. Burnet's book *Genocide Lives in Us* (2012). These vignettes, excerpts from the lives of different minorities, will highlight diverse points of intersection and divergence in their historical memories and everyday experiences, offering glimpses into the larger story this book aims to tell about minorities.

Acknowledgments

I wrote this book to provide a space for the Turkish Muslim minorities in Greece and the Greek Orthodox minorities in Turkey to express themselves regarding the concepts of nation, nationhood, belongingness, loyalty, history, memory, and their minority identity. My interest in exploring these concepts in the context of the minorities in Greece and Turkey emerged when I was writing my PhD dissertation at the Carter School for Peace and Conflict Resolution at George Mason University. I am indebted to the many people who supported me during the writing of my dissertation and while I transformed it into a book.

I am grateful to everyone who participated in this project for generously welcoming me into their worlds, and for sharing their time and energy. Their faith in my work and their encouragement throughout this process were what motivated me during this challenging yet fulfilling experience. I would like to express the deepest thanks to my PhD dissertation committee chair and mentor, Professor Karina V. Korostelina, for her unending guidance and encouragement. She is the person who sparked an interest in me to study and research the connections between history, memory, and identity in conflict environments. I would also like to thank Professor Daniel Rothbart and Professor Steven Barnes for their insights, feedback, and perspectives during the writing of my dissertation.

I am deeply grateful to the community members from the Turkish Muslim minority in Western Thrace, Greece, and the Greek Orthodox minority in Istanbul, Turkey, for their invaluable contributions and assistance. Their stories are the foundation of this book, which would not exist without them. This project also owes its realization to the intellectual, material, and emotional support of colleagues, mentors, and minority community leaders. My thanks go to professors Baskın Oran, İlay Örs Romain, Dimitris Kamouzis, Samim Akgönül, Elçin Macar, Vemund Aarbakke, Kostas Tsitselikis, Şule Toktaş, Ali Hüseyinoğlu, Dr. Dimostenis Yağcıoğlu, as well as to Yorgo Benlisoy, Koray Bağdatlı, Cemil Kabza, Ozan Ahmetoğlu, Kornilia Tsevik Bayvertyan, Abdülhalim Dede, Davut Melih Dede, Yanni Demircioğlu, Mikail Hannutoğlu, Koray Hasan, Laki Vingas, Mihail Vasiliadis, Minas Vasiliadis, Andonis Parizyanos, Ari Çokona, and many others who served as bridges to the Greek and Turkish minority communities and offered substantial feedback on my dissertation with invaluable comments. I am especially thankful to Professor Hercules Millas, who reviewed an earlier version of the book during its dissertation stage, offering critiques that helped refine and expand my ideas. My gratitude extends to Professor Vamık Volkan, who met with me several times during this research project and provided essential guidance and feedback. I am profoundly thankful to Professor Zuhal Mert Uzuner for her continuous encouragement and insights.

Finally, I am thankful to my family for believing in me, for supporting me, and for bearing with me. To my spouse Gürol, my children Atlas and Derin, my mother Münevver, father Sedat, and sister Ayşe, I am thankful for believing in my love of understanding how to build constructive peace. Without their constant support, love, and patience, I would not have been able to complete this book.

Foreword

Vamık Volkan

Constantinople, present-day Istanbul, fell to the Ottoman Turks on May 29, 1453. Even before the fall of Constantinople, some areas of present-day Greece had come under Ottoman domination. After the fall of Constantinople, the total Greek world eventually became part of the Ottoman Empire. For over 375 years, from 1453 until the emergence of an independent Greece in the 1830s, Greeks and Turks, under the Ottoman umbrella, lived together.

The Ottoman Empire was a multireligious, multilingual, and multicultural conglomeration with the sultan as its supreme ruler. Identity in the Ottoman Empire derived from one's religious affiliation. It surprises many that it was not until the sixteenth century, when the Ottomans conquered the Arab world, that the Ottoman Empire became a society in which Muslims held the majority. However, Christians and Jews, as well as their religions, were protected in the empire and were included in the *millet* system. The word *millet* came to mean nation in the nineteenth century, but it earlier referred to an organized religious community whose head was responsible to the Ottoman government for the good behavior of its members, payment of the *cizye* (special capitation) tax, and other obliga-

---

Vamık Volkan is Emeritus Professor of Psychiatry at the University of Virginia, and past president of the Virginia Psychoanalytic Society, the Turkish-American Neuropsychiatric Society, the International Society of Political Psychology, the American College of Psychoanalysts, and the International Dialogue Initiative.

tions. There was the Orthodox Millet, the Jewish Millet, and the Armenian Millet. The Muslims constituted the *Ummah*, the community of God or of Muhammad.

The Greeks belonged to the Orthodox Millet or Millet-i Rum (Roman Millet). Also under this category were Serbs, Vlachs, and others, but the Greeks were dominant in the Orthodox Church's hierarchy. Over time, Turkish words entered the Greek language. The resulting dialect could only be understood by those who had a knowledge of both languages. Many Greeks also became Turcophone, speaking Turkish, but writing it in Greek letters (Itzkowitz 1972).

Many Ottomans of Greek origin (and many more of Greek Orthodox origin, e.g., Serbs and Bosniaks) had been levied and educated through the *devşirme* to hold office in the Ottoman establishment. *Devşirme* refers to a process through which a Christian youth, taken away from his family, becomes a Muslim and receives an education to serve the sultan. Other Greeks retained their Christian religion while working for the Ottoman state. Some served as translators for the Ottoman government, some even served as governors of Moldavia and Walachia in the eighteenth century.

During the last century of the Ottoman Empire, things went badly for the Ottomans, and from the 1850s on the empire was seen as "the sick man of Europe." The Greek War of Independence started in 1821, and it eventually led to the formation of an independent Greek state. Nonetheless, even after a Greek state had been carved out of the Ottoman Empire, many Greeks still remained within Ottoman territory. A few of them would serve as Ottoman ambassadors to Athens, London, and St. Petersburg and another governed what is now southern Bulgaria. Alexander Caratheodry, an Ottoman Greek, represented the sultan at the Congress of Berlin (1878).

Andrew Mango (1987), who had deep knowledge about the Turkish and Greek histories, stated that during the Ottoman period, Turks and Greeks cooperated more than they fought. It would be a mistake, however, to consider the Greeks and Turks of the Ottoman Empire congenial brothers and sisters. Although conquerors and conquered had mingled blood throughout four centuries of "togetherness," they had differences in large-group identities (Itzkowitz 1972; Volkan and Itzkowitz 1994, 1997).

Unlike character and personality, which are observed and perceived by others, identity refers to an individual's inner working model—this person, not an outsider, senses and experiences it. Erik Erikson (1956) defined the subjective experience of individual identity that slowly evolves from childhood as a persistent sense of sameness within oneself, while sharing some characteristics with other individuals. According to Salman Akhtar (1999), the sustained feeling of inner sameness is accompanied by a temporal continuity in the self-experience: the past, the present, and the future are integrated into a smooth continuum of remembered, felt, and expected existence for the individual. I described how large-group identity develops and how it becomes linked to ethnic, national, religious, and even ideological identity in childhood. I also recognized large-group identities that develop in adulthood, such as membership to a religious cult or a terrorist organization (Volkan 1988, 2020). In everyday language we refer to large-group identities by saying, for example, "we are Catalan," "we are French," "we are Sunni Muslims," or "we are white supremacists in the United States."

Following the defeat of the Ottomans in World War I, parts of their empire were occupied and partitioned. Greeks entered Anatolia in May 1919. The Greco-Turkish War between Greece and the Turkish National Movement ended in October 1922 and Greeks returned to their pre–World War I borders. After the independence of the Republic of Turkey was recognized a population exchange took place between Greece and Turkey. However, some Greeks and some Turks remained in their original birthplaces as minorities.

This book carefully examines the present-day Turkish Muslim minority community in Western Thrace, Greece, and Greek Orthodox (Rum) minority in Istanbul, Turkey. It provides information about the relationships between two neighboring national large groups, Greece and Turkey. The author tells us how both the Turkish and Greek minorities hold on to two major and interconnected identities. One identity is based on the minorities' ethnicity, religion, language, and culture and the second identity is due to their citizenship status. She also focuses on how the emergence of deadly troubles between Cypriot Greeks and Cypriot Turks and the continuing efforts to find a solution for the so-called Cyprus conflict are influencing the Greek minority in Turkey and the Turkish minority in Greece.

Since the early 1570s, when Cyprus became an Ottoman island, Greeks and Turks began to live together there. Cyprus was first "leased" to the British in 1878 and then it became a British colony after World War I. When Cyprus became a republic in 1960 (after a period of terrorism carried out by Cypriot Greeks against the British rulers), the constitution divided power on the island between Cypriot Greeks and Cypriot Turks. According to the constitution, the president of the new republic would be a Cypriot Greek and the vice-president a Cypriot Turk. The Cypriot Greeks, however, perceived this new situation as a step toward *enosis* (union with Greece) (Markides 1977).

Three years after the establishment of the Republic of Cyprus, Cypriot Turks began to live in enclaves under subhuman conditions. While earlier the Cypriot Turks had owned 35 percent of the island, they were then squeezed onto 3 percent of the land. In 1974 a Cypriot Greek coup materialized and threatened the existence of the Cypriot Turkish community. A Turkish military intervention resulted in a de facto partitioning of the island into northern Cypriot Turkish and southern Cypriot Greek sections (Volkan 1979). The Greek minority in Turkey emotionally sided with the Cypriot Greeks and the Turkish minority in Greece supported the Cypriot Turks.

I was born to Cypriot Turkish parents in 1932 when Cyprus was a British colony. After attending medical school in Turkey as a newly graduated physician I went to the United States in 1957. I was able to develop a comfortable biculturalism and continued my emotional relationship with my family members and friends on the island. I have been spending my summer months in north Cyprus for decades.

My personal emotional factors related to the Cyprus conflict made this book of special interest to me. This book informs the reader about the investment of humans in their ethnic, national, religious, or ideological large groups. It illustrates how new shared traumas, especially those at the hand of the Other, inflame the images of previous historical events. When new threats against a large group occur, the members of this large group knowingly or sometimes unconsciously become preoccupied with maintaining and protecting their large-group identities. Minorities' "second identity," which is due to their citizenship status, becomes complicated.

I am reminded of Sigmund Freud's remarks on the psychology of communities with adjoining territories and the narcissism of minor differences. In 1917 Freud wrote: "It is always possible to bind together a considerable number of people in love, so long as there are other people left over to receive the manifestation of their aggressiveness" (114). He went on to describe how communities "with adjoining territories" such as the Spaniards and the Portuguese, the north Germans and the south Germans, or the English and Scotch, are engaged in feuds and ridicule each other. Freud added that the narcissism of minor differences "is a convenient and relatively harmless satisfaction of the inclination to aggression, by means of which cohesion between the members of the community is made easier" (114).

In 1988 my late friend David Werman, a psychoanalyst at Duke University in Durham, North Carolina, reviewed Freud's description of the "narcissism of minor differences." He wrote that "in contrast to Freud's observation that the narcissism of minor differences is relatively harmless, I suggest that in the social sphere it harbors the potential for a pernicious escalation into hostile and destructive actions on a widespread scale" (451). I agree with Werman's conclusion. There are examples in the literature to support Werman's remarks. For example, law and political science professor Donald Horowitz (1985) described how Sinhalese mobs in the Sri Lankan riots of 1958 relied on a variety of subtle indicators—such as the presence of earring holes in the ear or the manner in which a shirt was worn—to identify their enemy, Tamils, whom they then attacked or killed. In Cyprus, Cypriot Greek and Cypriot Turkish shepherds used to dress in an identical manner, except that a Cypriot Greek shepherd's cloth belt was blue and the Cypriot Turkish shepherd's belt was red. During their ethnic conflict, this minor difference sometimes would invite death (Volkan 1979).

Since Freud's times the description of communities and countries "with adjoining territories" has changed drastically. When empires and colonialism existed, one large group's administrators ruled territory inhabited by indigenous people. At the present time, neighbor-like psychology, regardless of actual physical proximity, is a reality all over the world between independent countries. Because of the incredible proliferation of communication, travel, military technologies, electronic commerce, and other new factors a neighbor-like relationship, regardless of actual physical proximity, is a reality all over the world between independent countries. For example, North Korea's missiles and the United States Navy's activities in the Yellow Sea or the Sea of Japan, in a psychological sense, make the United States and North Korea neighbors. The United States and Iran can behave like two rivals living next door to each other (Suistola and Volkan 2017). Also, the incredible increase of refugees worldwide is bringing our attention to minority groups in many locations.

This book reminded me of one political leader's reference to communities "with adjoining territories" that became known worldwide and urged academicians to pay attention to the psychology of neighboring large groups. On November 19, 1977, Egyptian president Anwar Sadat went to Israel. During his speech at the Knesset, he referred to a "psychological wall" accounting for 70 percent of the problems between Arabs and Israelis. Sadat's speech illustrates how physical borders are also "psychological borders" (Volkan 1988, 2020).

This book is an excellent example of the study of psychological borders. It also brings to our attention the dilemmas minority groups face behind such borders, gives us ideas on how to examine the realistic and emotional situations of such communities, and reminds us to find humane ways to help them.

Introduction

This book centers on the stories of the Greek Orthodox minority in Istanbul, Turkey, and the Turkish Muslim minority in Western Thrace, Greece. Elias,[1] a member of the Greek Orthodox minority, lives on the island of Tenedos (Bozcaada in Turkish) in Turkey. When we spoke in the summer of 2018, he shared the story you are about to read. He spoke of his life experiences as a minority. Much of what he shared is also reflected in the stories of other minority members, particularly from Istanbul's Greek Orthodox minority community.

> I WAS BORN ON TENEDOS (also known as Bozcaada)[2] in 1959. My father and grandfather were born there, too. My roots go back seven centuries. In the past, everybody knew each other by their nicknames like the son of the Drummer Nikholas (Davulcu Nikolas'ın oğlu), Arab Yorgo (Arap Yorgo), Kanarya, etc. Being from the island was part of our identity. Today, when I ask someone on the island who they are, what their nickname is, they don't know it. This shows that the island has transformed a lot over time. When someone says they belong to a certain community, there must be a history behind it. Therefore, when I say I am from Tenedos (Bozcaada), I mean I belong to this place, and it is mine. I am a local of this place. . . . It is a feeling that nobody can take from your heart, no politician, no law, no regulation. . . .
>
> Our identity had been mixed with Greek Cypriots for years. After the conflict in Cyprus, everybody in Turkey began to think

> that what happened in Cyprus is because of us (the Greek Orthodox people of Turkey). They preferred to believe that we, the Greek Orthodox minority, were responsible for the atrocities against Turks in Cyprus. This is bullshit. Yes, we share the same religion, but I am not a Greek Cypriot and I have no common culture with them. However, I was forced to leave Tenedos (Bozcaada) in 1975, when I was about sixteen, due to the conflict. When the conflict was at its peak, people were treating the Greek Orthodox minority very negatively in Istanbul, Imbros (also known as Gökçeada), and Tenedos (Bozcaada). . . . During those difficult years, there was no electricity in Tenedos (Bozcaada). I was working at the tailor's shop. We had to use generators. At night, around 11:55 p.m., the signals were given and then the lights were gone. I remember that the kids from my class were waiting for me in a dark corner of the street with scissors to cut my hair. We were exposed to so much discrimination at that time. . . . So, we had to leave.
>
> When I went to Greece, they did not treat us well either. I remember one day in 1981 . . . I went to a bank and the lady who was working there looked at my Greek work permit (because I was not a Greek citizen, but I had a work permit) and threw it in my face in anger. She said: "What are you doing here, Turkish seed?" Then, I had a huge argument with her because I was so disappointed and angry! We, the Greek Orthodox people, are Turkish in Greece and Greek in Turkey. . . . After living in Greece for thirty-seven years, I returned to Turkey in 2012. I have never experienced any adaptation problems. This land is my home. I am from here and this territory is mine.
>
> —Elias, Greek Orthodox minority member,
> Tenedos (Bozcaada), 2018

Through this book, minorities share their stories of everyday challenges similar to the one described above. Their narratives reveal deep wounds that are vulnerable to reopening, particularly if an incident were to occur (no matter how small) that is connected to their communities' historical traumas. By examining their narratives, it is possible to understand how these challenges and traumas construct their minority identity.

For Elias, Tenedos (Bozcaada) is where he felt he belonged. Irrespective of where he has lived, he has always dreamt about the land where he was born. When people are born and live in the same area all their lives, they are unlikely to ever feel conflicted about where they want to be buried.

They are unlikely to think about whether they want to spend the rest of their lives in another country. Our land is our home. It is where we belong and feel secure. But if you are a member of an ethnoreligious minority living in a particular country, seemingly simple questions such as "Where do you feel you belong?" may occupy your mind daily. Elias was clear about where he felt he belonged. For him, he belonged where he was born—Tenedos (Bozcaada). However, his personal journey of becoming a minority was filled with many challenges. He and his father fled from Turkey to Greece in a small boat in 1975. When they were crossing the Aegean Sea, they were fleeing their home in Turkey for somewhere they did not know or felt they belonged.

Involuntary displacement leaves scars on the human psyche. Ai Weiwei's documentary *Human Flow* (2018) opens with scenes of a vast blue sea with no one except a boat of refugees. Weiwei successfully captures the emptiness, uncertainty, and sorrow refugees experience. Since 2014, the Aegean Sea has been the backdrop for groups of traumatized refugees. Critically, while contemporary images of refugees fleeing their home countries now flash across our television screens or on social media, these very same images were present nearly a century ago as multinational empires were dissolving or more recently in the 1970s when people like Elias and his father fled both Greece and Turkey for opposite sides of the Aegean.

The movement of people raises several important questions about identity, belonging, and adaptation. The effects of massive flows of people are significant for everyone affected. Those who migrate or those who host newcomers are not the only ones affected by migration. Those who are left behind also experience difficulties. This flow of people can take several forms. It can be unconscious (the movement of the first man), voluntary (movement within one's own country or to another for economic reasons), or involuntary (forced migration or internal displacement, or both). Although scholars largely agree that involuntary migration stems from the likes of internal armed conflict and political persecution, little is still known about the consequences of these flows of people. As Elias emphasized, the negative consequences of his own migration continue to live with him in his memories. He has lived in a psychological state of *in-between* for his whole life. During different periods in time and contexts in Greece and Turkey, the states and majority populations have viewed him as an outsider. Even in his sixties, he still lives with negative memories of his past. Even though he has returned to Turkey, he states that he is ready to leave at any moment should the state dictate such a move. Similar feelings were raised by some of Istanbul's Greek Orthodox minority and the Turkish Muslim minority of Western Thrace. Despite these feelings, it is a stark contrast with the current reality that is characterized by limited minority migration from Turkey to Greece and vice versa.

The myriad challenges and complex emotions faced by individuals like Elias, caught in the web of migration and its aftermath, mirror a larger, more pervasive issue that underscores the strained relations between Greece and Turkey. The historical context not only shapes individual lives but also casts a long shadow over the minority communities within these nations' borders. Greece and Turkey have long been entangled in historical enmity, which is reflected in negative perceptions and ongoing conflicts. It is essential to recognize the impact of this tumultuous history on minority communities residing within their borders. Decades of institutional practices, such as forced migration, discriminatory citizenship policies, and political pressures, have left minority members in Istanbul and Western Thrace in a psychological state akin to Elias's. Their daily lives are steeped in memories of the past, as their identities are intricately tied to these collective experiences. They grapple with the pervasive perception of being outsiders, even enemies, perpetuated by state ideologies.

Despite periodic rapprochements, such as those seen in the aftermaths of natural disasters that occurred in 1999 and 2023, Turkey and Greece continue to navigate their complex relationship, often overshadowed by historical grievances. However, amid these broader geopolitical dynamics, it's essential to shift our focus to the minority communities themselves. Beyond the headlines of political tensions lie the narratives of Istanbul's Greek Orthodox and Western Thrace's Turkish Muslim minorities, each grappling with their unique historical and social contexts. Before delving into their stories and their significance in shaping our understanding of history, memory, and identity relations, it is pertinent to explore the terminology these minorities use to define themselves.

Some members of Istanbul's Greek Orthodox minority community I spoke with referred to their Eastern Roman roots, which trace back centuries. As Alexis Alexandris explains, the term *Rum* derives from *Romios*, meaning "from (Eastern) Rome" (1992, 17). İlay Romain Örs (2006, 2018, 2024) uses the phrase *Rum Polites of Istanbul*; Panagiotis C. Poulos (2014) uses the terms *Constantinopolitan Rum* and *Istanbul Rum* to describe these community members. Other scholarly works refer to them as the *Greek Orthodox community of Istanbul* or the *Greek Orthodox minority of Istanbul* (Kamouzis 2020; Prodromou 2005; Onar and Özgüneş 2010). Throughout this book, I use the term *Greek Orthodox minority of Istanbul* to refer to the Istanbul *Rum* community, whose presence in the city spans centuries.

In the book, I also occasionally refer to the Antakya Arab Orthodox community. Some people belonging to this minority group live in Antakya, Turkey, at the eastern end of Turkey's Mediterranean coast. Some have migrated to Istanbul and have—to a certain extent—integrated into Istanbul's Greek Orthodox minority. The Arab Orthodox minority of Istanbul, however, do not speak Greek. In chapter 3, I briefly discuss the internal controversies of their adaptation and integration process. Both the Greek Orthodox and the Arab Orthodox minority brought up internal issues during our conversations and both see the Arab Orthodox community as important for the Greek Orthodox minority group's survival. The stories of Greek Orthodox minorities who live on the islands of Tenedos (Bozcaada) and Imbros (Gökçeada) in Turkey, such as Elias, are also included in this book. Although these individuals do not live in Istanbul, some of Istanbul's Greek Orthodox minority community spoke of connections between themselves and the islanders. Including their stories allows us to understand the experiences of those who were subjected to traumatic events but also understand the perspectives of those who learned about these past incidents from family members.

The second minority community analyzed in this book is the Turkish Muslim minority of Western Thrace. Here, it should be highlighted that the Turkish Muslim minority and the Greek state differ in their use of ethnic descriptor. The Greek state argues that the Lausanne Treaty (1923) defined all their minorities, whether they are ethnically Turkish, Pomak (Bulgarian-speaking Muslims), or Roma, as a *Muslim minority* and, thus, any ethnic descriptor used to characterize the Western Thrace minority is unacceptable. Although there are Turkish, Pomak, and Roma minorities living in Western Thrace, the literature suggests that, among these minorities, some define themselves as "Turkish Muslim" regardless of their Pomak or Roma roots, for several reasons (e.g., they may do this due to their lack of access to opportunities, as Mantouvolu [2009] states).

Importantly, however, this book is not about Pomaks or Romas.[3] Rather, this book focuses specifically on minority members who define themselves as Turkish and Muslim. Although the official narrative in Greece is different, this official narrative has changed several times over the years. From 1923 to the mid-1950s, Greece referred to all the minority groups living in Thrace as the "Turkish minority." From the mid-1950s, Greece referred to these minorities collectively as the "Muslim minority." Currently, these minority communities are referred to as the "minority with three language groups Turkish, Pomak, and Roma" (Tsitselikis 2012; Huseyinoglu 2018).

This book acknowledges that there are different minority groups under the "Minority in Greece" title. However, this research focuses specifically on the Turkish Muslim minority based on their self-definition.[4]

Beyond elucidating the terminology associated with Istanbul's Greek Orthodox minority and the Turkish Muslim minority in Greece, this book primarily revolves around the narratives of these minority communities. Through their stories, it delves into two fundamental inquiries: First, why do these minorities frame their struggle for needs and rights in ways in which history and memory play key roles? Second, how do understandings of nation, nationhood, identity, belongingness, and loyalty—in an environment where one state has a minority that is kin to the majority of the other state—complicate bilateral state relations? It is crucial to study these two communities comparatively because they share mutual historical experiences that have influenced and helped construct their identities. However, they also differ significantly in religious, ethnic, and socioeconomic terms, which will be discussed in more detail in the forthcoming chapters.

Here, however, it's important to note that both minority communities experienced difficulties in the past and face contemporary challenges due to who they are. Many of them are also still strongly attached to their minority identity. However, demographically, they are dramatically different. While the Turkish Muslim minority in Western Thrace numbers around 120,000–150,000 people, Istanbul's Greek Orthodox minority numbers around 2,000–3,000 people. Therefore, what the members of these two minority communities prioritize in their stories, as well as the struggles they face, are different but there are some similarities, as discussed in detail in what follows. Hence, this book starts with a comparative look at the two minority communities, both of which were exempt from the Population Exchange of 1923.

As the Ottoman Empire (hereafter the empire) was dissolving, smaller national groups—once part of this fallen empire—began to establish their own nations. However, these nations were neither ethnically homogenous nor did they have a national identity. The leaders and political elites of these new nations embarked on population exchanges at the beginning of the twentieth century to increase the homogeneity of their nation-states. The Greek Orthodox people of Turkey and the Turkish Muslim people of Greece were at the center of the 1923 Population Exchange.

Although the 1923 Population Exchange resulted in human tragedies, it was a relatively successful example of unmixing almost two million people to achieve so-called ethnic homogeneity. While these policies appeared necessary at the national level and timely given the conditions in which they were created, these population exchange policies and similar population movements were devastating at the community level. In their wake, they left significant trauma that persists today. Although population homogeneity was the desired aim, leaders and political elites were unable to achieve their desired homogeneity due to the empire's interethnic and religious legacy. Another challenge included the inability of the exchanged populations to adapt quickly to their new countries despite sharing the same ethnic and religious identity as the existing population. Equally, for those people who were excluded from the exchange, they were unable to adapt to their new minority status easily and lost access to their social networks with the movement of many of their friends and relatives in the exchange process.

Despite these historical commonalities, minority experiences in Greece and Turkey are not a mirror image of each other. The characteristics and historical experiences of these two countries are authentic to them. However, the processes of nation-building in both Greece and Turkey have brought these minority communities together as two sides of a unique historical narrative about what happens to people who end up on the wrong side of an arbitrary border.

Given this backdrop of diverse challenges and demographics, this book embarks on a nuanced exploration that bridges the gap left by previous studies. Despite the existence of several studies on religious minorities in Turkey and Greece, only a handful of scholarly works examine Istanbul's Greek Orthodox minority and the Turkish Muslim minority from Western Thrace in Greece comparatively (Akgönül 2007, 2008; Chousein 2009; Hirschon 2003, 2009; Dayıoğlu and Aslım 2015; Kurban and Tsitselikis 2010; Aarbakke 2008; Tsitselikis 2008; Oran 2008; Anagnostou and Triandafyllidou 2006; Lytra 2014; Taskin 2019; Mylonas 2012). Most extant literature examines Greek-Turkish relations by focusing on the principle of reciprocity. Literature on these minorities is limited to an analysis of the processes and dynamics of minority identity formation, in addition to how these processes influenced national becoming, minority-majority and in-group out-group relations, and collective memory formation. The micro-level analysis of minorities at the heart of this book sheds light on the historical and psychological roots of the conflict structuring Greek-Turkish relations.

Although this book builds on the existing literature, the discussion is uniquely centered on the narratives of members of these two minority communities, government officials, and experts in Greece and Turkey. Their stories underscore how nationalization policies in both countries (as well as minority-kin-state relations) affect the formation of minority identity. Their stories also emphasize how these policies have the potential to facilitate conflicts between states and their kin elsewhere as well as between states and their minority citizens.

Despite the visible effect of the negative past on minority memory and identity in Greece and Turkey, only a handful of studies discuss this topic (Lytra 2014; Gökçe and Sezgin 2017; Akgönül 2008; Millas 2004). The root causes of the hostility between Greece and Turkey and the distrustful relations between the minority and their states have received minimal attention (Grigoriadis 2008; Uzuner 2018; Millas 2002). Studies on minorities in Greece and Turkey, and particularly on the roots of contemporary conflicts between and within these two countries, also lack a profound examination of the perceptions, values, and aspirations of these minority groups. Taken together, contemporary relations between these countries and their minority are as fragile as Greek-Turkish bilateral relations. Any negative incident between the two countries has the potential to escalate into an active conflict that could cost the minority their fundamental rights.

Any study on minorities in Greece and Turkey, thus, requires a systematic examination of how historical nation-building processes, which included various challenges and trauma that have affected the members of these minority communities, have influenced minority memory and identity formation. Such an inquiry is significant to the future status of the minorities and state-led policy changes affecting them, as well as to fostering social harmony in Greece and Turkey.

In line with this literature and to better understand the impact of the incongruence between the geographical distribution of ethnoreligious groups and the physical borders of nation-states on minorities, I made several trips to Western Thrace in Greece where a majority of the Turkish Muslim minority live and to Istanbul in Turkey where most of the Greek Orthodox population are present. Members of these minority groups did not hesitate to share their feelings about where they felt they belonged and about their loyalty to their respective countries during our conversations. Land and, by extension, the country in which they live are decisive for those I spoke to when it came to articulating their love for a country. Being born in a territory and living there increased their attachment to the land. What was clear from their testimonies, however, was that despite being citizens of the countries in which they lived, they did not feel equal to the majority population. It is in this dichotomy of loving the land but feeling inferior within their societies more broadly that the incongruence arises between the geographical distribution of ethnic groups and the physical borders of nation-states.

The epistemological and methodological assumptions of this study were developed within the framework of social constructivism and the research for this book rests on a comparative case study of the Greek Orthodox and Turkish Muslim minority communities. Given the critical role language plays in building social reality, particularly within a social constructivist approach, I relied mainly on semi-structured interviews to gather data.

By employing semi-structured interviews,[5] I was able to search for traces of minority identity formation. By looking at the past through the narratives of the minority members, state officials, and experts on minority and minority affairs in Greece and Turkey, I was further able to illuminate the meanings that members of these minority groups give to nation, minority, national and minority identity, belongingness, and homeland. I also investigated the reproduction and transmission of social memories intergenerationally and the influence of state institutional practice on the minorities. Lastly, I examine how the minorities position themselves with regard to these policies and their past, and how this entire process helps construct their identities.

Using a combination of purposive and snowball sampling allowed me to generate a rich body of data from a sample of equal gender distribution and occupations among participants ranging between eighteen and sixty-five years old from both minority groups. I used purposive sampling to identify key figures within both minority communities and snowball sampling to identify experts and state officials.

To gather the information needed to create a comprehensive and in-depth understanding about these two minority cases, I spoke to minority community leaders including civil society representatives, schoolteachers, academics, journalists, religious authorities, administrators, politicians, psychologists, and writers in Turkey and Greece. In addition to this core group of people, I also interviewed Greek and Turkish officials as well as experts on minority affairs in Greece and Turkey. I conducted sixty interviews in total between 2013 and 2021. Of these, fifty were conducted in-person in Istanbul, Ankara, Western Thrace, and Athens in 2013. Each interview lasted one to two hours. Due to the COVID-19 pandemic, I conducted an additional ten interviews online with minority members from both communities. In 2023, I conducted eight more interviews. Four of these interviews were with members of the Turkish Muslim minority and one with Prof. Vemund Aarbakke in Western Thrace. The remaining three were with members of the Greek Orthodox minority (one of which was with a member of the Arab Orthodox minority community in Istanbul). I conducted these additional interviews to supplement the earlier primary data and to highlight if there were any policy changes targeting both communities.

I found it useful to supplement the interview data with focus groups to examine the attitudes, beliefs, opinions, desires, and motivations of those who participated in their own social environments. I asked general questions to guide the discussion, and the duration of the focus groups was flexible and based on the needs of those who participated. I also observed interactions between participants to understand everyday discourse on minority-related issues. Lastly, this book is also informed by observations from public and community events hosted by both communities such as Christmas gatherings, art exhibitions, cultural festivals, and concerts. I observed community interactions in a non-positivistic sense and employed unstructured observation to understand and interpret cultural behavior. As a native Turkish speaker and a social scientist, I had cultural fluency in observing, understanding, and explaining the deeper meanings of the cultural behavior (Hall 1976; Avruch 2012; Geertz 1973) of the minorities.

To analyze the data, I used thematic analysis. Given the flexibility of thematic analysis, I was able to develop unique insights from the narratives of minority members, officials, and experts. This analytical approach allowed me to look beyond semantics to generate a deeper and more encompassing understanding of the narrative patterns in the stories the minorities shared. The first stage of data analysis included analyzing resources related to the history of both minority communities. I then focused on the narratives surrounding the tragic encounters the minorities experienced. I looked at the coherence of the stories and questioned why they were coherent. Norman K. Denzin (1989, 62) argues that individuals give coherence to their lives when they write or talk about themselves. Denzin continues, noting that "the sources of this coherence, the narratives that lie behind them, and the larger ideologies that structure them must be uncovered" (62). Therefore, while analyzing the data, I not only focused on what was said but I also looked at why those I was speaking to mentioned specific topics and what was the overarching ideational framework behind each story.

This book is separated into four chapters with each beginning with an ethnographic vignette that describes the life experiences of the Greek Orthodox and the Turkish Muslim minorities. This book relies heavily on the narratives of minorities and starting every chapter with these narrative descriptions enhances their stories. These vignettes are particularly effective in highlighting the emotional component in intergroup conflicts. As an author, I wanted to ensure that the conflict dynamics were adequately explained by providing more narrative space to the minorities, especially at the opening of each chapter. Chapter 1, "Minority Memory Space," lays out the theoretical framework needed to understand the role of collective memory and narrative in minority identity construction. Through the lens of collective memory and narrative analysis, I explored the characteristics, function, and dynamics of minority collective memory systems. This book defines collective minority memory as a form of social memory, constructed over time through interactions between members of a national minority group and the rest of society, including the state, nonstate actors, and international actors.

Through a discussion on nation-state building and nationalism, I explain how key turning points in the histories of both Greece and Turkey led these two nation-states to emerge while also creating a new form of governance for their respective minority community. Although these two countries followed similar paths in how they emerged as modern nation-states and experienced nationalism, Turkey and Greece cannot be viewed as two sides of the same coin, particularly in reference to how they treat their minority. Through a psychological analysis, I examine the social psychology of becoming and being a minority in Greece and Turkey. Due to the historical processes of becoming a nation, the Greek Orthodox minority and the Turkish Muslim minority formed their national minority identities in opposition to the national majority identity of their respective home (national) states, each with its own unique complexities. The concepts of "enemy other" or "significant other" are used to describe this process of (national) minority identity construction in both countries.

Chapter 2, "A Glance at Turkish-Greek Relations," contextualizes Greek-Turkish relations and how social boundaries emerge between various actors. The history of Greek-Turkish relations is important to examine because it provides us with the historical context of two nation-state-building processes. These two nation-building processes resulted in different national identity formations: the Greek Orthodox and the Turkish Muslim identities. Moving away from studies that only focus on the nation-state and identity formation in Greece and Turkey, this book analyzes the historically parallel identity formation processes of the Turkish Muslim and Greek Orthodox minority.

The role of the Ottoman Empire is crucial in the historical and political development processes of Greece and Turkey, as discussed in chapter 2. The empire became the political framework within which Greeks and

Turks, as well as many other ethnic-religious groups, lived and operated for centuries. To some, these different groups lived side-by-side in peace, while others view this appearance of harmony and coexistence as a false perception. Credence was given to the latter with the nationalist uprisings beginning at the end of the nineteenth century.

From here on, the chapter analyzes how the process from the Ottoman Empire to a nation-state created sociopsychological boundaries between various communities. These boundaries have shifted and transformed over time, which has affected the identities of these communities. National identity formation is a complex process that involves institutional practices, power dynamics, national narratives, myths, and culture. This process goes hand in hand with boundary formation between various identities in a nation. In addition, I analyze the social boundary formation of the Greek and the Turkish minorities. To that end, I examine in-group and out-group relations during the nation-building process to explain the unconventional meanings the minorities use for the concepts of nation, nationhood, citizenship, and loyalty. This chapter ends with an analysis of a press conference given by the Turkish and Greek foreign ministers in April 2021. Examining this case study underscores how memories continue to be present in contemporary everyday interactions and active boundary changes.

Chapter 3, "The Greek State and the Turkish Muslim Minority Memory," puts the Turkish Muslim minority community at the center of the analysis. First, it examines the Greek state's minority policies that affected the Turkish Muslim minority in a historical context and, second, it analyzes how the Turkish Muslim minority remembers the past. This chapter examines why the Turkish Muslim minority of Western Thrace places the issue of identity recognition at the heart of their relationship with the Greek state and the Greek majority. It also discusses how the issue of identity complicates Greek-Turkish bilateral relations. This chapter deepens our understanding of how the Turkish Muslim minority community gives meaning to the concepts of nation, nationhood, citizenship, EU membership, being kin-people of Turkey, and loyalty to Greece within the framework of history and memory. This chapter underscores the significance of the struggles of the communities regarding their needs and rights (especially in the areas of education, religion, and minority associations), which are believed to be critical for the survival of their community and identity in Western Thrace. This chapter highlights that the Turkish Muslim minority community's act of remembering the negative past is existential for the minority community. When the minority members demand their rights, they do so by reminding the Greek state of its past wrongdoing. However, remembering the negative past is a double-edged sword. Although remembering may empower the minority, it also activates threat perceptions, hardens the positions and attitudes of the minority and the state toward each other, and solidifies the image of the enemy other. Consequently, the act of remembering only serves to deepen existing social boundaries, which were formed through historical categorization and social identity processes, between the minority and majority, the minority and the state, and Greece and Turkey. This section ends with a discussion on youth perspectives about who they are, how their everyday challenges differ from the traumas of their parents, and how these relate to the future of Greece.

Chapter 4, "The Turkish State and the Greek Orthodox Minority Memory," focuses on Istanbul's Greek Orthodox minority. First, it elaborates on the Turkish state's minority policies that affected the Greek Orthodox minority in a historical context and, second, it analyzes how the minority remembers the past. The issue of demographic loss comes to the surface as a major concern for the minority. This issue is central to their relations with the state, the majority, and with their own community members. This fear has mobilized the minority community to conduct memory work around major incidents such as the incidents surrounding September 6–7, 1955 and 1964 due to their direct effect on the size of the minority demographically. By remembering this negative past, younger generations learn about their community's past, and the minority reminds successive governments as well as the majority about the historic institutional practices that led to various injustices in the minority's lives. Therefore, while memory work is essential for minorities in Istanbul, it also brings up past injustices and the state-enforced discrimination they have experienced.

The process of remembering has the potential to complicate the minority's relationship with the Turkish state and the majority. The minority employ historical narratives about the past in their contemporary struggles for their rights and to have their needs met. In doing so, they make meaning around what happened to them in the past, why these incidents happened, and how they continue to struggle due to the negative effects of past incidents. These meaning-making processes are important to explain because they complicate the relations between the two states as they both include the kin-people of the other as a minority. The minority community's historical narratives and how they utilize memory space are, therefore, crucial to better understand their struggle for existence as a minority community despite demographic erosion.

The concluding chapter, "Restructuring the Memory Space," provides examples of when and how the minority use minority memory space and how it could be restructured as a system that helps them deal with the past without deepening social divides. This chapter also discusses how minority memory space could be used to strengthen good governance in both Greece and Turkey. Based on the historical narratives of the minority, experts, and officials, it must be understood that the memory work of the minority can be viewed as an instrument used to legitimize their demands and preserve their goal to exist as a minority.

In both Greece and Turkey, minority memory work is contested. It is a reaction to the dominant memory forms of the state and the majority. Further, it is also based on the minorities' unmet needs and the injustices they continue to experience. A contested memory space, however, could be reconstructed through multi-actor and multidisciplinary processes that are not only comprehensive and complementary but also based on the will of the minority and the states to work toward a peaceful future. Such a process has no start or end point. Various interventions are already present in both countries. This book highlights that the overall goal of the actors who work toward peaceful neighborly and bilateral relations between Greece and Turkey must center the agency of the minority in every initiative. Doing so is imperative to the construction of a better society where the rights and needs of the minority are met and their inclusion and equality are achieved in both countries.

ONE

Minority Memory Space

I AM A *heimatlos* (stateless). I live with no citizenship in this world. Greece deprived me of my Greek citizenship in 1992 under Article 19 of the former Greek Citizenship Law. I was born in Pamforon (also known as Ambarköy) in Western Thrace. I went to the elementary school there. Since that time, I have traveled back and forth between Turkey and Greece. I went to middle school and high school in Turkey. I quit university in Ankara, [Turkey,] and then returned to my village in Greece in 1980. I got married in 1985 and had my son in 1986. Then, we decided to move back to Turkey in 1989 to open a new business but we were not successful and closed the business.

One day, I received a letter that said I was no longer a citizen of Greece. The problem was that Turkey had not given me citizenship either. Since 1992, I have been living on temporary *heimatlos* visas to visit my extended family in Greece. There is a certain law for the stateless people in Turkey and based on this I kept applying for temporary (one month, three months, etc.) visas and went back and forth between Greece and Turkey. You cannot imagine how difficult this can be. Sometimes, the Greek consulate just doesn't issue the temporary visa on purpose; they delay or reject your application. Although all of these are everyday challenges, we are used to it now.

We also experienced traumas that deeply affected us. These are the ones that we cannot forget. One of them was when I learned that my mother had died. My mom had cancer for some time. And one day, my brother in Greece called me and said, "Brother, we lost our mother." I went to the consulate to apply for an emergency visa for the funeral, but they did not give me the visa to attend my mother's burial. It was the hardest day on earth for me. The political problems between the two countries prevented me from performing my last duty to my mother.

Another time was my twin brother's wedding ceremony in Greece. That time I was dealing with business in Turkey and could not go to the wedding. But I said to my wife that at least she should go. I dropped her and my son at the checkpoint at İpsala, Edirne, at the border between Turkey and Greece. My daughter was ten months old at the time and she stayed with me. We thought their visit would not take long, and my wife would come back after the wedding. I did not think anything would happen to her. So, I left them there and headed home. Then, I learn that the officers at the Greek checkpoint didn't not allow her in the country, saying that they did not have citizenship although she had valid visa from Turkey. Then, she went to the Turkish checkpoint to come back home and this time they said, "If Greece won't let you in, we cannot [let you in] either." My wife literally stayed in limbo for some time, going back and forth between checkpoints. Eventually, Greece allowed her and my son to enter the country for the wedding, but my wife got official word that they [the authorities] would return their Greek passports to the governorate in Komotini (because they were not considered Greek citizens anymore). They had to stay in Komotini (also known as Gümülcine) for three months to deal with this passport issue. When my wife came back to Turkey, my daughter did not remember her. When my wife went, my daughter was still breastfeeding. After three months, my daughter had to stop that too and my wife was in pains there in Greece because of this process. . . .

I can talk for hours about how miserable our life is without citizenship, on temporary visas. I am sixty years old now and hate both countries because I have talked to everyone in Turkey and Greece to regain my Greek citizenship or get Turkish citizenship. Nobody responded.

—Mehmet, Turkish Muslim minority of Western Thrace,
Turkey, 2013

Mehmet's story painfully captures both the need and the importance of examining how memories of the past shape the identity of minorities. For ordinary people, what matters most is what they experience, how they make sense of their experiences, and the feelings of security or insecurity they have connected to their identity. As Mehmet notes, he remembers certain incidents, and it is these incidents that can be characterized as identifiers of his memory space. These personal experiences are his traumas. Yet there are many other minority members who share similar experiences, and it is their shared experiences that bring them together in one memory space, as discussed in this chapter.

Memory space is a fluid space where a social group's identities are formed through social interactions, narratives, and cultural products related to certain historical incidents. Remembering certain past events is both a political act and an everyday act for those who have less societal power and whose rights and needs are deprived by their states. When the existence of a person's identity is at stake, remembering the past becomes significant. Remembering the past is how social group members deal with the identity insecurities they experience. Mehmet's memory space is created in connection to the memory spaces of others in his collective—that is, how minority members interact with others in their minority community is based on their shared (remembered) experiences that provide members of a minority group with a perceived sense of identity security and self-confidence.

In Mehmet's case, he views himself as a former Greek citizen who hopes to regain that citizenship one day. Mehmet also continues to apply for Turkish citizenship because of his perceived sense of belonging to the Turkish identity. Although he does not compare his identities, he carries many emotions related to them due to the negative treatment he suffered in the past. As a result, Mehmet does, at times, indicate his dislike for both countries. As an individual and a minority member he does not feel valued as part of either Greece or Turkey. Further, he is acutely aware of the disconnect between his experiences, felt at the individual and social group levels, and how the state evaluates minorities' experiences. As with Mehmet, Murat has also lived as a *heimatlos* for forty years. During this time, and as a direct result of his *heimatlos* status, he lives in neither social, economic, nor political security (Anonymous 2019). He and his family feel totally insecure about their life and future.

Even if remembering the past acts like living with an open wound, minorities still engage in processes of remembering to sustain their identities and struggle for their rights and needs. Remembering the past must, therefore, be understood as a tool that minorities employ to remember who they were in the past, who they are in the present, and who they will be in the future. They place their experiences at the core of their narratives to advocate for and demand their rights.

These minority stories are present in both Turkey and Greece. However, this does not mean the Greek Orthodox minority in Istanbul and the Turkish Muslim minority of Western Thrace are identical. They are unique in how they construct the meaning of nation, nationhood, identity, belonging, and loyalty. Their similarities as minorities stem from their connections to their homelands through kinship ties. To some extent, it is these kinship ties that complicate Greek-Turkish bilateral relations. The Greek Orthodox minority of Istanbul is the Greek state's kin whereas the Turkish Muslim minority of Western Thrace is the Turkish state's kin. Although the Istanbul Greek Orthodox community differentiates itself from the majority Greek population in Greece (Hellenic Greeks), especially based on their belonging to the city of Istanbul, their shared language is a significant tie.

For the Turkish Muslim minority, although the connection to their kin-country is quite strong, some among the younger generations differentiate between the two based on the way of life in Turkey and Greece. Despite the generalizations contained in their narratives, they nevertheless view life in Turkey to be more conservative, particularly in terms of the freedoms they perceive that young people have available in public spaces in Greece in comparison to Turkey. Even though there are some differences in the connections between the minorities' identity and the kin-state's identity, both countries have politicized this kin relationship throughout history, which has deepened the divides between the minorities and their host (national) states.[1]

Most of the minority stories included in this book concern the struggles of minorities to regain lost rights and have their respective states address their unmet needs. These minorities employ history and memory to support their demands in their communications with state officials. Their identities have become embedded in historical narratives about past injustices and discrimination. Therefore, when we investigate how these minorities identify themselves and feel about their home countries (kin), their host countries (national), and their position in between them, we begin a journey into the minorities' memory space.

Examining the historical and political nation-building processes[2] of Greece and Turkey reveals how these processes affected minorities, what historical incidents minority members select to be remembered, how and why minorities sustain and transfer their memories of the past as tools to be used in their contemporary struggle for rights and needs, and how this remembering complicates Greek-Turkish bilateral relations. Both nation-state-building processes emerged after the Lausanne Peace Treaty (1923) that concluded the war between Greeks and Turks after the Ottoman

Empire collapsed. As part of this treaty, based on the Convention Concerning the Exchange of Greek and Turkish Populations signed in Lausanne on January 30, 1923, the Greek Orthodox people of Turkey and the Turkish Muslim people of Greece were exchanged in an attempt to achieve religiously and ethnically homogenous nation-states.

However, the Greek Orthodox people of Istanbul (as well as the two islands of Imbros and Tenedos) and the Turkish Muslim people in Western Thrace were excluded from the Population Exchange. Articles 37–45 of the Treaty of Lausanne define how Greece and Turkey should treat these remaining minorities. Specifically, both states should implement policies guaranteeing the security, rights, and needs of the remaining minorities in reciprocity. In practice, however, the Lausanne Treaty was not fully implemented due to the changing dynamics of Greek-Turkish bilateral relations and factors such as the Cyprus conflict. Today, these minorities conduct memory work to remind their states of their rights, as embedded in the Lausanne Treaty and other international agreements,[3] and to advocate for their unmet needs as citizens.

Minority memory work is needs based. However, memory work and sustaining the memory space are inherently political. Often, the act of remembering places more emphasis on the past injustices the state enacted through institutional policies against the minorities than practices perceived to be more just. Remembering these injustices complicates and frustrates minority-state relations, relations between minorities and the majority, as well as relations between the host (national) state and the minority's kin-state. Therefore, discussing the effect of memory on group identity is complex. To advance the discussion, this chapter employs theories of nationalism, nationhood, identity, collective memory, and narrative practice, which serve to shape a framework for analysis.

Returning to Mehmet's story is instructive for several reasons. Considering how the state stripped him of his Greek citizenship, how he and his family have suffered for decades due to negative policies, and how he frames his current needs and demands relevant to insecurities concerning his identity serve to explain

- how nationalism functions in practice;
- how the concepts of citizenship, belonging, and loyalty are questioned and reframed based on experiences;
- how subjective historical storytelling and meaning making sustain the memory of past injustices; and
- how all these practices facilitate the demands and needs to

eliminate the insecurities a person experiences regarding his, her, or their identity.

This book seeks to explain the significance of minority memory in a nation-state system where minorities are both the citizens of their host states and the kin of nearby home states. Caught between their host and home state, minorities try to form, sustain, and transfer their identities to younger generations. Minorities perceive this work as essential for their continued existence. Minority memory is, therefore, like any other form of group memory. However, minority memory's uniqueness comes from the factors affecting its structure, the processes through which it is constructed, and how minority memory functions.

Minority memory is composed of connections between past state policies and practices and contemporary minority struggles around their needs and rights. Theories of collective memory explain this connection between the past and present. As human beings, we are the product of what we remember and how we make sense of what we remember in our social milieu. Therefore, remembering the past is remembering our identities. Understanding how social groups define themselves is much more related to how these groups' memories form and what types of interactions occur in each memory space.

Remembering a certain past, as an identity group, is also a narrative act. Theories of narrative and nation-building provide us with the necessary narrative tools and historical depth to understand how minority groups construct meaning out of the past, how minority memory is formed, and how remembering this past affects the minority group. Lastly, theories of social identity and categorization help us to understand what types of identity-forming mechanisms create different identity groups, how they interact in memory spaces, and how these processes work toward the creation of a new minority identity group.

Collective Memory

Being part of a social group means members must learn the identity markers, values, myths, priorities, and ways of behaving associated with group membership and interacting with other groups. History and memory are essential parts of this membership process. Remembering certain past traumas or glories, commemorating events, writing memoirs, collecting testimonies, and generating media related to that past are all part of how minorities create, strengthen, and sustain identity. When examining the memories of a group, it is important to note that remembering the past serves multiple functions.

The Greek Orthodox minority and the Turkish Muslim minority are just two examples of social groups living through their memories. As Aleida Assmann (2006, 201) argues, research on memory investigates how social groups are haunted by memories of the past as well as how they use, and abuse, them. Similarly, minorities in Turkey and Greece live with the past to sustain their minority identity in addition to reminding the state about its past injustices. This process of reminding the state may trigger a multitude of tensions not only between the state and the minority but also at the interstate level between the host state and the neighboring kin-state. A minority's home state can view the act of remembering past injustices as a threat, which may also make the kin-country intervene in discussions to defend the rights of their kin minorities. Though perhaps understandable, this can create interstate tension, leading to more destructive relations based on the demands or the narratives various actors employ. Building on this point, Stephen Saideman and William Ayres argue that the "most virulent and damaging form" of nationalism stems from countries making territorial claims based on the presence of their ethnic kin residing in another country (2008, 2).

However, despite the potential consequences of remembering the past, a minority group's identity is focused on preserving its group memory. When they work to resurrect history, they do this by remembering the past through the lens of the present. Doing so sustains a sense of self, defines the framework of relations between social groups, and is a mechanism through which minorities can demand their rights and needs from their respective governments. This form of memory work can be referred to as the memory of the collective. It is this memory of the collective that operates to keep the past active in order to form group identities (Olick and Robbins 1998). Whatever is remembered about the past also defines who these groups want to be and how they will treat other groups around them.

In addition to actively remembering the past, collective memory also includes active forgetting. What minorities select to remember and forget becomes political. The contemporary use of the term *collective memory* dates back to Maurice Halbwachs' *Social Frameworks of Memory*, published in 1925 (Halbwachs 1992). Art historians, psychologists, anthropologists, and sociologists interested in collective memory began defining its various elements, including remembering and nationalism, memory and commemoration, memory and identity, memory and history, and mourning

(Billig 1990; Bodnar 1992; Cole 1998; 2001; Confino 1997; Crane 1994; Gillis 1994; Middleton and Edwards 1990; Schwartz 1990). Memory, in these works, began to differentiate itself from history. While history was described in its simplest terms as "the written record of the past" (Cubitt 2007, 43), collective memory in the work of Halbwachs and others is seen as unwritten and attached to a specific group. This form of memory evolves dialectically, between forgetting and remembering as well as appropriating and manipulating experiences and present and future expectations (Nora and Kritzman 1996; Olick, Vinitzky-Seroussi, and Levy 2011; Schwartz 1982). Collective memory is also educative for new generations, helping them to learn who they are through memory work. Specifically, collective memory creates "a sense of shared continuity on the part of successive generations of a given unit of population" (Smith 1991, 25).

Memory and history are viewed as the same field of research, which suggests that it is important to highlight the differences more explicitly. The field of memory allows researchers to explore the linkages between the past and present in an organic way, while the field of history is oftentimes more rigid, separating the past from the present. The effect of a past event on the identity of a group cannot be analyzed only by studying history. While history may provide some direction, the stories attached to an identity group are where the memories of that social group are found. Further, while history concerns "the reconstruction, always problematic and incomplete, of what is no longer" (Nora and Kritzman 1996, 1–3), the past, present, and future converge in the memory space, bringing it alive. Memory provides a space for memory transmitters to weave from the past to the present and in the future. As a result, what identity groups experience in the past does not stay in memory space, it is carried to the present through stories about how the past affected certain identity groups. Crucially, while history belongs to everyone, memory belongs solely to those who create it. Therefore, memory is vulnerable to criticism. As opposed to history, which is based on "facts" produced through intellectual effort, memory is open to manipulation.

The discussions with minorities, state officials, and experts, which form the basis of the forthcoming analysis, also underscore that there are certain historical incidents everyone remembers. However, how each group remembers the past differs. Sometimes, narratives about the past include contested and competing discourses due to the varied opinions, actors, and ways of remembering what certain incidents mean that can exist in any one community. Further, due to its subjectivity, a memory space generally belongs to communities more than the state. Different social groups remember some past incidents fairly well at the individual and community level, while silence prevails about these same incidents institutionally. In consideration of collective memory, it is important to first look at the general characteristics and functions of this form of memory before turning to examine the collective memory of nations and minorities. To highlight the uniqueness of minority memory, in comparison to national memory, the proceeding discussion starts by examining the meanings of collective memory.

Characteristics and Functions of Collective Memory

In addition to being a collective action, collective memory construction is also a mediated action. Various "cultural tools," including language and narrative texts, mediate the way human beings form their identities without externalizing their agency (Wertsch 2002, 6). Therefore, "memory—both individual and collective—is viewed as 'distributed' between agent and texts, and the task becomes one of listening for the texts and the voices behind them, as well as the voices of the particular individual using these texts in particular settings" (Wertsch 2002, 6).

Memory work is also based on multiple narratives. When a person narrates a historical event, the narration has multiple voices. It is reflected in texts and the voices behind these texts as well as the individual storyteller's voice. The agency of a person plays a significant role here because what is selected to be narrated and how it is narrated both depend on the person narrating the past.

Collective memory plays a dualistic role: it becomes both a goal to reach and an instrument in the identity construction process. The collective construction of the past is a voluntary, conscious, and political process. Group members remember past incidents, as taught to them by their group or community leaders, and then selectively use and often distort or delete pieces of information to serve their purpose of constructing the present. As Pierre Nora and Lawrence Kritzman note, "memory is unconscious of its successive deformations" (1996, 1–3). Therefore, collective memories are not written by historians and based on historical facts, but by elites or the community leaders of social groups who think they know what should be included and excluded from the overall story. More simply, they dictate what should be memorialized or glossed over in order to strengthen the formation of national identities. The events that serve the purpose of creating a national historical consciousness and collective mind in a society are selective. From these perspectives, the memory space becomes a goal to reach.

Memory is also an instrument. National myths and official memories help construct and sustain a nation's emotional and historical attachment to newly built nation-states (Anderson 2006; Hobsbawm and Ranger 1984; Smith 1986, 1999). Events are either distorted or deleted from a nation-building process if they do not serve this purpose. If certain events serve no purpose in line with the goals of the social group, these events are not used in the nation's memory space. Through various mediums like education and the media, the past elites sketch serves as an identity signifier for a social group. In societies where national identity is built on "ethnic oneness," all alternative memory forms that disrupt the linearity of this "true" form of official memory are rejected or falsified through similar mechanisms.

Conversely, in multicultural societies, there is not one narrative or the same tendency toward one narrative about the meaning of the nation. Rather, national identity emerges out of "an alternative means of national solidarity from nationally specific interpretations of constitutional principles to cultural or ethnic nationalistic sentiments" (Korostelina 2014, 22). Individuals make their decisions about which narratives fit their identity better than others with the help of political agents and state representatives using structural mechanisms including laws, bureaucratic procedures, educational structures, and social rituals (Korostelina 2014, 22).

Constructing collective memories is both an individual and a social process. Individuals are part of social groups and due to their voluntary attachment to their social groups, they cannot remember the past in a coherent and persistent fashion outside of their group environment. As they engage in interactions with group members, memories of the past are transferred to them through community rituals, commemorations, education, and other traditions. Because an individual's appropriation of the past comes from his or her internalized experiences with other group members, this process happens in a "deeply visceral and subconscious way" (Nora and Kritzman 1996, 1–3).

Members of social groups incorporate their choices and control their loyalty to the group based on their memories and identities. According to this psychoanalytic explanation, members of the group can even produce memories about individual events they have never experienced in any direct sense. Similar to Benedict Anderson's notion of imagined communities, Vamık Volkan (2006) argues that members of a large group who come together under one "tent," such as an ethnic identity, will feel, act, and project their future in similar ways even if these individuals have never met or will never meet. Thus, minority communities can be seen as a microcosm of nation-states because the communities are also created upon an idea of oneness. Even if every minority member does not know the other members of their group directly, they develop a minority identity and memory space of the past. Even if individual members of a large group such as a minority group or nation-state did not experience past incidents directly, some of them strongly internalize the memories of these events that group leaders produce, promote, and teach. It is not hard, then, to understand why younger generations feel so strongly about memories of their group's past.

Collective memory is also transmitted generationally (Volkan 1997, 2001). The concept of generational memory sheds partial light to the fluidity of memory between past and present generations, which creates the background for different generations to cultivate their group identities in response to traumatic or formative events that demand the sharing of memories. The sociability of young generations and how they share experiences also produce an affective basis for their generational identity (Misztal 2003, 88).

In sum, memory space is crucial for the survival of any social group, including minority communities. It is created through a collective group effort, mediated between group members, and reflected in the group's texts and narratives. There is continuity in the production and reproduction of memories of the past by group members. This is an especially critical process for minorities who face policies targeting their minority identity. The memory space is also a space in which interactions between identity groups are internalized, are learned from, and reflected upon. This three-dimensional process creates the basis for memory work and building group identities. In memory work, the agency of individuals and the interactions within social groups play significant roles. Further, collective memory is both a goal to reach (nation builders create the past they believe best serves the needs of their members in the present) and an instrument to legitimize positions, solidify in-group bonds, and increase safety, security, and group attachment. Finally, the intergenerational transmission of memories is integral, especially in helping to build the identities of newer generations. Even if they have not experienced certain historical incidents firsthand, they are taught to remember the past in a similar way to how they learn about their culture.

Collective Memory of Nations

This book focuses on the collective memory of national minorities and its effect on their contemporary identities. It is impossible, however, to discuss national minorities without understanding how nation-building projects create the national collective memory space needed to form a nation. A national memory space can be associated with two levels of activity. First, the nation-state system is accepted as given. Due to the changing historical and political context, national memory-building processes serve the needs of elites in the nation-building process as one aspect of national identity building. First, while the national memory space begins to create the context for fellow members of a new nation to feel secure and attached to the new nation-state, elites begin to create legitimacy for the new system through the will of the citizens. In turn, elites gain authority to rule over the larger population. Second, as the authority of the state is guaranteed, the link between the past and the future is established, and the new system is legitimized.

However, how do people's beliefs about their belonging to a nation emerge? Is it a conscious or subconscious process? How do they define themselves as part of a nation and act based on this feeling? How do they conclude it is a better idea to draw boundaries between themselves and others rather than living without boundaries? How are they sure there is a political and social system, or that the authorities will safeguard their needs and interests under any circumstances? To answer these questions, it is important to turn to key sociopsychological processes that function to create identity groups.

According to John Hutchinson and Anthony Smith (1994), national identity is produced through ethnic history and identity continuity, religion, and a belief system, as well as a dominant ideology and conscious manipulation through commemorations, ideology, and symbolism. The need for community also plays a significant sociopsychological role in national identity formation (Korostelina 2007a, 181). Other than through a common territory, national identity is acquired through various processes. First "the adoption of the specific elements of the national identity, including shared beliefs, history, values, assumptions, and expectations; (2) the development of an orientation to the nation itself; and (3) self-definition as members of the nation" (Korostelina 2007a, 182). Crucially, the national memory space supports this sociopsychological national identity formation process in which individual units of the nation feel they are inherently part of the nation. National memory space provides a context that presents a more orderly view of the past, which serves the needs of the community in the future. A nation's elite can consciously select, distort, or change the past in a nation's memory space through different cultural tools and mechanisms until the individual units of the nation believe they are already part of what has been created based on their history. Therefore, they see this past as a legitimate basis for future beliefs and acts. The national memory space functions like a national identity, binding members of the nation together.

Collective Memory of Minorities (Minority Memory)

As a group, minorities form part of nations, but are not typically part of the dominant identity group in nation-states. Categorically, minorities exist in opposition to the majority.[4] In a majority of cases, the identities and memories of minorities are formed along with nation-building processes, but not in parallel. Given that historical and sociopsychological processes form a collective national memory, a national minority also develops its own parallel yet divergent minority memory space. The civil war history of Greece serves as an apt example. In this case, the national memory of the majority and the minority memory around how they experienced and perceived the civil war were similar due to their shared views of the civil war period. Regarding the Cyprus conflict, however, how the majority and minority perceive and construct meanings about this conflict differs. The Turkish Muslim minority has kinship ties to Turkish Cypriots, which led them to support them as well as the Turkish state. Conversely, the Greek majority sided with Greek Cypriots and supported the Greek government in its approach to the conflict. Therefore, two different communities can construct different meanings about the same past incident based on their group identities.

We know the nation-state system is exclusionary at its core because it is founded upon societal homogeneity. It is this homogeneity that sidelines certain identities automatically because they do not belong to the core identity. Given that minorities categorically are not part of the dominant identity system in a new nation-state, they develop their own counternarratives around how they perceive the past during the nation-building process. Here I suggest the term *minority memory* to explain what happens to minorities while core identity groups form their own memory space.

The terms *minority memory*, *minority memory space*, and *minority memory work* are interrelated. Minority memory space is a fluid area in which minority community leaders interact with actors related to them (minority community members, majority community members, state representatives, kin-state actors and communities, minorities in diaspora, and international actors) about their needs and rights. While minority leaders interact with these actors, they remember past injustices and raise concerns about current state policies. Memory work is intimately tied to minorities' sense of self and existence—that is, for the continuation of their identity and perceived sense of security. This interactive and fluid space where minorities conduct memory work is their minority memory space.

How these related parties perceive each other in this space is related to how the parties use identity mechanisms, which is discussed in more detail in this chapter's final section. Identity mechanisms, including boundary interactions, othering, threat narratives, positioning, stereotypes, collective axiology, chosen traumas and glories, and projection are activated during interactions between and among actors in a memory space. When minorities remember past injustices they suffered, this may activate threat perceptions and the state may use threat narratives.

The narratives minorities use when they remember this unjust past may also include certain axiological stances, othering, or stereotyping. When the parties perceive each other from an in-group and out-group perspective, the use of these mechanisms is not viewed as unusual. These identity mechanisms serve to disrupt any clear vision of the future and, by extension, constructive relations between the parties. Memory and identity function together, particularly when social groups perceive each other through a historical lens. Negative perceptions and historical memories that activate identity mechanisms feed each other over decades and sustain divides between social groups.

This divergence is best seen in state-minority relations. Although Greece and Turkey perceive their minorities as citizens of their nation-states, when minorities make policy demands on their states, these states often perceive them as extensions of their kin-states (enemy nations). As a result, both they and their demands are perceived as illegitimate and, more often than not, are ignored. The government's negative perceptions are heightened when the kin-state intervenes to support the kin minority's demands. States can often view minority memory work and related demands not as existential but as the propaganda generated by minority leaders and elites who are viewed as an extension of the kin-state. This process of demanding rights and needs make minorities a target. These perceptions are sustained through identity mechanisms and memory work, which make governments perceive minorities' demands as illegitimate due to sociopsychological dynamics as well as the historical past between these states and their minorities.

The term *minority memory* indicates a type of memory that differs from other collective memory forms such as official memory or national memory. The dominant or official memory space is formal and static, while minority memory space is informal and active. Further, while the past is not at the forefront of the everyday lives of members of the dominant memory space, the opposite can be said for minorities. Minority memory space is alive and present in the everyday lives of members of that space. Conversely, for those who are part of the dominant memory space, they need not remember the past beyond the existence of specific acts or cultural products such as official holidays, commemorations, or national museums. In the dominant memory space, the past is remembered if there is an external threat, but in minority memory space, an external threat is not essential to conduct memory work because the past is embedded in this identity group's present and the future. Minority members' desire to conduct memory work daily stems from the connection between the past and their identity's survival. If there is no sense of urgency over the loss of identity, as in the dominant identity case, there is no need to resurrect memories of the past in daily conversations.

Minority Memory System

When memories are placed at the center of minority group interactions, they create the basis for group identity. Cultural activities are integral for minority communities to reproduce and sustain their minority identity. For instance, the Greek Orthodox minority in Istanbul celebrates religious holidays, organizes festivals (e.g., Baklahorani), and exhibitions (e.g., 20 Dollars 20 Kilos), while the Turkish Muslim minority in Western Thrace gathers for events such as religious holidays, musicals, theater productions, and charity bazaars (*kermes*) in Turkish Muslim villages throughout the region. During these events, interactions between group members create and deepen their in-group bond. These cultural activities form, transform, and re-form group memories. During these gatherings, minority members learn and reflect on their cultural products, internalizing them as memories and identity markers.

The memory work national minorities conduct can be better understood with reference to the various levels of nested interaction in which minorities engage. Expanding on Rogers Brubaker's triadic configurations of the relationships between the nationalizing state, the minority, and the homeland in newly independent or newly reconfigured states (Brubaker 1996), a minority's memory space includes interactions with

- the nationalizing state through official, institutional channels
- the majority through unofficial channels
- between minority group members with the minority group itself (minority groups are diverse in terms of their political views about the group's fate)
- diaspora members of the minority group
- international organizations
- the kin nearby (ethno-religious homeland).

How a minority constructs meaning about and reflects on past policies is completely different from how officials construct the meaning of the past. As a government official noted during one of our conversations in Turkey, the 1964 expulsion of Greek citizens was carried out due to the context of the historical period, namely, to put pressure on the Greek government during negotiations related to the Cyprus conflict. The current Turkish administration can, therefore, not be held responsible for this policy.

The Greek Orthodox minority expelled from Turkey and transferred to Greece in 1964 continues to suffer in Greece.[5] The Turkish government asked Greek citizens to leave the country, but these Greek citizens were often married to Greek Orthodox minority members of Istanbul. Therefore, the minority who were married to Greek citizens had to either leave Turkey with their spouses or be separated. The implications of the policy on both those who had to leave and on those who were forced to break up their families were very real and exist today.

Similar to Turkey's 1964 policy, there are thousands of Turkish Muslim minority members in Greece who lost their citizenship with the implementation of Article 19 of the Greek citizenship law, as mentioned in Mehmet's story. As a result of being stateless, they continue to exist in an absolute state of insecurity wherever they live.[6] The legacy of the past and the implications of past policies on the people who experienced them have real and significant repercussions in the present. It is for this reason that minority memory work is so significant. *Heimatlos* minority members remind the Greek state, Turkey, and international actors at every possible moment that they did not deserve this policy and the suffering they continue to experience.

Minority memory evidently functions as a double-edged sword. While assisting minorities to keep the past alive to make demands on their states for what they have lost, remembering the past creates political, social, and economic burdens on current governments that did not cause the suffering directly. Further, exposing the state's past wrongdoing is an uncomfortable position for current governments, which could function to trigger tension or even conflict between the home (kin-state) and host states (national states) of the minority. Nevertheless, contemporary governments do bear a degree of responsibility for not addressing the suffering of their minority citizens or meeting their needs.

Although Rogers Brubaker does not directly address why this tension emerges, he explains the interlinkages between nationalizing states, minorities, and homeland states, which provides some insight into why these linkages are established in a structurally contradictory way (Brubaker 1996). According to Brubaker, a newly independent or newly reconfigured state utilizes policies that are supported with a nationalizing nationalism approach to build the nation-state. Based on this idea, the state aims to nationalize its population as much as possible to create one nation by focusing on the core nation/nationality. It is this core nation that, in turn, is understood as the legitimate owner of the nation-state. In doing so, the core nation is constructed upon an ethno-cultural identity and is distinguished from the citizenry as a whole (Brubaker 1996, 5).

In the case of Turkey, Sunni Muslim Turks form the core nation. In the case of Greece, Greek Orthodox people form the core nation. Others excluded from this circle of privilege form each country's minority groups, even if they are officially recognized as citizens. This new state positions itself as economically, culturally, and demographically weak, which means it must work on policies Brubaker refers to as "remedial" or "compensatory" (Brubaker 1996, 5). The aim behind this revivalist rebirth of the core nation is to promote the interests of its members. In line with this, the state's projects focus on "the language, cultural flourishing, demographic predominance, economic welfare, or political hegemony of the core nation" (Brubaker 1996, 83). The idea behind nationalizing nationalism, in our case, therefore, takes the shape of policies targeted toward homogenizing, assimilating, discriminating, or excluding those (religious minority groups) who do not have access to the core nation group in both Greece and Turkey.

Brubaker's second typology, "transborder nationalism," refers to the nationalist tendencies of the kin-states (or external national homelands) for nationals who live in a neighboring country (Brubaker 1996, 8). Thus, Greece is the kin-state of Greek minorities in Turkey, while Turkey is the kin-state of Turks in Greece. This type of nationalism directly challenges the idea of nationalizing nationalism since it becomes interventionist and conflicting. The term *homeland* here carries a political rather than an ethnographical meaning. As Brubaker argues,

> a state becomes an external national "homeland" when cultural or political elites construe certain residents and citizens of other states as co-nationals, as fellow members of a single transborder nation, and when they assert that this shared nationhood makes the state responsible, in some sense, not only for its own citizens but also for ethnic co-nationals who live in other states and possess other citizenships. (Brubaker 1996, 5)

Therefore, homeland nationalism can take a contending, interventionist, or—in extreme cases—an irredentist position. In this case, the homeland argues that the interests and rights of the kin-people are endangered by the policies of the nationalizing state and, as the kin nearby, they have the right to intervene and save its kin-people living in the neighboring country.

Saideman and Ayres (2008) argue that the dependent relationship between the homeland and the minority is related to internal political competition in each country. With the examples of Serbia's support for Serbs in Bosnia and Croatia and Somalia's interventions in Ethiopia and Kenya, they argue that if the political elites of the homeland are dependent on the kin-people who live nearby, they would support irredentist policies, even invasion in extreme cases. If dependency is not salient, there would be few real efforts to intervene in the domestic affairs of the other country (Saideman and Ayres 2008, 14). Alternatively, the approach of the external homeland can be reconciliatory. It can monitor and assess the condition of its conationals, and—in communication with the minority and their government—provide constructive criticism or suggestions, but it does not see the minority as a stepping-stone to become involved in the domestic affairs of the neighboring country. This attitude must be supported by the minority itself. The minority must show political will to decide on the extent of the power of the homeland state in kin minority affairs.

The political will of minorities, their power and agency in decision-making processes regarding their own fate, and relations with the national and home states are all related to how they construct meaning around their identity as citizens, minorities, and as kin-people. Brubaker's third typology, "national minority nationalism," discusses this point (Brubaker 1996,

11). He refers to how minorities shape their position in a national state and toward their external homeland. The minority community tries to maintain a balance between two opposing poles of authority given that they "shar[e] citizenship but not (ethnocultural) nationality with the nationalizing state, and nationality but not citizenship with the external national homeland" (Brubaker 1996, 11). Maintaining this balance is not easy to achieve especially when minority-majority categorization emerges in nation-building processes.

This book departs from other studies that focus on either nationalizing nationalism or homeland nationalism. It focuses more on the minority communities' meaning making and how they balance their relationships with other actors as well as the effect of minority memory on their identities. The following section discusses factors including power dynamics and perceptions of relative deprivation that affect the structure of minority memory.

Factors Affecting the Structure of Minority Memory

Minorities conduct memory work in reaction to the majority or dominant memory work. In the case of Turkey and Greece's nation-building processes, the *millets* of the Muslim and Orthodox communities in the Ottoman Empire became Turkey and Greece, respectively. However, those not included in the Population Exchange, such as the Muslims in Greece and the Orthodox of Istanbul, became minorities.[7] The members of these formerly equal parts of bigger social units (the *millets*) transformed into smaller, "inferior" pieces of the new political and bureaucratic formations as "minorities" who are socially and politically placed at the periphery. This categorical, social, and historical transformation (from being a member of *millet* to a minority) resulted in different power dynamics between the majority and the minority, as well as the deprivation of several needs that the minorities continue to experience today. These have become major factors motivating minorities to conduct memory work.

Power Dynamics

Power manifests itself in all social relations and particularly in intergroup relations structured around a power asymmetry. Power relations are also at the heart of a collective memory space because memory is a relational space where actors interact, including the minority-majority, minority-state, minority-kin, minority-diaspora, and the minorities and international stakeholders. What is remembered, how it is remembered, and how the remembered incidents work to alter power dynamics between actors is very much related to perceived power structures in a given society.

Minority memory strengthens the position of the minority in response to the majority. Rather than feeling helpless, minority communities are empowered through the act of remembering. When minorities make demands, remembering past wrongdoings helps them to defend their rights from a stronger starting position. If the nationalizing state does not accommodate the minorities' needs and the kin in close proximity behave in a threatening way to the national state, conflict between the kin-state and the national state is inescapable.

According to Erin K. Jenne's model of ethnic bargaining, a kin-state's interventionist stance can worsen the situation. She suggests that the parties need to deal with their issues separately at the state-to-state level and at the level of majority-to-minority interactions rather than trapping relations in a destructive triangle of minority, national state, and kin-state interactions (Jenne 2007, 2). In the case of Greece and Turkey, this suggests minority communities need to decide how to bargain for their rights and how to respond to the interventionist stances their homelands adopt.

Here, it becomes important to understand what meanings minorities give to the power dynamics between all of the related actors that affect their own identity. To that end, it is necessary to think beyond traditional conceptualizations of power that largely conceive of social power as the capacity of powerful agents to influence other people through resource control.[8] Rather, it is important to think of power as the will of one or some over the will of others, which is perceived as either empowering or disempowering. We know that in many minority-majority relations, the will of the majority supersedes the will of others in the form of domination and the imposition of force through policies, discourses, or social practices.[9]

Citizens of modern democratic states prefer that power holders rule them using a "power to" (the empowerment of the people in the system) rather than a "power over" approach (domination and imposition of the power holders' will). In other words, people want to be ruled through their own will, not by force. Broadly speaking, the legitimacy of power holders is established via voluntary relationships. However, if citizens view power holders as dominating, then this relationship is not established voluntarily. The legitimacy of power is an interesting concept, especially in terms of minority-majority relations. The majority's acceptance and adaptation to power becomes natural because if the majority approves of the power holder that then creates legitimate power.

While the majority endorses the status quo and legitimizes the ruler, how does the minority accept the legitimacy and adapt to the status quo? Karina Korostelina mentions that "theories of justice and theories of legitimacy of power describe legitimacy as the acceptance of the structure (system of power), as 'right' by both advantaged and disadvantaged groups" (2014, 35). She also adds that this adaptation among low-status or less advantaged groups results "in conflict with the discriminating system and they must deal with this incompatibility" (Korostelina 2014, 35).

According to the social identity perspective, less advantaged and low status groups are exposed to various belief systems about their societal status from structural inequality to legitimizing ideology (O'Brien and Major 2009; Ridgeway 2001). In the meaning making processes of low status groups about their status, social and psychological justification systems function (Jost and Banaji 1994) whereby they internalize their status as "inferior" because they accept the legitimacy of the status differences between social groups, endorse the impossibility of changing this status quo (Tajfel 1978, 1982; Tajfel and Turner 1986), and learn ways to tolerate injustice (Martin 1986; Olson and Hafer 2001). John Turner argues that the standard theory of power "fails to deal adequately with the role of psychological group membership and the facts of social and historical change as well as with the nature of persuasion and coercion" (2005, 5). As such, how minorities make sense of persuasion, authority, and coercion in social identity formation must be analyzed to understand how different forms of power result in different types of in-group dynamics.

In every social identity group, systems of power play a significant role in in-group dynamics. This system is based on a mutual process of consent, whereby group members agree that other group members govern them, which requires choosing and elevating certain group members to authority positions. Turner describes this leadership and the use of persuasion, authority, and coercion to convince group members about certain stimulus situations (social or physical objectives). According to Turner, there are two forms of power: power "over" and power "through" (similarly to the "power to" idea discussed previously) (2005, 10). *Persuading* group members to create one voice to some stimulus situation emerges as power "through." In this process, group members need to influence each other to reach a consensus over a stimulus situation. Among group members, some are perceived by others within the group as relatively prototypical of the emerging consensus. When these prototypical figures persuade other group members, the latter relinquish their will and authorize these persuasive figures to make decisions in the interests of the group (Turner 2005, 10). In some cases, group members cannot be persuaded about the validity of a stimulus situation and, in this case, "power through" turns into "power over" in two forms. The first is the emergence of legitimate *authority*, which becomes "the power to control in-group members because they are persuaded that it is right for a certain person to control them in certain matters" (Turner 2005, 10). The second form is *coercion*, which is a form of power used without consent and against the will of the other group members.

This book suggests that in the cases of Turkey and Greece, "power over" and "power through" take different forms during conflict periods regarding interactions between national minorities, nation-states, and neighboring/kin countries. If we assume less advantaged groups (minorities) endorse the legitimacy of power that governs them and the status quo during periods of nondirect conflict that structures state-minority relations, periods of conflict become episodes during which the minorities question the status quo and the power holder's legitimacy. In turn, the authority turns to coercion. Minorities remember conflict periods, viewed as historical traumas, negatively and persistently. The act of remembering creates a basis for memory work that provides support for in-group identity (in-group solidarity, increased identity salience, self-esteem, in-group support, metacontrast, and in-group favoritism) and legitimacy to the minority's narratives in response to dominant narratives. Therefore, less advantaged groups remember conflict periods as a reaction to the system of power that governs them.

Deprivation of Needs

Minorities feel the effect of power dynamics most concretely when they think their state is stripping them of their rights and depriving them of their needs, while the rest of the society is not exposed to similar policies. Needs deprivation is a significant concept because of its connection to violent behavior. As Ted Gurr argues, deprivation can be defined as an individual's or group's "perception of discrepancy between their value expectations and their value capabilities" (1970, 24). Power inconsistencies between the majority and minority may lead minority community members to think they are receiving less than they deserve due to state-implemented policies. The deprivation of the needs of minorities is relevant to their personal and social suffering in comparison to the rest of the society who are seen as legitimate actors who have an established right to access resources and opportunities.

Johan Galtung uses the term *structural violence* to define harm, disadvantage, and inequality emerging from the systematic implementation of policies on certain parts of a society. Structural violence can be latent or manifest (Galtung 1969). In the case of the Greek Orthodox and Turkish Muslim minorities, respectively, a latent version of structural violence exists. During the nation-state-building process of Greece and Turkey, in particular, social, political, economic, and cultural policies created disadvantages for these minorities regarding their access to resources and opportunity within their states. The policy constraints placed around minorities' agency prevent them from achieving self-fulfillment and impede their chances of becoming an equal part of their national societies.

This lack of a sense of equality and belonging in a society has been shown to trigger societal frustration. Building on this, Gurr suggests that when levels of frustration increase from relative deprivation, parties justify the use of violence (1970, 24). For minorities, feelings of relative deprivation have resulted in a highly salient minority identity. This highly salient minority identity strengthens the boundaries between the majority and the minority. Minority group members have become focused on building a minority memory space and winning against the state. As John Gillis argues, memory and identity not only complement each other, they also work to sustain "certain subjective positions, social boundaries, and, of course, power" (1994, 4). In the case of minorities in Turkey and Greece, we see that relative deprivation has not resulted in violent conflict between the states and their minorities, but past deprivations have laid the foundation for the minority memory work seen today. Therefore, the memory space has become a platform from which the states and minorities fight for power to change, sustain, or degrade minority social status.

The Process of Minority Memory Construction

Minority memory space is a fluid space that changes based on how meaning is ascribed to past incidents and how the space is framed and reframed through narrative, the interactions between the myths and culture belonging to a group, and through changing power dynamics, legitimization, and conflict. Table 1 summarizes the level of contrast between the memory space content of the Turkish Muslim minority, the Istanbul Greek Orthodox minority, Greece, and Turkey. Minority memory and national (official) memory exhibit little contrast or contrary images of the past. This is due to the times of conflict or historical traumas where the minorities question the legitimacy of the status quo and compare the past and the current relative deprivation of their group. Conversely, minority memory work and the kin-country memory space exhibit a high degree of contrast in their meaning making of the past due to their in-group status (see table 1).

In the process of experiencing myths and culture, minority and national memory spaces have less commonality than minority and kin-country memory spaces. To justify or validate past victimizations, minorities use myths and cultural forms similar to the way in which the kin-country experiences myth and culture in relation to the past and differently from the way their home state experiences myth and culture. Finally, in terms of how a memory space becomes a realm of power, legitimization, and conflict, minorities conduct memory work about current injustices and discrimination related to the past. Minorities stress how, during times of conflict, national authorities tried to power over them through the use of coercion and manifest domination, depriving them of their needs.

Concurrently, the kin-state tries to use power through persuasion and authority and power over through implicit domination to affect the power relations between the minorities and their nation-states. Therefore, the minority memory space becomes, as Duncan Bell aptly suggests, an arena of "a counter-hegemonic site of resistance" and "a space of political opposition" (2003, 66). In this space, minorities use narratives and acts against different forms of power other actors use over them and create demands for either a change in the status quo or to certain policies, and to make identity demands.

Meaning Making

Memory construction is a dynamic and malleable process. The historical incidents social groups remember, reconstruct, distort, and forget can change for pragmatic reasons to serve the interests of group members in the present and for the future. Group members who participate in memory-building processes choose the events that create an orderly view of the past to build a more meaningful present. This process is the same for every type of identity group engaged in building a memory space. The difference is when power dynamics change and deprivation occurs.

Minority memory construction is largely a meaning-making process

TABLE 1. Memory Contrast between the National and Kin-Country by Memory Processes

	Relations between Actors	
Processes	*Ethnic or religious minority and national country*	*Ethnic religious minority and kin-country*
Meaning making of the past	Low contrast	High contrast
Myths and culture	Less commonality	High commonality
Power, legitimization, conflict	Power over (coercion, "manifest" domination)	Power through (persuasion and authority)

that occurs contrary to dominant meaning-making processes. When situations give rise to power inconsistencies and relative deprivation, the events chosen, and the meanings given to these events, differ dramatically for different groups according to how they form their memory space. Therefore, constructing the meaning of the past is one of the biggest differences in minority and national memory spaces.

Some of the characteristics of meaning making and how narratives work to create meaning can be summarized as follows. First, meaning-making processes are accomplished through narratives. Similar to memory processes, narratives are at once dynamic and malleable (Rothbart and Korostelina 2006), constructive and destructive (Ross 2001; Rouhana and Bar-Tal 1998), and interactional and interpersonal (De Fina 2012). In every relationship, individuals conceptualize their feelings, perceptions, and positions through narratives. In the context of history, narratives are the instruments through which societies shape their collective memories and identities. They transmit the past to the present and future. Narratives, action, and meaning-making processes work in a cycle. Individuals use stories to act and the meanings they give to these acts in turn create new stories, and so on. This is how narratives, action, and meaning making work toward forming memory and identity.

Second, the function of narratives varies based on the nature of a relationship. If relationships in a society are based on binary forms and categories like gender roles or dualistic race forms (black and white) between two ethnic or religious groups, this type of relationship encapsulates contentious narratives based on the meaning given to this relationship. As a consequence, narratives function as *boundary builders* between these binary identity forms and affect conflicting relations. This also establishes that narratives can be transformed and used to destabilize and erase these boundaries to transform the conflict toward reconciliation. As Rothbart and Korostelina (2006) argue, given narratives are dynamic and malleable, the narratives that fuel conflicts can be transformed into peaceful narratives. Narratives that assist in the construction of boundaries can also be contending or peaceful.

Third, because of the role of narratives in constructing the meaning of the past and building boundaries, narratives also *stabilize power inconsistencies* between binary identity forms in society. As Somers (1994) argues, narratives are not automatically embedded in the self. Our social environment rests on social and institutional practices, and through these practices, individuals employ certain types of narratives. More critically, from a Foucauldian perspective, this embedded process is accomplished through domination (a version of power over) of individuals through social and institutional practices, particularly in the form of discourses (Foucault 1981). Therefore, structures create narratives, and these narratives strengthen and solidify the structures in a similar way to how memories function. In the case of national identity formation, national narratives are shaped by both institutional and social practices, and they also function to legitimize those practices through memory work. If power inconsistencies exist between identity groups, the more dominant identity group has more dominant narratives and may dominate the memory space of the less-dominant group to sustain its power.

Culture and Myth

Myths and cultural practices are integral parts of memory construction work. The literature on the concept of myth is quite large and composed by philosophers, ethnologists, anthropologists, psychologists, and sociologists.[10] From a modern anthropological perspective, myth can be analyzed from functionalist, symbolist, and structuralist modes. While their boundaries are blurred, as Nigel Rapport and Joanna Overing note, they are best analyzed from a Durkheimian or Straussian perspective (2000, 276). From a Durkheimian point of view, the role of myths is directly related to social order. Myths maintain a given social order by reinforcing social cohesion and unity. By presenting and justifying traditional order and reminding the community of its identity, myths work through the public process of specifying and defining a group's distinctive social norms (Rapport and Overing 2000, 276). Similarly to Émile Durkheim, Bronisław Malinowski believes that myths have social power. When social and moral rules or issues relevant to politics need to be legitimized, myths emerge in a society to strengthen people's belief in them (Malinowski 1954, 84). From this perspective, the nation-building process is achieved using national myths that create and sustain national order. They then become national identity reminders through certain public processes that specify and define a nation's norms. During the nation-building process, minorities also begin their own myth-making process, which runs parallel to dominant myths in some areas and differs in others, based on the context.

Importantly, memory- and myth-making processes do not have to exist in parallel. During a minority community's memory work process the events they remember and their myths differ. While both memory work and myths strengthen minority identity, they differ from each other at certain times in a community's history. Bell supports this idea by noting that

> the memories that are privileged in the minds of individuals (whether they like it or not) or are recalled through ceremonies of collective remembrance, may not be the ones that are privileged in mythology, conceivably due to the highly personal nature of the incident being recalled, or because it happens to conflict with the self-image embodied in the various mythical narratives. It could be a memory recounting lost battles, participation in horrific illegal events, or the daily grind of living under a despotic regime. (2003, 76–77)

In societies where binary forms of identity shape social relations, in particular, as is the case in minority and majority interactions in nation-states, culture also occupies a highly significant role in a memory process. In these societies, the axiological order between social identity groups compels these identity groups to use their cultural practices as identity markers. Culture is a contested, sensitive, and hard-to-explain term. One of the most systematic attempts to explain the term comes from Kevin Avruch. For Avruch, the term refers to "the derivatives of experience, more or less organized, learned or created by individuals of a population, including those images or encodements and their interpretations (meanings) transmitted from past generations, from contemporaries, or formed by individuals themselves" (2012, 10).

Culture's significance in minority memory work stems from its emphasis on the meaning given to historical and social experiences as well as the organized transmission of these experiences into the future. Cultural practices, which include all types of traditions and normative systems (beliefs, values, and social norms), help build a social group's memory space. As Avruch argues, "Social identity refers to the social uses of cultural markers to claim, achieve, or ascribe group identity" (Avruch 2012, 15). While culture contributes to a group identity, culture also contributes to the memory space. Like narratives, culture also transmits the past to the future. Cultural practices, as well as a group's normative system, draw the boundaries of this group, differentiating the members from others. Therefore, like narratives, they also function to form boundaries in which memory work and identity formation are achieved.

Like culture, myths also build boundaries between identity groups, justifying and legitimizing positions, monopolizing certain ideas and dictating group rules, and developing an in-group/out-group axiological normative system. Myths achieve this by referring to past historical incidents and the group's origins, which justify the group's everlasting existence (Rapport and Overing 2000; Korostelina 2014). An analysis of the historical validation of the myths the groups in this study use is beyond the scope of this book, but, as Korostelina mentions, "the beliefs that constitute the criteria of goodness, legitimate participation, and exclusion/inclusion" (Korostelina 2014, 28) is discussed.

In the case of minority memory construction, I analyze minority myths, rather than dominant/national mythic constructions, to understand which meanings minorities generate about the past, how these meanings strengthen and legitimize the minority's position in society relative to others, and how these meanings eventually form the minority's memory space. Korostelina underscores the monopolistic function of myths that dictate certain worldviews and rules ordering the world. As such, myths function like narratives and memories that set the context for in-group members to own a shared identity. In the case of minorities in a nation-state, it is also necessary to analyze national and kin-country myths to see commonalities and differences in the identity formation (Korostelina 2014, 28).

Here, the theory of collective axiology provides insights on how a system of myths works to create boundaries between identity groups.

> A collective axiology defines boundaries and relations among groups and establishes criteria for in-group/out-group membership. Through its collective axiology, a group traces its development from a sacred past, extracted from mythic episodes beyond the life of mortals, and seeks permanence. Transcending the finitude of individual life, a collective axiology extends retrospectively from the salient episodes of the past to a prospective vision, presumably into the otherwise uncertain future. (Rothbart and Korostelina 2006, 4)

Myths also provide the context groups use to identify a common enemy and determine the negative values attributed to them in connection with threat perceptions as well as positive values that legitimize the in-group. Every identity group achieves its unity through the categories of right and wrong, good and bad, virtues and vices. These categories are passed on through storytelling practices, and are used to justify, rationalize, condemn, and denounce specific actions. In recounting episodes of violence and impending threat, storytellers often dwell on values. Negative valuation, inherent within a threat, is inseparable from its significance for the threatened group (Rothbart and Korostelina 2006, 3).

Both the majority and minority employ negative valuation about past incidents to justify, condemn, or rationalize their position over the other. When a minority community faces injustice, the minority condemns the majority and tries to rationalize their underprivileged position in society. At the same time, the majority also tries to justify past actions and to rationalize current policies and behavior. Normative forms of "othering" along with ethnic and religious divides in both Greece and Turkey have contributed to the creation of boundaries between social groups. The mythical narratives over the "othering" process frame the context that appropriates or rejects certain positions of these groups about their past experiences in society. Narratives of minority victimization and marginalization, in particular, delegitimize the position adopted by the other while justifying the in-group identity. Here, it is vital to underscore the role of mythic narratives, which are an essential part of the minority memory space. More specifically, the moral boundaries of the in-group and out-group are a strengthening factor of identity.

Power, Legitimization, and Conflict

The reciprocal zone, which characterizes Greek-Turkish relations, consists of the kin minority of both. This zone can function positively or negatively. During times of peace, when the reciprocal zone functions constructively, the kin minorities benefit mutually. With the emergence of auxiliary factors, the reciprocal zone is transformed negatively. Auxiliary factors include events such as the Cyprus conflict, government change or a regime change (or both) that bring about a more nationalistic government or a junta regime. The destructive functioning of the reciprocal zone results in a mutual loss for both minority communities. Therefore, existing polarization and social boundaries between national actors (Greece and Turkey) may seem invisible during peacetime. Parties do not hesitate to display reciprocal moves that are generally seen as conciliatory signs or positive policies, or they use constructive rhetoric to create mutual benefit for the

TABLE 2. Transformation in the Reciprocal Zone in Times of Conflict and Peace

Auxiliary Conflict Factors	No Conflict Factors
Conflict emerges	Constructive reciprocal moves
Activation of memory work	Betterment in the position of minorities
Activation of perceptions	
Negative reciprocal moves	
Loss of rights/deprivation of needs	

minorities of both countries. Therefore, a positive reciprocal zone leads to mutual benefit.

However, the emergence of an auxiliary factor creates a negative reciprocal zone of mutual loss and triggers projector conflicts and projector policies. These emerge as a reflection of events that resulted in a mutual loss for the minorities. As an example, even if the states do not admit there is a link, the minorities I spoke to associate auxiliary factors with reciprocal loss for their communities: for example, the Cyprus conflict triggered the 1955 incidents, the 1964 deportations from Turkey, and the deprivation of minority citizenship through Article 19 of Greece's citizenship law.

The consequences of the reciprocal zone transforming negatively are manifold. There is a deepening polarization between the two countries bilaterally and a loss of ground gained during the positive reciprocal zone period (see table 2).

The leaders of nation-states are dominant societal actors who do not hesitate to use coercion to suppress alternative voices when the reciprocal zone functions negatively. When this happens, the needs of nondominant identity groups such as minorities are deprived, which eventually disrupts relations between community members and social harmony more broadly.

Identity Mechanisms and Minority Memory

Boundary Making and "Othering"

Creating and sustaining boundaries are crucial for a social group's identity and memory space. Boundaries provide fundamental information about the differences between people or social groups and how these differences function. From a sociopsychological perspective, they tell us about how social groups form identities by providing information on their internal relations and their relations with out-groups. While symbolic boundaries are conceptual categories formed through narratives, social boundaries are "objectified forms of social differences" (Lamont and Molnár 2002, 168). Social boundaries are, therefore, more procedural and concrete. We can observe them if a group of people lack equal access to any type of resource or social opportunity. Social boundaries emerge through imposition when authorities draw lines where they did not previously exist (Tilly 2005, 137–45).

Powerful actors draw these social boundaries to categorize individuals and social groups based on their characteristics, including race, ethnicity, and language, their cultural practices, and any other criteria. Through symbolic boundaries, individuals gain group membership identity and boundaries become a way to gain status and monopolize resources. Therefore, boundaries can be beneficial to some social identity groups and individuals while they become disadvantageous for some others (e.g., certain races and language groups, indigenous peoples, and ethnic or religious minorities).

The actors in the boundary zone determine the boundaries categorically, historically, and institutionally. Boundary categories may change over time through institutional practices, social interactions between members of the same social group, between actors of different boundary zones, how these actors perceive their internal and external relationships, and how they construct meaning out of their encounters. As Charles Tilly emphasizes, "People everywhere organize a significant part of their social interaction around the formation, transformation, activation, and suppression of social boundaries" (2005, 132). These social boundaries can also exhibit within-boundary and cross-boundary interaction. Groups living side by side in peace one day can become enemies the next. Feelings of fear and survival become existential and social boundaries become more salient, categories deepen, and polarization occurs. This context may lead to the development of conflict-generating attitudes. In some cases, an us-them dichotomy may shift, and old enemies can become allies. In such cases, the boundaries between enemies dissolve, categories shift, and parties view each other differently (Tilly 2005, 132).

Boundary salience may also change from one period or environment to the next. When a natural disaster occurs in a country, minority-majority identities become less salient and every member of the state becomes one, working to stem the fallout of any given disaster. Even the boundaries between countries can dissolve during states of emergency. Turkey and Greece's rapprochement during and after the 1999 earthquake speaks to this softening of boundaries. However, when a minority leader resurrects past injustices, emphasizing the ways in which the state deprived minorities of their needs, boundaries regain their salience between the state and the minority group as well as between the minority and the majority. When this happens, parties find it increasingly difficult to develop constructive solutions to their problems. Therefore, boundaries can dissolve or become more salient based on the context and the actions of key stakeholders.

At each boundary zone and cross-boundary zone, the interaction and stories of individuals may change, based on differing identity forms. As Tilly mentions, "on either side of the boundary, people maintain relations with each other . . . they also carry on relations across the boundary . . . finally they create collective stories about the boundary" (2005, 7). Those stories usually differ from one side of the boundary to another and often influence each other. Changes in boundaries affect interactions between members of different social groups.

Tilly's writings on social boundaries are instructive for understanding how social boundaries change and how these changes affect social groups. Tilly questions how former enemies become friends or how former friends become enemies by discussing the mechanisms that precipitate (2005, 137–42) and constitute boundaries (142–45). Further, as Tilly underscores, boundaries are not static. They change over time, from one context to another, and through the actions of a social group's members. More specifically, Tilly highlights the importance of precipitating and constituting boundary mechanisms for boundary change (2005, 142–45). He argues that boundary changes are incremental processes and that shifts in relations, perceptions, emotions, and the discourse of actors in a positive or negative direction evolve step by step. As this book suggests, boundaries and memories are intertwined and affect each other during identity formation processes.

According to Tilly's framework, *imposition* begins when institutions draw lines between categories (2005, 139). Imposition would, for example, include distinguishing citizens from noncitizens. The process of minority-majority categorization and states treating each group differently is an important example of how the imposition of boundaries functions in practice. One of the best examples of how social boundaries have an effect can be observed in the narratives of minorities in Turkey and Greece concerning the lack of a well-structured minority rights framework, their inability to secure their rights, and their needs deprivation. Therefore, minorities use narratives of boundary imposition and how they are perceived as inferior socially in their memory work.

Tilly also mentions another mechanism of boundary work, *conversation*. This mechanism enables information exchange and relations to be modified through signals, symbols, actions, reactions, and emotions as well as words (Tilly 2005, 140). This mechanism is also significant to explain minority memory and identity formation because the more minorities conduct memory work, the more they are brought into conversation within and across their boundaries. It is one of the major tools used to transform memories over time and transfer memories from one generation to another. Tilly's precipitating boundary mechanisms explain boundary changes, but they do not explain what constitutes this change.

He explains various constituting mechanisms but *inscription and erasure* relate to the importance of the boundary and intergroup relations (Tilly 2005, 143). In the former, these elements become more important and, in the latter, the importance decreases. As discussed previously, when a natural disaster occurs, minority and majority categorization become less important, and they can even be replaced by a common identity of just being human. The boundaries are erased naturally. However, when minorities conduct memory work to demand their rights as a group, the importance of the boundaries increases between the minority and the state. Similarly, through *activation* and *deactivation* mechanisms, the salience of the boundary and intergroup relations increases or decreases (Tilly 2005, 143–44).

When minorities conduct memory work, they use boundary mechanisms in their narratives, seeking to legitimize their position in their societies relative to other actors. In the case where the categorizations between social groups are based on historically and institutionally formed boundaries, actors can gain legitimacy by positioning the opposing party as a threat or what Anna Triandafyllidou describes as a "significant other" (1998, 600). Greece's and Turkey's perceptions of their minorities as a national threat explains how the boundaries between these actors are historically and institutionally constructed. In cases like Turkey and Greece where kin relations exist on the other side of the boundary zone, Triandafyllidou's notion of significant other provides insights into why one party's memories relate to the memories of the other. "The notion of 'significant other' refers to another nation or ethnic group that is territorially close to, or indeed within, the national community and threatens, or rather is perceived to threaten, its ethnic and/or cultural purity and/or its independence" (Triandafyllidou 1998, 600).

A significant other can be seen as internal or external relative to territorial boundaries and historical ties. Triandafyllidou observes that "for a nation which is in possession of its own state or which forms the dominant national majority within a quasi-nation-state, an internal significant other may be an ethnic minority or an immigrant community" (Triandafyllidou 1998, 602). External significant others, on the other hand, appear in three forms:

> the dominant nation or ethnic group of a multinational state from which the in-group seeks to liberate and/or distinguish, rival nations (or nation-states); neighbors of the in-group, which contest some part of the in-group's homeland or are in possession of lands that the in-group claims to be part of its own territory; [and finally], nations, nation-states or ethnic groups which are territorially close to the in-group but do not contest its territorial boundaries. (Triandafyllidou 1998, 602)

In the case of nation-building, in-group national identification can be solidified through biases, prejudices, and negative stereotypes toward out-groups. During this process, intergroup differences deepen and other nations derogate (Mummendey et al. 1999). To emphasize the *Turkish Muslim* identity in Western Thrace or the *Greek Orthodox* identity in Istanbul, significant others must be identified and highlighted. This othering process can affect boundary changes and legitimize the policies power holders develop. For example, tougher national policies targeting the Greek Orthodox minority or the Turkish Muslim minority can strain the boundaries between external others (Turkey and Greece) and internal others (Turkey and its Greek Orthodox community and Greece and its Turkish Muslim community).

This results in somewhat of a "cause-effect" cycle. When a kin-country's nationalist moves rise, the boundaries shift again. When Greece perceives the relations between Turkey and Turkish Muslim communities as a threat, the boundaries between Greece's external significant other (Turkey) and internal significant other (Turkish Muslim community) shift. This can then affect the relations between Turkey and its internal significant other (Greek Orthodox community). As Harris Mylonas argues, external support for minority groups or antigovernment minority group mobilization can result in the perception of threat on the part of the host country during a nation-building process (Mylonas 2012). This threat perception is among the reasons why minorities are seen as "agents" of the kin-country.

Boundaries can also shift when a state needs to legitimize a policy. The significant other is seen as a societal threat and the state implements discriminatory policies that reflect this. The state can then legitimize these policies by activating threat perceptions and narratives. During the implementation of the Capital Tax in 1942, the Turkish government claimed minorities were profiting from increasing inflation during World War II and needed to be taxed on what they earned during that time. The state perceived the minorities' increasing wealth as a threat and as unfair for the rest of the population—the majority Turkish Muslim population—and the minorities were burdened with a heavy wealth tax. The wealth tax evolved into an antiminority tax because its express purpose was to deprive the minorities of a certain level of economic status (Aktar 2009). When minorities talk about such discriminatory policies from the past and remind contemporary governments, there is the potential that the state will (once again) perceive them as a threat. And so the cycle goes on.

Threat, Positioning, Collective Axiology

In a nation-state system, the majority's memories and those of the minorities are built on historical experiences that are remembered in connection with national or minority identity. When social groups conduct memory work, it may or may not include threat narratives, but it contains certain attitudes and an axiological-moral order. These provide legitimacy to minorities in their struggles for rights and needs. For the majority, as the dominant actor in a society, memory work is not existential. If there is a threat perception, they conduct memory work, and they use threat perceptions and narratives. Boundaries and the existence of a significant other create suitable ground for the majority's activation of threat perceptions and threat narratives to position themselves against the minority. Threat narratives and moral denigration of the other provide the legitimacy of power to community leaders and elites to establish their authority and gain consent from in-group members.

This process may also trigger conflict under suitable circumstances. When parties begin to view each other as a threat and view themselves as morally superior, they seek to eliminate the threat to survival. Threat narratives focus on the source of danger, a person, a group, or a situation, and the ability or intent of a threat agent to adversely affect a specific target. In addition, threat narratives—whether the threat is real or perceived—about out-groups or a significant other are dangerous because they have the potential to affect the behavior of in-group members in the direction of conflict (Korostelina 2007a, 207).

Nation-state-building process necessitate a common enemy and a common identity group. Threat narratives facilitate the creation of this enemy or significant other(s); they solidify the nation's moral superiority over others, strengthen in-group bonds, and strengthen the positions of fellow members of a new nation. Threat narratives are based on uncertainty. They draw on thoughts about an uncertain fear with uncertain outcomes. Whether this fear is real or fabricated, "storytellers strive towards, but rarely attain, a single coherent framework for explaining and predicting violence, and for charting a path from past to future" (Rothbart and Korostelina 2006, 33).

Both the parties who generally employ threat narratives (mostly more powerful actors) and parties who are perceived as threats need to position themselves in a reciprocal relationship. When the state use threat narratives against minorities, the state positions itself against the minority and the minority also positions itself against the state. In this type of interaction, as in every social interaction, actors construct their personal stories in response to the positioning of the other in the conversation to legitimize their utterances and actions.[11] Social groups typically position themselves according to moral orders, a system of rights, obligations, and duties in which they perform social actions (Harré 1986). For instance, state and minority relations already contain a system of rights, obligations, and duties. However, positioning can take dramatically unexpected routes when a real or perceived threat is involved in the interaction process.

Therefore, any act or narrative that is seen as a threat can change a relationship's regular rhythm. When a minority reminds the state of some of its past injustices, the state may perceive this as a threat and position itself against the group. Threat narratives always provide morally justified positions in response to an *evil* other, again, to legitimize their acts and ideas. Minorities can also directly employ threat narratives to prove they are better morally, which deepens boundaries between actors and makes resolving problems and reconciling actors nearly impossible.

In a less moderate form, actors may use the perception of a security dilemma as a reason to discriminate and exclude those they view as threat socially and morally inferior. John Herz (1950) was the first to discuss the term *security dilemma* in international affairs to describe the dilemma of nation-states increasing their security structures to protect themselves against a potential threat. This, in turn, makes other nation-states increase their security structures to prepare for conflict situations. This perception of threat causes an increase in the overall security system, which is an undesirable situation because, to live in peace, nation-states increase their war preparation capabilities, creating an increasingly insecure and uncertain environment.

When this is applied to social psychology at the level of in-group and out-group relations, the dilemma of providing security in a society can make certain social groups think others may attempt to attack, subject, dominate, or annihilate them. This concern about the intent of others can lead to some acquiring "more and more power in order to escape the impact of the power of others" (Herz 1950, 157). A dominant group's threat narratives about the intent of out-groups can be analyzed in this framework to see how threat perceptions cause more insecurity for all social groups and strengthen social boundaries.

In Turkish-Greek relations, the policy of reciprocity is a key example of how parties' position and justify themselves based on their threat perceptions and narratives about the other. In peacetime, any positive policy implemented for one country's minority may motivate the other country to implement similarly positive policies. This positive reciprocal move can help dissolve boundaries between all actors. However, any negative move can trigger a negative move reciprocally by the other. As described, Greek and Turkish relations were developed historically around categorizations and identity processes of enemy perceptions, the use of threat narratives, and axiological stances. History is replete with examples of the consequences of this dynamic, including majority attacks against minorities, incidents, and the deprivation of minority needs and rights. Though minority memory is significant for minorities, states and the majority regard it as a process that sustains and deepens boundaries. Minority memory work reactivates these threat perceptions and traps intergroup relations in negative cycles. This, in turn, feeds an unproductive process for the minorities in their struggle for their rights and needs.

Chosen Traumas and Glories, Projections, and Suitable Targets of Externalization

It is also possible to analyze individual and group identity formation, as well as the relationships between different social groups, from a psychodynamic perspective. In this regard, Vamık Volkan's contributions to the literature cannot be ignored. Volkan (2006) argues that people who come together under one tent, such as an ethnic identity, feel the same, act in a similar way, and project their future in a similar way even if these individuals have never met or will never meet. This argument is pertinent because it gives us insight into how the individual "self" transforms into a member of a "collective" identity group and how intergroup relations emerge. In that sense, nations, as an idea or perception, can be seen as one of these "tents" under which groups of people who feel ethnically, religiously, linguistically, or racially similar come together. Through their perceived or real past, they obtain their large-group identity, which is a national identity in this case. Whether it is a Turkish or a Greek identity, both are established based on "the subjective experience of millions of people who are linked by a persistent sense of sameness while sharing some characteristics with others in foreign groups" (Volkan and Itzkowitz 2000, 227).

This feeling of sameness is best seen in the memory space. When members of a nation talk about their independence, they narrate it as if they were the ones who fought against the enemy and built the country. Volkan argues that chosen traumas and chosen glories help these large national identity groups (whether minority or majority) strengthen their in-group bonds and create a sense of security for every group member. The members of a large group who experience these traumatic incidents also transmit, or teach, their memories to their descendants. When victims of violence cannot address certain psychological issues, they begin to place this psychological burden on the shoulders of newer generations, along with the conscious and subconscious notion that the next generation will solve outstanding issues. Therefore, studying the past's effects on newer generations helps us to examine how this transmission occurs, and whether it creates sociopsychological damage, frustration, or the will to resolve the psychological traumas their ancestors experienced. Volkan also argues that

> when an event turns into a chosen trauma, what becomes important is the fact that the group carries the mental representation of the traumatic event—along with associated shared feelings of hurt and shame, as well as mental defenses against perceived shared conflicts that these feelings initiate—from generation to generation. During this transgenerational transmission, the mental representation of the event emerges as a significant large-group marker; the group draws the shared mythologized mental representation of the traumatic event into its very identity. The chosen trauma functions primarily to link the members of the large group together as if it were an invisible spider's web. (2004, 5)

In addition to the chosen traumas, Volkan also discusses chosen glories, which are important historical events that create shared feelings of success and triumph (Volkan 2006). These events increase in-group bonds, self-esteem, and feelings of security and safety. Chosen glory narratives affect identity groups differently. Triandafyllidou gives an example of in-group/out-group comparisons by talking about the Ottoman conquest of Constantinople in 1453 and the end of the Byzantine Empire. Triandafyllidou notes that it "symbolizes for the Greeks the age-long struggle between Greeks and Turks and the intrinsically evil nature of the latter" (1998, 598). In that sense, while the conquest of Istanbul is a chosen glory for the Turkish people (for those who have strong bonds with the Ottoman past), it is a chosen trauma for Greek people. Similarly, the minority communities of both countries can perceive the incident differently. The 1919–22 Greco-Turkish War is a chosen glory for Turks, but it is a chosen trauma for Greeks.

The existence of chosen traumas and glories for a nation is undeniable. But how nation builders employ them in a national identity process is a pertinent question. As Korostelina aptly notes, "suitable targets of externalization" (STEs) such as flags, songs, special dishes, places of worship, religious icons, memorials, certain animals, and people as well as groups of people provide cultural tools that help solidify the idea of traumas and glories during the nation-building process (2007a, 28). These STEs are divided into positive and negative elements, and negative STEs are mostly projected on the "other," or the enemy. "Minorities can easily become suitable targets for the externalization (or projection) of the negative feelings and images of majorities" (Korostelina 2007a, 28; Volkan 1988). It works like metacontrast and in-group favoritism whereby every negative is attributed to the out-group.

Volkan's analysis of modern Greek identity underscores how Greeks projected negative STEs toward Turks, retaining positive STEs for themselves. For Volkan, as Greece gained independence from the Ottomans, it needed to establish a nation that was culturally homogenous and cleansed of all unwanted aspects of the centuries-long togetherness they shared with the Turks (Volkan 2001). As such, "upon 'separating' from the Turks," write Vamık Volkan and Norman Itzkowitz, "Greeks wanted to retain only the 'good' and civilized aspects of their former 'togetherness,' which could fit into Hellenism, and to dispose of the 'bad' or oriental aspects by externalizing and projecting them onto the closest reservoir" (2000, 231).

During Turkey's nation-building process, the use of STEs against Greeks and others who were thought of as "enemies" was relatively different. The new nation's elite planned to establish a nation that was "Western" and "Turkish," which meant that they could not fully externalize or project all the negativities onto the West (the main enemy during the independence war) (Volkan and Itzkowitz 2000, 231). Instead, the unwanted element was Islam's role in the public sphere, which was thought to have caused the Ottoman Empire's collapse. Elites aimed negative projections at Ottoman royalty such as the sultan, the caliph, religious leaders, and the population's traditional and conservative segments (Volkan and Itzkowitz 2000, 231). However, the Cyprus conflict, Greece's irredentist desire to implement the *Megali Idea* to merge the island with Greece, and conflicts over the Aegean islands also changed the feelings Turkey had toward Greece, and Greece became one of the main targets of Turkey's negative projections.

In conclusion, minorities hold two major and interconnected identities related to their minority status: a minority identity (based on their culture, ethnicity, religion, race, and language, among other characteristics) and a national identity (based on their citizenship status). When minorities are not part of a new nation-state's dominant identity group, they develop their own counternarratives around how they perceive their minority status and their relations with the majority. Nation-state-building policies that strengthen the majority's national identity become instruments that weaken the national identity of minority groups and strengthen minority identity salience. When a state treats its minority group negatively, a minority's in-group identity salience is heightened, while their national identity salience decreases. Minorities can feel *sentimentally* and *instrumentally* attached to the in-group more than they can to the state. In addition, minorities can exhibit strong *rule orientation* in relation to following citizenship-related rules and feeling obliged to adhere to them, but low attachment to the nation-state, low commitment to the nation, low role identification orientation, and low emotional involvement in national roles supporting the nation-state.

Discriminatory nation-state-building policies as well as the unjust treatment of minorities related to identity during conflict periods serve to strengthen a minority's in-group identity, while weakening their national citizenry identity. Minority memory space becomes an interactional (remembering past incidents in relation to certain actors) and a fluid space (there are no defined boundaries or rules governing past remembering) in which minorities remember injustices they experienced in the past, as a means through which to bolster their contemporary demands for their rights and needs to be met from state actors.

Every identity group engages in processes of remembering and memory making, and minorities are no exception. Minority memory space is a space in which several mechanisms, dynamics, and factors intersect to form minority identity. Minority memory work functions to create and preserve minority identity under changing conditions and legitimizes the positions of minority groups. Power imbalances and the deprivation of needs are two major factors that worsen relations between the minority in relation to the state and the majority. The state's use of different forms of power (persuasion, authority, coercion) in minority-majority relations are mechanisms that a state uses to legitimize its behavior.

Minority memories of structural violence and relative deprivation serve as the foundation for their memory work, enabling them to advocate for their rights and address their needs. Memory work becomes particularly important for social groups that do not have secessionist and irredentist demands but that have demands around their rights and needs as both citizens and minorities. These demands may revolve around cultural rights related to the use of a minority language, being equal citizens (both in rhetoric and practice), receiving justice for past injustices, and more inclusivity and having an equal voice in society. As a result of structural violence and relative deprivation, minority groups channel their frustrations toward nonviolent struggles of remembering the negative past and using it to serve their social group's needs.

Various mechanisms of social categorization and identity formation affect a minority's memory space. The most important of these sociopsychological and psychodynamic mechanisms are boundary making (constituting and precipitating), "othering," threat, positioning, collective axiology, stereotyping, chosen traumas/glories, projection, and STEs. Identities are formed in dynamic, malleable, and interactional ways, and an identity group's memory work supports these processes directly and naturally. Memory work provides insight into where the contradictions exist, which deepen the boundaries between identity groups, and how working in and between societal memory spaces they can be transformed into peaceful forms.

Minorities conduct memory work through meaning-making processes related to their historical experiences, narratives, cultural and mythical tools, and meanings given to power structures. Minority communities may have high contrast with their kin-country about how they both construct the meaning of the past, including which shared myths and cultural tools they use to construct meaning, and how the kin minority view the use of different power structures (like the kin-country's use of persuasion and authority) as legitimate in conflict situations. Conversely, a minority's lack of kin relations and shared culture and values with the host (national) state may result in low contrast in meaning making about the past, less commonality in using myths and cultural tools, and the minority group viewing the state's use of power in conflict situations as a form of coercion.

TWO

A Glance at Turkish-Greek Relations

I AM A THIRD-GENERATION Asia Minor Greek. My parents and grandparents experienced the trauma of being uprooted and the difficulty of resettling and starting a new life in Greece after the Asia Minor catastrophe between 1919 and 1922. When I look at Greek-Turkish relations, I see the nature of their relations as violence and trauma. Once, I heard a story of a Greek, a Turk, and an Asia-Minor refugee. The Greek and the Turk were fighting over who was responsible for what happened in İzmir (also known as Smyrna) during the Asia Minor catastrophe. The Turk was saying to the Greek, "You came and landed in Smyrna to take over the Ottoman Empire." The Greek was saying to the Turk, "Yes, but you committed violence, you killed and set Smyrna on fire." And, listening to them both, the Asia Minor Greek refugee turned to them and said: "Did I lose my home? I don't care who was responsible." At the end of the day, what stays in the mind is the trauma of violence.

Another problem is the official narrative. Greece and Turkey don't want the official national narratives to change, especially in the field of education. Last year, there was the celebration of [the] Greek Revolution on March 25 that is accepted as the beginning of the Greek uprising against the Ottoman Empire. At my daughter's school, they celebrated by reciting poems and learning about the Greek struggle against the Ottomans, and so on. About a week later, I met a Turkish friend. I met with my friend and went back home. I was talking to my wife about the meeting. My daughter in the room who was in second grade at the time said, shocked, "Do you have Turkish friends!?" It was an incredible moment of reflection for me. I said: "Yeah, of course I have Turkish friends!" She said: "But Turks are the enemy and we fought against them!" That happened a week after the March 25 celebrations. Can you imagine the contradiction in the mind of my daughter between the official narrative and the narrative of her dad normalizing Turks? Even though history is my profession, and I am working on Greek-Turkish relations, I still experience this kind of a moment. It is very difficult to change the official narrative unless ordinary people decide to read alternative perspectives, unless they travel to Turkey for education, workshops, or for a vacation. Interestingly though, Greeks nowadays watch more Turkish series and realize that Turks are not aliens!

Narratives about [Greek-Turkish] relations need to change but the problem is that people who can change the narrative, like historians and political scientists, have the least power to do that! I don't see Greek-Turkish relations as black and white. It is gray to me as opposed to the average Greek perspective would be. Because . . . [I am] . . . an Asia Minor Greek and [having] listened to the stories of the family and oral history, I realize the relations are in a gray zone. Both sides construct a lot of stereotypes, but these do not represent the truth. They represent the constructed truth. A lot of people are asking me what it is like to be an Asia Minor Greek. My generation managed to integrate the Asia Minor Greek identity and Greek national identity. But my mom couldn't. She was born in 1941 when Germans entered Athens. Then, it was 1959. One guy interviewed her, and the guy said, "Where are you from?" My mom said, "from Athens." "What part of Athens?" "Nea Philadelfia," she replied (predominantly an Asia Minor Greek settlement area). The guy said: "So, you are a refugee girl!" She still remembers that incident. That stigma follows the first and the second generations.

—Georgios, Asia Minor Greek, 3rd generation, Greece, October 2019

Collective trauma as well as negative historical and official narratives continue to exist in Greece and Turkey. We cannot understand contemporary Greek-Turkish relations without understanding these communities' narratives of the past. As Georgios notes, the Turkish War of Independence, as described in Turkish historiography, is referred to as the Asia Minor catastrophe in Greek historiography. Experiencing a life with parents and grandparents who went through a collective trauma of this kind in the past that included war, a population exchange, and forced migration is challenging. We realize this from Georgios' story regarding his conversation with his daughter regarding the dichotomy between the "enemy Turk," on the one hand, and the "friend Turk," on the other. This dichotomy is an example of how historical traumas are transmitted intergenerationally. They evolve, take different forms, and pass from generation to generation as chosen traumas (Volkan 2001).

Chosen traumas leave marks on individuals and the collective identity of a community. Today, minorities who live in Greece and Turkey as well as their relatives and friends who were part of the Population Exchange, or who migrated for other reasons, express themselves based on these historical incidents. They connect the past to the present constantly. Analyzing the history underpinning Greek-Turkish bilateral relations, therefore, is central to any understanding of how minorities construct the meaning of their identity in both countries. Any positive or negative fluctuations in their relations make the traumas minorities hold increase in salience. As one minority member highlighted regarding the tension developing between Turkey and Greece in the Mediterranean Sea in 2020, minorities watch TV channels or follow social media constantly to see if there is breaking news that will affect their lives. This is a powerful feeling and very real for those who experienced these types of issues in the past. Minorities refer to this as living on a knife's edge.

In what follows, I explain the nature of Greek-Turkish relations, situating these interactions in their historical context. Although Greek-Turkish relations were relatively positive in the 1930s, their interactions can be generally characterized as in a constant state of negative peace[1] that is marked by the absence of direct violence such as interstate war. Negative peace has become the norm and there is little political will to work toward positive peace and reconciliation. This means minorities will most likely continue (at least in the near future) to feel as if they are living on a knife's edge. I then elaborate on how key historical turning points in Greek-Turkish relations facilitated the boundary formation between the two states, between the minority and the state, and between the minority and the majority.

Atatürk and Venizelos's Rapprochement and the Longest Negative Peace

Irrespective of the general state of negative peace between Greece and Turkey, there was a time when they engaged in open dialogue and cooperation. After the war of 1919–22, the leaders of both countries, Eleftherios

Kyriakou Venizelos and Mustafa Kemal Atatürk, decided to open a new and peaceful chapter in their relations—driven by the strategic need for collaboration during the interwar period as neighboring nations, as well as by humanistic motivations to heal the wounds of the past, which they achieved to some extent during their rule. In his Nobel Price nomination letter for Atatürk on January 12, 1934, Venizelos highlighted the bloody past of the Near East, blaming Ottoman rule, and appreciating Atatürk for building modern Turkey. He referred to the rapprochement between the two countries beginning in the 1930s, noting that

> this shows that even peoples divided by the most serious differences can come closer to each other when they become filled with the sincere desire for peace, which was beneficial both for the two countries involved and for keeping the peace in the Near East. (Colston 2017)

After exchanging Greek Orthodox and Turkish Muslim populations in the Lausanne process, both countries continued to work together to solve issues that emerged from the exchange such as *etabli* status,[2] the limits of the Patriarchate's authority, and indemnity issues (Demirözü 2008). Against the backdrop of the strategic collaboration required during the interwar period, they maintained open communication channels, leading to the signing of the Ankara Convention of 1930, briefly known as the Friendship Agreement. After signing the Convention, Venizelos visited Ankara and Greeks who were living in Turkey at that time welcomed him. Turks chanted and flew Greek and Turkish flags in welcome (Demirözü 2008, 324). Such scenes in Ankara would be rather surreal in contemporary Greece or Turkey. Despite being former enemies who fought a bloody war against each other between 1919 and 1922, Greece and Turkey demonstrated the political will to build healthy relations where peace and reconciliation would be front and center.

Relations between the two countries were relatively peaceful until the mid-1950s. Since then, however, their interactions have been fractious and unstable, punctuated by fleeting moments of friendship. Despite the periods of mutual friendship, the overall tendency has been toward enmity. Except for the recent rapprochement between the two states starting in the aftermath of the 2023 earthquake in Turkey, their relations were strained during the writing of this book (2017–23) due to tensions in the Mediterranean Sea, as discussed later in this chapter. The question we must ask, therefore, is, Why do we mostly define contemporary Greek-Turkish relations with words such as "tension," "dispute," "brink of war," "hostility," "confrontation," and "mistrust"? Why were these neighbors unable to overcome their past to build a peaceful future? Instead, war and conflict have prevailed.

Today, the image of these two neighbors toward each other is quite *Clausewitzian*, constantly cautious and suspicious of the actions of the other. There is little hesitation about coming to the brink of war and the desire to win over the other. Greece and Turkey have existed in a state of negative peace for almost a century now. Johan Galtung (1969) argues that in order to talk about peace, we first need to understand violence. According to Galtung, violence has two forms: direct and indirect. Direct violence is present and causes the death of those targeted. Indirect violence is latent and can be thought of as attitudes, institutions, or structures that result in social injustice for someone or for a community. What he suggests is that human beings should work toward the ideal as much as possible by eliminating direct violence and the conditions that cause indirect violence for equitable and harmonious relationships to emerge.

This, however, is easier said than done. There is little prospect for positive peace in Greece-Turkish relations in the short term at least. These formerly conflicting parties have not yet dealt with their past, built trust, or achieved reconciliation. They continue to view the other as a threat, which makes building trust challenging. This does not mean there is no dialogue between the two countries. Greece and Turkey communicate through "exploratory talks" that were originally developed in 2002 by George Papandreou (Greece) and İsmail Cem (Turkey), the former foreign ministers of their respective countries. After the Kardak crisis (1996), discussed in more detail later in this chapter, and the capture of the leader of the Kurdistan Workers' Party in Nairobi who had been sheltering at the Greek ambassador's residence (Demirtaş 2021), the two countries decided to communicate more regularly. It was hoped this method of light conflict prevention would increase confidence between the parties and stop smaller issues from escalating into bigger conflicts.

Exploratory talks can play a similar role in preventing serious bilateral conflicts from erupting. However, these talks cannot generate sustainable changes over the longer term due to the lack of a broader reconciliatory framework. Dealing with Greece's and Turkey's past is particularly important for the two countries' kin minorities. Some romanticize the existence of minorities in Turkey and Greece, arguing that the minorities were inherited from the past and need to be treated well. In reality, however, Greece and Turkey perceived them as burdens their states must shoulder. Further, the kin states treat the minorities as an instrument to use as a means through which to gain advantage over their rival state.

A central question, therefore, is the following: How could Greece and Turkey move from violence to negative peace, as evidenced in the 100 years of no violence following the war of 1919–22, but not move from negative peace to a state of affairs more characterized as positive peace? In an environment of positive peace, the two countries' attitudes and structures would also transform, creating a more equitable and harmonious relationship. Similarly, how do the national states and their minorities experience negative peace where there is no violence between the parties, but there is lack of development and a significant gap regarding the state meeting the minorities' needs?

To answer these questions and analyze the effect of interstate relations on the minorities in Greece and Turkey, respectively, I discuss two phenomena that are at the heart of their conflicting relations. First, Greek and Turkish communities experienced *systemic change* with the rise of nationalism and the Ottoman Empire's collapse. Second, the minorities experienced *collective trauma* from the Population Exchange and the Cyprus conflict. At the interstate level, it is clear that Turkey and Greece have a contentious relationship resulting from the likes of the Aegean Sea disputes, the Kardak crisis, the refugee crisis, and issues in the Mediterranean Sea, among other disputes. For the minorities, however, none of these have directly affected them, their minority memory space, and their identity formation. Conversely, the systemic change and traumas they experienced had a profound and long-standing effect on them as individuals and communities.

Systemic Change: Fall of the Ottoman Empire and the Rise of Nationalism

There are various opinions about the history of Greeks and Turks. According to one opinion, Greeks and Turks first encountered each other during the Trojan War. During this war, "the 'Greek invaders' deviously—by using the Trojan Horse—succumbing the valiant Trojans, presumably the ancestors of today's Turks" (Heraclides 2010, 12). According to others, Greek-Turkish relations date back to the defeat of the Byzantines in eastern Asia Minor/Anatolian Peninsula by the Seljuk Turks in the Malazgirt (Manzikert) War (1071). After this defeat, the Ottoman Turk victors defeated the Byzantines in 1453 during the siege of Constantinople (Istanbul). This incident became one of the most significant historical traumas in Greek history.

According to Alexis Heraclides, Greeks and Turks describe the period between 1453 to 1821 in opposing ways. For Greeks, this period was felt as "400 years of Turkish yoke." Conversely, for Turks, it was an era represented by a model of tolerance during which the Greek Orthodox community developed far better than other non-Muslim communities (2010, 5). Yet it was this minority community that was the first to revolt against Ottoman rule. The siege of Istanbul in 1453 by the Ottomans created the *millet* system under which non-Muslims began to coexist with the broader Muslim community. This system was largely premised on the belief that Muslims were first-class subjects of the Ottoman Empire. The Greek Orthodox community was perceived as second-class subjects followed by Gregorian and Catholic Armenians, and then the Jewish Millet. While each non-Muslim community had rights to regulate their own religious affairs, they paid taxes to the Ottoman administration and were all loyal subjects of the empire. Though the Lausanne Treaty ushered in some modifications to this system, it largely continued with the creation of the Turkish Republic.

Even if there is a narrative in Turkey that non-Muslim and Muslim communities lived side-by-side for centuries, this does not mean they were brothers and sisters. As Vamık Volkan and Norman Itzkowitz write,

> Although conquerors and conquered had mingled blood throughout four centuries of "togetherness," differences in large-group identity depend more upon historical processes, belief systems, shared traumas, glories, myths, than on blood ties and cooperation in administrative matters. (2000, 229)

National Awakening within the Ottoman Empire

With the rise of nationalist movements between the end of the eighteenth century and beginning of the nineteenth, the national awakening of various nations under the Ottoman Empire saw them break away from the empire. Greek and Turkish national awakening was completely different in terms of their aims and the conditions under which they emerged. Greek national awakening emerged from a desire to break away from the "sinking ship" or "the sick man of Europe" that was the Ottoman Empire. As with other Balkan nations, Greek nationalism was premised on Westernist and modernist ideas. Conversely, Turkish nationalism was the outcome of ill-fated attempts to save the ship (Özkırımlı and Sofos 2008, 17–18). In a similar vein, "both Greek and Turkish nation states," Hercules Millas writes, "were founded through a proclaimed process of negating the

Ottoman Empire: Greece by rejecting the Ottoman legacy, and Turkey by transforming it" (2004, 34).

Theoretically, nation-building is a similar process irrespective of where and when the process occurs. State actors initiate a deliberate process to unify the people living under the state framework through mechanisms and products such as national ideology, national language(s), an education system, myths, flags, and an anthem among other elements. However, nation-building processes can also be unique, particularly in cases in which the process is premised on a national identity that is embedded in either religious or ethnic values.

Nation-building, therefore, is a technical process in which certain tools are used to construct national identity. Millas stresses that one of these instruments as "national founding myths," arguing that

> irrespective of the degree of practical success of the "rejection" and "transformation" [the author refers to the Ottoman past]—and in spite of the common past that the two societies shared—the national founding myths of the two countries, which were used to legitimize their new political formations, differ and at some domains are even almost opposed to each other. (2004, 34)

Taken together, the nation-building processes in Greece and Turkey were "parallel monologues," as Umut Özkırımlı and Spyros A. Sofos argue. These two nation states

> relentlessly emphasiz[ed] their differences yet [were] painfully aware of their similarities . . . two countries have been trying over the past two centuries to purify the national body politic from each other's contaminating presence, and even from each other's memory, while yet maintaining an intense interest in the relationship between themselves, one expects to find a vibrant comparative literature on nationalist imaginaries in Greece and Turkey. (Özkırımlı and Sofos 2008, 2)

Comparing Greece's and Turkey's nation-building processes generates insights regarding how these two nations tried to manage the creation of a national identity. This was achieved by cleansing the legacy of the Ottoman past and the presence of the *other* from their national memory space. Since the Greek Orthodox minority and the Turkish Muslim minority are part of this legacy, the process of forming a national identity and national memory created a challenging situation, especially for the minorities. The relationship between these two countries and their minorities, therefore, should be analyzed seriously because their minorities are the kin of the other state, and they are largely regarded by their own states as the other side's representatives who must be approached with suspicion. Perhaps more severely, minorities in both present-day Turkey and Greece are perceived by their states as a failure for their nation-building processes. Prior to explaining the unmourned traumas associated with the nation-building processes of both countries, I next examine how Greek and Turkish elites developed their respective national identities, which mobilized a collective to form newly independent national organizations that came to be known as modern-day Greece and Turkey.

Greek National Awareness

As part of their respective nation-building processes, Greece and Turkey had to address the issue of how to deal with the Ottoman past. Central to this issue was whether Greece and Turkey should disentangle themselves from the Ottoman Empire altogether or recognize it in their new national identities. Specific to the Greek national awareness process, there was a clash of views among those who preferred to reject any recognition of the Ottoman past and those who thought acknowledging that past was crucial.

Adamantios Korais, a prominent nationalist thinker of the Greek Enlightenment, advanced the narrative that modern-day Greeks are the descendants of Ancient Greeks and their link between Ancient and Modern Greece was interrupted by a series of invasions from Macedonians, the Romans, the Byzantines, and finally by the Turks (cited in Heraclides 2010, 6). By creating a tie between their ancient past and a modern Greek nation-state, the Greek uprising against the Ottomans in 1821 was framed as a metaphorical and tangible resurrection of Greekness (cited in Heraclides 2010, 6). For Greeks, the Ottoman past is seen as "a reactionary force that had held back and corrupted Greeks. A return to original, pure Greek values was thus crucial to the modern achievement of Greek national independence" (Breuilly 2010, 3).

In contrast, Constantine Paparrigopoulos's "Hellenic Christian Synthesis" narrative became more popular among Greeks in the mid-nineteenth century. This narrative claimed Modern Greek history was built on various forms of Hellenism (Ancient, Macedonian, Christian, Medieval, and Modern), which created the contemporary Greece we know today. This ideal, purified image of Greek history gave more power and legitimacy to the nation builders and members of the new nation. This narrative is based on "the idea of 3000 years of uninterrupted Greek 'national history'" (Heraclides 2010, 6). This image enabled elites to bring "rights" from the past and apply them to the present (Heraclides 2010, 6).

Creating a link between Ancient Greece and Byzantium was a hard project for nineteenth-century Greek intelligentsia because the European Enlightenment treated the Byzantine Empire as unworthy (Heraclides 2010, 6) but they nevertheless succeeded. This was crucial because crafting a link between modern Greeks and the Byzantines would give Greeks historical rights to the claim of being a successor state of an empire that governed the Balkans and Asia Minor many centuries before the "Turks" (Heraclides 2010, 6–7).

In addition to the legitimizing effect of building connections between Ancient and Modern Greece, it was also an outcome of domestic interest and desires, as well as an externally directed ideology. Domestically, the primary defenders and builders of Neo-Hellenic Greece were the diasporic Greek intelligentsia and the emerging mercantile middle class. To guarantee their interests in the modernization process, they worked to exclude and displace alternative representations, and effectively silenced competing interpretations of the past and aspirations for the future. This new and rising interest group had to fight with traditionalists whose authority was threatened by this new project (Özkırımlı and Sofos 2008, 25–26).

There were alternative voices in addition to those who were pushing these historical and ahistorical narratives of Greek history that focused on a more natural and dynamic development of a nation and its identity. According to John A. Petropoulos, for instance, Modern Greek identity was under the influence of Hellenic as well as Byzantine and Ottoman cultures. Modern Greece tries to continuously suppress the hallmarks of its Ottoman past, which are still present in society, because they are seen as signs of "backwardness" and "barbarism" (Heraclides, 2010, 9).

In sum, the main aim of Greek intellectuals' nationalist independence project was to bond more closely to the West by purifying themselves and their societies from the "backwardness" and "barbarism" of the Ottoman Empire. Association with the West could only be achieved, however, by referring back to Greece's ancient past, which was also admired by the West. However, the extent to which this linkage between the ancient past and modernism—then called Neo-Hellenic Enlightenment—could be established is not above questioning. As Umut Özkırımlı and Spyros Sofos argue, "This potent mixture of classicism and modernism was however incapable of totally erasing the resistance of a lived, Romaic culture carrying in it remnants of a fading cultural memory of Ottomanism" (2008, 97).

Turkish National Awareness

The process of Turkish national identity formation also transitioned through different ideological experiences. Similar to Greece, Turkey also rejected its Ottoman past. A more recent political trend in Turkey with the AK Party (Justice and Development Party) government, however, is a turn toward the Ottoman past through the idea of Neo-Ottomanism. As the Ottoman Empire was dissolving due to the rise of nationalist movements, the first project Ottoman elites launched to save the empire was *Ottomanism*. This involved emphasizing loyalty to the land and Ottoman citizenry, which were the themes that had kept all of the identity groups together within the empire for centuries. When this failed and nationalist awakening in the Balkans became prominent, intellectuals and politicians replaced Ottomanism with another project, namely, *Islamism* or Islamic unity against Westernization from 1887 under the rule of Abdulhamit II. The stage was already set for Islamism in an environment where involuntary and Western-imposed reform packages such as *Tanzimat* and *Islahat* had created resentment.

However, none of these approaches were as influential as that of *Turkism* developed by two intellectuals, Yusuf Akçura and Ziya Gökalp. This view was seen by most as a break with the ideals of Islamism and Ottomanism to save the empire. According to Akçura's ethnic-nationalist approach, the purpose of Turkism was "to unify all the Turks who, being spread over a great portion of Asia and over the eastern parts of Europe, belong to the same language groups, the same ethnicity and mostly the same religion" (cited in Özkırımlı and Sofos 2008, 33). Gökalp, on the other hand, sought to merge Turkism with Islamism and modernism. In Gökalp's cultural approach to Turkism, the nation was not an ethno-racial entity, as Akçura had suggested. Rather, the nation was composed of people who experienced the same educational, linguistic, religious, moral, and aesthetic processes. According to Gökalp, culture was a natural process composed of "sentiments which cannot be developed artificially and cannot be transmitted from nation to nation." It is "the sum total of the value judgments that constitute those of a people—hence it is unique" (cited in Özkırımlı and Sofos 2008, 34).

Both the Greek and Turkish national projects were a product of their time as well as their sociohistorical environment. In the Greek case, the Neo-Hellenic Enlightenment project of tying Ancient Greek civilization and modernism gained more support among the diasporic intelligentsia and the rising mercantile middle class in Western civilization. In the Turkish case, Turkism became one of the inescapable outcomes of geographical and population shifts when non-Turkic elements left the empire, and the remaining Turkic population homogenized in Anatolia. While Turkish nationalism originated from an idea to save the empire, it then turned into the ethno-religious and modernist project of the Turkish Republic. Greek nationalism, in contrast, was based on separation from the empire and purifying the Greek nation of "backward" and "barbarian" Ottoman influence.

To understand Greek-Turkish relations and the position of the minorities within their states, it is important to recognize the role and position of the Patriarchate and the Greek Orthodox Church in the Greek nationalist project. It is also crucial to understand Turks' perceptions of the Patriarchate and of the role of Islam in the Turkish nationalist project. As the empire dissolved, the Ottoman administration legitimized the authority of the Patriarchate in an attempt to retain this authority as an ally as Balkan nations and, particularly the Greek nation, began to respond to nationalist waves. The Greek nationalist project was also based on the appropriation of Orthodoxy into the Greek national identity. The status of the Greek Orthodox Church became important in the political independence process of Greek nation-building. Specifically, the Greek church disentangled itself from the Patriarchate to allow for ecclesiastical independence and to break from the authority of the Ottoman Empire.

Today, the church and the Patriarchate are two independent authorities, but the Greek church has reaffirmed its spiritual union with the Patriarchate (Özkırımlı and Sofos 2008). Many in Turkey have always questioned the role of the Patriarchate in Istanbul as well as in other countries. Turkey's early republican rulers wanted to control the Patriarchate's power in politics and the political sphere more generally. The Turkish state wanted to limit the Patriarchate's role due to its proximity to Greek nationalism and the *Megali Idea*, which was the irredentist Greek ideology created in mid-nineteenth-century Greece that aimed to reunite Greek populations in Western Anatolia as well as in the Aegean and Eastern Mediterranean (i.e., Cyprus). To that end, during the Lausanne Treaty[3] negotiations, the parties agreed to keep the Patriarchate in Turkey by limiting its role to ecclesiastical affairs within its own Greek Orthodox community.

Somewhat ironically, even though Turkish officials did not trust the Patriarchate, it was nonetheless expected to ally with Turkey in regional or international affairs. During the Cold War, the US expected the Patriarchate to be an active "moral force" among Christian communities in and around Turkey to countervail the Soviet communist wave. Turkey also expected the Patriarchate to "discipline" those involved in the mobilization of Greek Cypriots against Turkish Cypriots during the Cyprus conflict (Şeker 2013, 283). Within the Istanbul minority itself, variation exists in terms of their engagement with religion. While there are community members who are more conservative, there are others who do not engage in religious events.

Similarly, the minority in Western Thrace differs in terms of their proximity to religion and specifically to Islam. While some minority members are strict adherents of Islam, others are not. This divide also stems from the sociopolitical changes Turkey experienced during its nation-building process. During the Independence War period, Islam was a bonding mechanism, pulling together various ethnic groups, from the Kurds and the Circassians, to the Arabs and the Turks. This did not last. Rather, a prominent secular ideology established a sharp divide between religion and politics, which also served to distance modern Turkey from its Ottoman past. In contrast to the Greek state's approval of the Orthodoxy in politics, there was a strict separation of religion and state in Turkey at least until the era of the multiparty political system.

After Turkey's transition from a single-party to a multiparty system at the end of the 1940s, initial reaction to the state's secular ideology came in the form of an electoral victory for the center-right Democratic Party that had correctly understood the discontent of rural Anatolia toward the Republican Party's revolutionary policies. Whatever Turkey experienced in terms of contention over the role of the religion in society, the Western Thrace minority also experienced it to some degree. The minority in Western Thrace gained its minority rights based on being a religious minority. Today, the Turkish Muslim minority are also fighting for ethnic identity recognition. To date, the Greek government has rejected their demands. According to the state, the minority gained its minority status based on religion, as suggested in the Lausanne Treaty. While we can say religion is a significant part of identity in Western Thrace, as well as for the Istanbul Greek Orthodox community, the minorities' Turkish language and ethnic identity are at the heart of their sense of self.

Unmourned Collective Traumas

Greece and Turkey are in conflict with each other over bilateral, regional, and international issues, including disputes in the Aegean Sea, which are aerial and sea sovereignty disputes, European Union (EU) membership and NATO related issues, contestation over drilling for hydrocarbons in the Eastern Mediterranean, and sea delimitation topics. Notwithstanding these areas of conflict, only certain events have created collective traumas and become identity markers for their minority communities. Among all of these, two events (and how Turkey and Greece reacted) became collective traumas for minority communities in Greece and Turkey: the Population Exchange and the Cyprus conflict.

The Population Exchange and Becoming a Minority

Nation-states used population exchanges in the twentieth century to increase the homogeneity of their nations. Though nation-states found this tool useful, for those subjected to and those left behind in these exchanges, these processes were inhumane. Overnight, people who had been part of the empire were uprooted and sent to a place they had never lived but were expected to call home. This was not only the experience of Asia Minor Greeks and Greece's Muslim Turks in 1923, but it has also become part of their collective trauma.[4] While this was traumatic for the people who were uprooted, those who were exempt from the Population Exchange, as in the case of Istanbul's Greek Orthodox community and Muslim Turks of the Western Thrace, also experienced trauma.

The agreement that emerged from the Lausanne Peace Conference of 1922–23, which was signed by Greece and Turkey, as well as allied countries, ended the Turkish War of Independence. During the conference, those present at Lausanne also signed the Convention and Protocol on the Exchange of Greek and Turkish Populations (the Population Exchange). This convention emerged as the major instrument both Greece and Turkey used to justify (and continue to justify) their treatment of their minority populations.

Section III of the Lausanne Peace Agreement contains Articles 37–44, each of which guarantees the protection of non-Muslim minorities in Turkey. Article 45 emphasizes that the same rights will be similarly conferred by Greece on the Muslim minority in its territory.[5] The provisions relative to minorities in the treaty reflect the limited interpretation of minority protection under the League of Nations system. However, while these provisions do not comply with today's international standards around minority protection under the more expansive United Nations system, both Greece and Turkey still refer to the treaty as they try to find solutions to deal with contemporary minority affairs through the principle of reciprocity.

Principle of Reciprocity

There is agreement among scholars that when one analyzes the wider implementation of the Lausanne Treaty's minority clauses, it is not difficult to see a lack of implementation on both sides (Akgönül 2008; Oran 2003; Toktaş and Aras 2009). Minorities who had to stay and, as a result, were not part of the Population Exchange experienced different difficulties and, in some cases, relatively more difficulties than those who were forced to leave. As Baskin Oran argues, "Although those who had to leave under Article 1 suffered a great deal, their problems were more or less limited to one generation. These problems diminished considerably, and even faded away altogether as the 1923 expellees adapted to their respective new countries" (2003, 101).

This book examines the difficulties experienced by those who had to stay and, thus, gained minority status from one day to the next. This is achieved by listening to their meaning making about the past in their own narratives to find answers to the questions of how the past does and does not make sense for them and how the past is and is not part of their identity. According to Oran (2003), these minority populations were discriminated against physically, psychologically, and emotionally. They were isolated from the public sphere in different ways and their respective states never considered these minorities to be fully part of the nation-state, as citizens. The passage of time has done little to settle the negative perceptions shared by both Greece and Turkey toward each other and their minority communities. Since the mid-1950s, and particularly due to the Cyprus conflict, negative images of the *other* in both countries have crystallized.

Many members of the minority communities in Western Thrace and in Istanbul shared the fate of those forced to leave their countries through the Population Exchange when they had to leave their territory amid institutional injustices. Further, and despite its original intent, the policy of reciprocity became the instrument through which both Greece and Turkey enacted a series of injustices against their minorities. More directly, when one state acted unfairly toward its national minority, the kin minority community in the other country was subjected to similarly unfair treatment (Oran 2003, 101). Through this form of governance, known as reciprocity, both minority populations essentially became pawns for their respective states to control, manipulate, and use.

Before providing more examples of how reciprocity functions in Greek-Turkish relations, it is necessary to first discuss the term *reciprocity* more broadly. From a realist perspective, all states are equal sovereigns that seek to maximize their power. They only seek to fulfil their own interests in their conduct of international relations. In this anarchic Hobbesian world order, the norms of international law suggest that cooperation among states is limited through the principle of reciprocity (Keohane 1986). As the term reciprocity suggests, state behavior is a mirror of that of other states, or, in short, "people should meet smiles with smiles and lies with treachery" (Keohane 1986, 6). Therefore, the term generally implies an equivalence of benefits or an equivalence of damages, which indicates "the actions of each party are contingent on the prior actions of the others in such a way that good is returned for good, and bad for bad" (Keohane 1986, 8).

The classical Prisoner's Dilemma model in conflict resolution theory also relies on reciprocity. As Robert Axelrod explains, while cooperation is the most desired outcome, people choose to defect, thinking the other party will choose to cooperate. If reciprocal behavior starts out negatively, cooperation cannot be achieved as long as both persist with this strategy (Keohane 1986, 8–10). From a sociological perspective, reciprocity and its implementation are reminiscent of blood feuds between members of different tribes as "it was meant to prevent killings with the threat that it would set off a chain of killings" (Oran 2008, 36). Unfortunately, the implementation of reciprocity in Turkish-Greek relations has been predominately framed as more of a tit-for-tat or blood feud relationship in which contention rather than cooperation triumphs. Therefore, although there have been some positive reciprocal steps taken by both states regarding the treatment of their minorities, the minorities' treatment can be largely described as a form of negative reciprocity.

While the term is used as an outdated, nonhumanistic, and Machiavellian nation-state instrument in how states manage their relations with other states, its implementation in minority communities creates more damage than benefit for these states. Reciprocal moves in international relations may make sense to some extent to guarantee these states' power. However, when reciprocity applies to a group of people whose ethnic, religious, or linguistic roots are in a neighboring country, reciprocal moves between neighboring states become a form of punishment, not a constructive or remedial approach.

When the Lausanne system established the principle of reciprocity as the means through which the states would govern their minorities in Greece and Turkey, both countries used this principle to make their minorities' lives better from 1923 until the 1950s. The major goal of the newly founded Turkish state was to restructure the state and not become involved in more conflicts. The founder of Turkey, Mustafa Kemal Atatürk, named this policy "peace at home, peace in the world." Forgetting past mistakes was the basis from which Greek-Turkish relations were to be reestablished and peaceful.

However, the deterioration of their relations over the Cyprus conflict facilitated a different governance system. Specifically, from that time on (the mid-1950s), the principle of positive reciprocity was largely forgotten by Greece and Turkey and replaced with a negative application of reciprocity to manage minority affairs. As Hercules Millas explains, "The reciprocity in Greek-Turkish relations has been practiced, not for cooperation, but for pressure, securing political advantage and/or as an act of retaliation. What is more problematic though is this policy and how it is understood also appropriated/internalized by most of the subjects of these states as a 'normal' approach in exercising minority policy" (2008, 40).

The effects of this change in approach are reflected in the lives and identities of minorities in Turkey and Greece and particularly in their negative memories and experiences regarding their in-group and out-group interactions. The boundaries, enemy depictions, prejudices, stereotyping, biases, threat narratives, distrust, and many other identity dynamics between minority and majority populations in Greece and Turkey are visible through this appropriation/internalization of reciprocity by the people who are also the policy's targets. As Dimostenis Yağcıoğlu reflects, "They [the states] see the concept of reciprocity in the treatment of minorities as the most convenient and most morally and politically acceptable tool for them in fulfilling their desire for revenge, and in dealing with what they see as a potential danger for their nation and the state they care for" (2008, 107).

This appropriation/internalization process was also natural because "once the individual is perceived as part of the group (a representative of the whole), the punishment of any individual of the other nation for the wrongdoing of the group seems normal and understandable" (Millas 2008, 43). For the Turkish majority, it is normal, therefore, to punish any Greek Orthodox minority member over what happened in Cyprus because those who harmed Turks in Cyprus were viewed as the same Istanbul Greek Orthodox minority community and vice-versa.

How reciprocity and (minority) memory intersect is also pertinent. Millas (2008) highlights the anachronistic use of reciprocity in Turkish-Greek relations. The argument is that without any national or international authority to question the reasons motivating either government to take certain reciprocal measures, measures can be taken now for acts that took place in the past. The states' reciprocal actions are tied to the memory space of both states and both minorities. As Millas argues, states can use history and memory as an instrument, applying reciprocity to incidents in "the past as recent or quite remote" (2008, 41) to manage minorities. Once the states accept the use of reciprocity as a legitimate action and means through which to deal with the minorities, there is no reason not to extend this past to any ancient period (2008, 41).

Reciprocity is not only anachronistic, but also random with regard to how Greece and Tukey craft and implement reciprocity policies. As Vemund Aarbakke argues, reciprocity is

> not a legal issue but a political and social fact, or if you like, a certain mentality, a way of life. It permeates the views of most people involved. In its simple form its various representatives are standing in the bazaar haggling over issues related to the minorities. What complicates the situation, however, is that there are no clear rules for what they are haggling about. The combined demands of internal nation building and relationship to kindred groups outside the borders—which follow different patterns in the two countries—make comparison of the two minorities extremely difficult. (2008, 122)

These characteristics of reciprocity and how states implement reciprocity policies underscore how minorities are not considered essential but inferior to the majority in the state system. They are not well treated, cared about, or particularly valued. In an appropriate and ideally functioning state system, minorities must be treated more positively (through positive discrimination) to not only elevate their position in society but make their social status equal to the majority. The historical experiences of both minority groups in Turkey and Greece highlight that they are viewed mostly as pawns, used as a trump card as interstate relations fluctuate. As Vemund Aarbakke argues, "Minorities are not considered proper citizens of the country in which they live, but as appendices of a neighboring state.

This may have different consequences depending on the period in question and may be both advantageous and disadvantageous for a minority member" (2008, 122).

Cyprus Conflict and Interlinked Traumas

In the 1950s, Greek Cypriots began their struggle first against British colonial rule and, thereafter, to unite with Greece. Cyprus finally gained its independence from Britain after a series of negotiations and the London and Zurich Agreements of 1959 were signed. Greece, Turkey, Britain, and Cypriots from both sides of the island were signatories to these agreements, which created a federal Cyprus in which both sides were represented.

However, Greek Cypriots were not in favor of this equity, as enshrined in the new constitution. Much of their opposition to this part of the agreements stemmed from the fact that Greek Cypriots were the majority on the Island and the prominence of the Greek Cypriot nationalist ideology of *enosis* (unification with Greece). This, coupled with the rise of the Turkish Cypriot nationalist ideology of *taksim* (the partition of Cyprus) in response, caused both Turkish Cypriots and Greek Cypriots to thwart the new state from functioning (An 2015; Asmussen 2015). "The outcome of independence," as Papadakis, Peristianis, and Welz (2006) write, "did not satisfy the aspirations of either of the ethnic groups." Over time, this constitutional crisis transformed into a conflict marked by intercommunal violence. In response, the United Nations deployed a UN peacekeeping force in Cyprus (UNFICYP) in accordance with UN Resolution 186 in 1964. As part of its mandate, UNFICYP established a buffer zone between the two communities, which came to be known as the Green Line.

The 1974 Greek Cypriot coup d'état marked another watershed moment in Cyprus's history. In the wake of the coup attempt to unite Cyprus with Greece, Turkey intervened militarily. In 1983, the Turkish Cypriot parliament declared independence for northern Cyprus and announced the establishment of the Turkish Republic of Northern Cyprus (TRNC). To date, this status is recognized internationally only by Turkey. Ever since 1983, both sides of the island have been negotiating their future, which includes discussion around creating a political system through bicommunal and bizonal federation or through a two-state solution (Bahcheli and Noel 2015; Akçalı 2015). They have yet to reach either a consensus or a solution.

The Cyprus conflict and the associated trauma was not only experienced by Cypriots but also by the minorities in Greece and Turkey. Successive governments in both countries used their minorities as scapegoats for the intercommunal violence Greek Cypriots and Turkish Cypriots perpetrated against each other. Cypriots were perceived as either *Greeks* or *Turks* and not as Greek Cypriots or Turkish Cypriots. This perception continues to haunt the memories of the Istanbul Greek Orthodox minority and the Turkish Muslim minority of Western Thrace. Whenever conflict erupted in Cyprus, governments in Greece and Turkey have sought revenge for the violence their kin communities suffered by punishing their respective national minorities.

Since the beginning of the conflict between Turkish and Greek Cypriots, minority communities in Istanbul and Western Thrace have experienced periodic threats of violence, forced migration, and discrimination. On September 6–7, 1955, ultranationalistic and clandestine groups looted and damaged the businesses, homes, schools, churches, and cemeteries of Istanbul's non-Muslim minority, particularly targeting the Greek Orthodox community as a means of revenge for Turkish Cypriot suffering. In 1964, Greeks who had been living in Turkey since the 1930 Friendship agreements signed between Atatürk and Venizelos were forced to leave Turkey.

These Greeks had been living in Turkey with Greek passports but many of them were married to members of Istanbul's Greek Orthodox community, which meant that Greeks left Turkey with their Istanbul Greek Orthodox minority family members. Many of the Istanbul Greek Orthodox minority members also emphasized during our discussions that the purpose of this policy was to reduce the number of Greek Orthodox in Istanbul due to their familial ties to Greeks living in Turkey at that time. Therefore, for them, the 1964 policy was not only meant to rid Istanbul of the remaining Greek Orthodox minority but also a means of revenge for the violence in Cyprus against Turkish Cypriots.

Similarly, between 1955 and 1998, Greece deprived its Turkish Muslim minority of Greek citizenship in accordance with what was then Greek citizenship law. The Turkish Muslim minority was also exposed to various discriminatory policies, as elaborated on in later chapters. This series of events and others continue to live on in the minorities' memories in Istanbul and Western Thrace as chosen traumas. By transmitting past traumas to newer generations, the children of these minorities also live with these chosen traumas, which continue to be unreconciled, as discussed in chapters 3 and 4.

While there was no manifest violence toward minorities in either

Greece or Turkey, both minorities suffered structural violence due to various state policies. The structural violence in certain policy areas continues socially, economically, and politically. Although examined in more detail in chapters 3 and 4, suffice it to say here that the purposeful underdevelopment and denial of minority identity are examples of how structural violence continues to exist in modern Greece and Turkey. This situation only serves to deepen the trauma experienced by Istanbul's Greek Orthodox community and the Turkish Muslim minority of Western Thrace.

Contemporary Greek-Turkish Relations and Their Minorities

The Kardak crisis of 1996 is a well-known example of the tension at the heart of Greek-Turkish bilateral relations. On December 26, 1995, a Turkish cargo ship ran aground on the uninhabited rocky islet of Kardak (also known as Imia) in the Southern Aegean. The issue of how and who would salvage the ship turned into an international crisis that brought these two NATO member states to the brink of war. This issue was eventually resolved through increased military pressure from Turkey and bilateral and international negotiations. Could they have launched an attack against each other? In short, yes.

Just as Greek-Turkish relations can be driven by reactionary political actions framed through the lens of rigid nationalist sentiments toward the other side, their relations have also comprised more cooperative elements. For example, a process of rapprochement began with the devastation brought on by the 1999 earthquake. Based on interviews and unofficial dialogues with influential individuals from the Greek and Turkish sides, Volkan discusses the power of natural disasters to bring together former adversaries for a period of friendship. More specifically, Volkan argues that unbendable ethnic sentiments can be softened "above and beyond realpolitik considerations, by deep, mostly unnoticed, psychological dynamics" (2006, 110).

For decades, various Greek and Turkish leaders have initiated and engaged in either rapprochement or antagonism toward each other. Since the Lausanne Treaty, Greece and Turkey have experienced various geopolitical, military, social, and economic issues domestically, bilaterally, and internationally. At the heart of contemporary Greek-Turkish relations is the Mediterranean Sea and, particularly Turkey's changing geopolitical priorities under the doctrine of Mavi Vatan (the Blue Homeland).[6]

After the Greek Cypriots' unilateral decision to search for and extract undersea hydrocarbon resources in the Eastern Mediterranean Sea, Turkish Cypriots and Turkey followed suit, also initiating the same search under the Mavi Vatan doctrine. According to Turkish and the Turkish Cypriot officials, Greek Cypriot officials did not take into consideration either the interests of Turkish Cypriots or Turkey before moving forward with their actions in the Eastern Mediterranean. As a result, Turkey adopted a more active diplomatic and military presence in the area under the new doctrine.

Turkey's more overt military, political, and economic role in the Eastern Mediterranean specifically and in the seas surrounding Turkey more generally are revitalizing historical traumas among current Greek leadership regarding the Asia Minor catastrophe and Turkish intervention in Cyprus. This, in turn, has motivated Greece to strengthen its alliances with countries that have experienced negative relations with Turkey. Indirectly, these actions have put more pressure on the Turkish Muslim minority in Western Thrace and affected the Istanbul Greek Orthodox community. As with every antagonistic encounter between Greece and Turkey, the shifting dynamics in the Eastern Mediterranean have created anxiety for these minorities around how their states might treat them. Minorities in Istanbul and Western Thrace are acutely aware that were Greece and Turkey to start marching toward the brink of war, they would become trapped, forced into taking sides.

While Greece and Turkey have both chosen to increase their armament in recent years, the security dilemma between these two states is also increasing. So, too, are threat perceptions about the other side. At the state level, these threat perceptions and the lack of trust have deep historical roots. First, Greeks were the first among all other ethnic and religious groups to separate from the Ottoman Empire. Greece continues to commemorate its independence as the Greek Revolution, which Georgios highlighted at the beginning of this chapter. As his words suggest, the narrative of an "enemy Turk" is not only emphasized by the Greek state but is also central to the Greek national identity. Second, this underscores that, even after more than a century, little has changed in the mindsets of officials regarding how they perceive the history of Greek-Turkish relations.

Interestingly, perceptions regarding the history of intercommunal relations are not as black and white as interstate relations. According to some, Greeks and Turks have lived side-by-side peacefully for centuries. For others, this appearance of harmonious coexistence is a false perception, as evidenced by the nationalist uprisings beginning at the end of the nineteenth century. Irrespective of the view people subscribe to, the effect of living side-by-side for centuries has created a space whereby interpersonal relations cannot be described as an absolute binary.

Vamık Volkan notes that during unofficial dialogues, Greek and Turkish delegates begin each day negatively and at night they hug each other, dance, and sing. Far from romanticizing Greek-Turkish relations, this reality highlights that for communities that have lived together for centuries, whether they liked each other or not, they began to develop a common culture.[7] A similar commonality is applicable to majority-minority relations. In reality, however, minorities are largely ignored in Greek-Turkish interstate relations. According to minorities, the state only listens to them intermittently, rather than being motivated to listen to address the very real suffering minorities continue to experience.

Minority rights in the fields of education, economy and property rights, religious affairs, and identity-related matters cannot be solved unless Greek and Turkish leaders along with minority leaders decide to embark on a process of deconstructing the sociopsychological boundaries between the two nations, between minorities and their national states, and between the minorities and the majorities. Minority-related issues are overlooked as realpolitik spreads throughout the region. In this environment, all of the relevant actors can only expect these social boundaries to become rigid, deepening interstate and intercommunal distrust and negative perceptions. In the following section, significant historical turning points in Greek-Turkish relations are examined in line with their effects on boundary formation.

Greek-Turkish Relations and Boundaries

As Kamouzis's story at the beginning of this chapter underscored, the effects of the Population Exchange were manifold on the people who were either part of the process or learned about the trauma surrounding this period. Memories have passed from generation to generation, influencing Greeks and Turks on either side of the Aegean Sea. These memories and the state policies enacted during this time of nation-building in both countries created the identities of those who were exchanged and those who were left behind (the minorities). As their identities formed, the boundaries crystallized between the minorities and the majority populations, as well as between the state and the minorities. This process did not occur overnight, but rather over decades, as discussed below.

Social boundaries are the outcomes of various types of interactions between different groups in any given society, which gives boundaries their relational character. They can emerge, transform, and disappear based on the nature of the relations on different sides of the boundary. Social boundaries are part of our memory system and help define our social identities. While some boundaries appear more set and objective, others appear changeable and subjective. When interactions in the boundary zone become significant enough to make changes to the boundaries, these events become part of the memory space of those involved. It is for this reason that wars or destructive conflicts between enemies, which are extreme interaction forms, leave scars on both sides. Therefore, the boundaries of us versus them become salient and crystallize with every conflict experience. Crucially, however, social boundaries are not fixed, but open to change.

From a sociopsychological point of view, boundaries aid social groups to construct meaning out of their in-group membership while also explaining the nature of the interactions between the in-group and out-groups. Social boundaries are generally drawn by the social actors who have power to decide social categories in certain historical contexts (e.g., minority-majority categories). Since social boundaries are "objectified forms of social differences" (Lamont and Molnár 2002, 168), as seen in binary national, racial, or ethnic boundaries, they are more than procedural. Therefore, boundaries are categorical, institutional, and historical.

While social boundaries are discussed at the intergroup and in-group levels, respectively, and are alternative means of contact and meaning making between the actors in the boundary zone, symbolic boundaries may emerge as cross-cutting categories and alternative forms of boundaries. Symbolic boundaries function at an intersubjective level and explain a "necessary but insufficient condition for the existence of social boundaries" (Lamont and Molnár 2002, 168). The existence of symbolic boundaries therefore only partially explains why social boundaries exist. Consequently, symbolic boundaries must be part of any analysis of minority memory work because of their potential to bring alternative narrative and interaction forms into social boundary discussions. Even before individuals engage in a process of categorization, they craft conceptual distinctions regarding objects, people, practices, and even time and space. The purpose of this alternative and cross-cutting boundary work can be to highlight new categories and make them salient. When some group members create these alternative and cross-cutting boundaries that are accepted by everyone, "they take on a constraining character and pattern social interaction in important ways" (Lamont and Molnár 2002, 168).

Throughout this book, I provide various narratives of the past and how the minorities, officials, and experts who work on Greek-Turkish relations and minority affairs make meaning of this past. These narratives imply that reconciliation between Greece and Turkey, as well as between the states and their minorities, is not yet an aim. Given the lack of closure, enmity and threat perceptions still dominate in how the parties perceive each other; the role of boundaries, and how they emerge, function, and deepen existing problems, is apparent. Without an understanding of these dynamics, it is more challenging to understand the root causes of the conflicts between the minorities and the majorities from a sociopsychological perspective.

In the forthcoming sections, I first highlight easily observable social boundaries and their effects on minority memory and identity in the case of the Greek and Turkish minorities. Second, I provide an example of how boundaries between Greece and Turkey change at the level of discourse and the states' behavior, respectively, both of which have consequences for how minorities experience their minority status and dual identity (citizen/minority identities).

Historical Turning Points, Social Categorization, and Emerging Boundaries

Minority demands on their states in both Greece and Turkey are rooted deeply in history and particularly in the emergence of hostile attitudes and perceptions between the two nations. These attitudes and perceptions are strongly correlated with boundary-making and changing processes brought about by different political and historical contextual changes as well as the varying goals of political actors. The minorities' narratives examined in this book associate certain historical episodes with different boundary forms and processes of social categorization or the lack thereof (see table 3). These are analyzed in detail below, but to summarize, the narratives are based on the relative peacefulness of boundaries between different social groupings (Muslims, Jews, Orthodox, Armenians) in the Ottoman *millet* system. During the Ottoman Empire, the *millet* system served as a form of conflict management between Ottoman minorities. Under this system, the Ottoman regime granted certain privileges to each religious group, which resulted in a lack of strong intergroup comparison or feelings of relative deprivation. It also fostered a degree of relative coexistence and nonthreatening boundary forms.

This relative intergroup peacefulness started to change as certain groups began to acknowledge their own national awareness and group elites from within the minorities advocated for their own nation-states. Among these, Greek *ethnies* (ethnic communities) were the first to fight for independence against Ottoman rule. For this group, they regarded the period under the empire as the dark ages and as an era of subordination. It should be noted that nationalist ideas did not reach to the Ottoman Empire until the eighteenth century. After the French Revolution, secularization and nationalism spread through the empire and resulted in a national awakening among the empire's *millets* (*ethnies*). Prior to the eighteenth century, religion was the boundary maker between different *ethnies*. The degree of independence they exerted in managing their own community affairs resulted in relative inter-*ethnie* coexistence.

In the wake of the successful Greek War of Independence (1821–32) against the Ottoman Empire, the relatively peaceful boundaries between Turkish Muslim and Greek Orthodox *millets* polarized. Increasing awareness of ethnonationalism became an ideological boundary-strengthening mechanism. The Greco-Turkish War (1919–22) revived negative images, hostile attitudes, and negative perceptions between Greeks and Turks. This conflict resulted in the emergence of new boundaries, as in-group–out-group relations became more visible and pronounced, and intergroup comparisons grew stronger.

The Lausanne Treaty is the landmark agreement in minority memory work that initiated boundary change. Old boundaries transformed as the empire dissolved and nation-states (Greece and Turkey) emerged. Through the treaty, clearer (though still not consolidated) boundaries appeared with the creation of minority-majority categories and in-group–out-group comparison continued. The Lausanne Treaty's effect on boundary change between the minority and the majority categories is evident in the minorities' memory work. State-minority and minority-majority boundary salience has fluctuated over time due to Greece and Turkey's reciprocal actions regarding institutional and narrative practices as well as contextual shifts (domestically, regionally, and internationally).

Greek and Turkish institutional practices related to their respective nation-building processes are not the only state actions that have consolidated the boundaries between the minorities and the majority. Their negative reciprocal actions in their management of minority affairs have also strengthened these boundaries. As noted previously, even if the Population Exchange was the most traumatic incident experienced by those who had to migrate, for those who stayed behind in either Greece or Turkey in their

TABLE 3. Boundary Forms and Social Categorization at Historical Turning Points

Historical Turning Points	Boundary Forms	Social Categorization
Ottoman *millet* system (conflict management)	Relatively peaceful religious boundaries	Peaceful coexistence with different social groups; no strong comparisons
National awakening (new ideologies) Greco-Turkish War (violent conflict)	Ethnic-religious boundaries Polarization and war	From relative coexistence to separation, categories strengthen; identification with categories strengthens
Lausanne Treaty (peacemaking) Population Exchange (conflict management)	New boundaries (i.e., minority-majority)	Categories become clearer, boundaries strengthen, comparisons continue
Nation-building (new ideologies) Nationalization policies/reciprocity (conflict management)	New boundaries consolidated	Categories are set; boundaries are certain; comparisons strong

new minority status, it was the process of becoming a minority that was painful due to the traumas experienced along the way.

Relative Coexistence with Peaceful Boundaries: The Ottoman *Millet* System as a Conflict Management Tool

Most of the minorities in both Istanbul and Western Thrace referred to the past as much as the past relates to their daily lives. Their everyday encounters involve interactions among and between community members and with the majority, state institutions, and the media. Being part of this larger group identity means that members of these minority communities raise the same concerns about past injustices repeatedly in their narratives as *memory markers* or as a shared history.

The Ottoman past is the period minorities refer to the least. Further, even those who refer to this period refer to it as an era of relative coexistence between different identity groups. This idea corresponds with Vamık Volkan and Norman Itzkowitz's (2000) argument that different *millets* in the Ottoman Empire lived peacefully but not as brothers and sisters. They add that the conquerors and the conquered populations mix over time and cooperated on administrative matters. Despite this cooperation, the empire's various *millets* did not share a large-group identity, which is actually much more about historical processes, belief systems, shared traumas, glories, and myths. Will Kymlicka (1995, 35–37) notes that the Ottoman *millet* system provided a substantial measure of self-government and official status to Christians, Jews, and Muslims, which created separation among peoples instead of unification. Though separated, they did not attempt to suppress each other. These boundaries produced fewer threat perceptions and less conflict, which then resulted in relatively humane and tolerant intergroup relations (Kymlicka 1995, 37).

The *millet* system can, therefore, be viewed as a conflict management system between different social groups structured around relatively non-threatening boundaries. Under this system, the emperor showed tolerance to each of these *millets*. The emergence of the modern Turkish state and the official narrative of tolerance toward minorities, however, has created confusion for minorities. Although the minorities do not have access to the same rights and freedoms experienced under the Ottoman Empire, they nevertheless feel they are treated similarly due to contemporary rhetoric around tolerance.

Nationalist Ideologies and the Greco-Turkish War in Boundary Formation

As discussed earlier, nation-building processes in Turkey and Greece can be seen as "'parallel monologues' . . . relentlessly emphasizing. . . . similarities" (Özkırımlı and Sofos 2008, 2). Further, while nation-building processes in both countries may have differed internally, they converge in the area of reciprocity regarding how Greece and Turkey have treated their minorities and how they consolidated the social boundaries bilaterally.

These national awakening processes among Ottoman *millets* precipitated the emergence of ethnic-religious boundaries. The literature reminds us that this ideological transformation in the Orthodox Millet began with the Enlightenment and the French Revolution. In the Greek case, Adamantios Korais's idea of "resurrecting" the Greek nation was rejected first by Spyridon Zambelios and then by Konstantinos Paparrigopoulos. Embedded in this understanding was the belief that the Greek nation had been the subjects of the Macedonians, the Romans, the Byzantines, and the Turks (Heraclides 2010). As an alternative, Zambelios and Paparrigopoulos focused on a "Hellenic-Christian Synthesis," which tried to reconcile Ancient Greek and Byzantine historical legacies (Grigoriadis 2013). The role of Paparrigopoulos' "Hellenic-Christian Synthesis" paved the way for contemporary Greece by emphasizing Greek Orthodoxy as a more encompassing element of new Greek nationhood (Grigoriadis 2013, 29). In doing so, they overlooked Greek language and ethnicity. This ethnic and religious boundary-making was also supported by the Orthodox Church of Greece. While the Church and the irredentist *Megali Idea* played a key role in building a Greek nation-state, the Ecumenical Patriarchate and Greek Orthodox community of Istanbul kept their distance from this goal and declared their loyalty to the Ottoman Empire. Consequently, it can be said that the minority's narratives of loyalty to the state voice their approval of the historical and cultural patterns between the Turkish political authority and the Greek Orthodox people.

With the wave of nationalism in Europe at the end of the eighteenth and at the beginning of the nineteenth centuries, the boundaries between religious communities that coexisted in the Ottoman Empire started to transform into an ethno-religious boundary. The Ottoman Empire's Greek Orthodox Millet's successful independence campaign and the Greco-Turkish War (1919–22) increased polarization between Greeks and Turks. These historical periods as well as others discussed below also created strong boundaries between these groups. Tilly argues that boundaries emerge through imposition from the top, by elites or political authorities (2005, 137–45). These newly imposed boundaries are activated through various nation-building policies that then help shape the memories and identities of communities.

As the story of Georgios at the beginning of the chapter reminds us, Greek independence from the Ottoman Empire (March 25, 1821) is remembered as a chosen glory. Conversely, the minorities' memory of losing a decisive war in Anatolia against Turkish nationalists during the Greco-Turkish War is remembered as a catastrophe. The trauma of Greek losses in Anatolia still plays a significant role in the historical narratives and attitudes of officials when the topic of the Turkish Muslim minority is raised. We can therefore describe the shift from being a *millet* in the empire to a Greek nation-state as a period of transition—moving from relative coexistence between identity groups to a state of separation whereby identity categorization becomes clearer and identification with these categorizations strengthens.

Due to these glories and past traumas, the Greek state perceives the ethnic identity demands of the Turkish Muslim minority as a threat and associates their demands with another narrative, namely, one of Turkish interventionism in Greek affairs through their kin minority in Western Thrace.[8] Relatedly, when the Turkish Muslim minority reminds the Greek state of past traumas, which is motivated by a lack of social mourning among the minorities for these past tragedies, this act also triggers the Greek state's fear of losing territory and authority more generally.

Similarly, the Treaty of Sèvres (1920), which partitioned Anatolia between the Allied powers during the fall of the Ottoman Empire, can be viewed as a similar type of trauma, which Turks experienced. In official discourse, it is not difficult to see how threat perceptions about Greeks and the minorities erupt when Turkish officials raise the topic of Greeks in late Ottoman history. Arguably, Turkey winning the Independence War in Anatolia healed the trauma of the Sèvres Treaty to some extent, because with independence, the Turks no longer implemented the treaty. However, even remembering this past evokes emotions of threat, anger, and frustration that activate social boundaries and categorization between Greece and Turkey.

The Lausanne Treaty and Beyond: Boundary Consolidation

The Lausanne Treaty and the Population Exchange of Turkey's Greek Orthodox people and Greece's Turkish Muslim people became cornerstones for how Greece and Turkey as well as their respective minorities began to perceive each other. The old boundary of being a religious community under the empire turned into a new boundary defined in ethnoreligious, nation-state terms. The Population Exchange provided a new majority-minority boundary categorization for the Turkish Muslim community in Western Thrace and for the Greek Orthodox community in Istanbul.

These parties have adapted to the new boundaries, and the salience of these boundaries has fluctuated over time due to the states' institutional actions and narrative practices. As Tilly (2005) argues, the relationships on either side of the boundary and across the boundary help the actors to form their collective stories about these relationships, which eventually form the identities of the actors in these boundary zones. Greek and Turkish institutional practices related to their respective nation-building processes not only consolidated the boundaries between the minority and the majority, so, too, did the state's (negative) reciprocal actions in how they have managed minority affairs.

This boundary consolidation is an incremental process and boundaries are dynamic. They shift due to the nature of the relationships, perceptions, emotions, and the discourses actors use. They can change positively or negatively and can evolve step by step (Tilly 2005). When interstate or minority-state relations and their corresponding perceptions, emotions, and discourses became more positive during times of rapprochement in Greek and Turkish relations, the boundaries between these actors are erased. The importance of the boundary diminishes or deactivates and the salience of the boundary decreases. However, when interstate relations sour, the boundary inscription (the importance of the boundary increases) or boundary activation (the salience of the boundary increases) become visible.

The Cyprus conflict triggered Greece and Turkey to engage in negative reciprocal behavior toward their respective minorities. These actions intensified existing polarization and boundaries between both countries' minorities and majorities. Most of the minority members referred to the conflict as another event that consolidated the boundary between their minority communities and the majority. According to the minorities, when the conflict emerged, the media and political authorities' use of negative rhetoric directed at the minorities created a situation in which Greece and Turkey made scapegoats out of their identity groups, legitimizing further discriminatory acts such as the 1955 and 1964 incidents in Istanbul or the implementation of Article 19 of the Greek Constitution. This resulted in mutual losses for both minorities as social divides deepened and Greece and Turkey increasingly used power over the minorities. Any gains made during periods in which Greece and Turkey applied positive reciprocity were also lost.

To a degree, Greece and Turkey projected their kin's suffering in Cyprus on their minorities as a form of structural violence that caused their minority citizens to be dehumanized. Various minority policies and institutional practices implemented by both countries created more inequality between the minorities and the rest of the population, systematically disadvantaged minorities, and constrained their self-fulfillment and individual agency. The minorities were not permitted to access resources and opportunities freely available to other Greeks and Turks. The policies favoring the ethnic and religious core (the majority) during the nation-building process eventually caused the emergence of negative stereotypes about out-groups (the minorities in this case). Therefore, perceiving the out-group as a threat became inescapable. As discussed in reference to minority youth in both Greece and Turkey, negative policies and their effects on minorities triggered the minorities to engage in intergroup comparison in the form of socioeconomic and political relative deprivation.

Regardless of ideology, therefore, any policy or institutional practice that places minority members—directly or indirectly—in an unequal position socioeconomically, politically, or in terms of their cultural life in comparison to the rest of the society can be viewed as state-led structural violence. This book's findings show that minorities' references to a fear of becoming lost, either through demographic policies or through the denial of ethnic identity, have direct connotations with the institutional practices, policies, or discourses that previously harmed their communities and disadvantaged them societally. As members of the minorities noted, they felt invisible for a long time. This invisibility also strengthened the social boundaries between them and their respective majorities. In this social environment, minorities experienced internal conflicts between their minority and citizenship identities.

By way of example, the laws forbidding minorities from working in certain sectors in Turkey had a huge effect on the minorities' sociopsychological and economic development. Greece and Turkey put their minorities in a disadvantaged position in comparison to the majority through the systematic implementation of a social policy (employment). This form of structural violence, which prevented the minorities from accessing specific jobs, also constrained their individual agency. The Turkish Muslim minority in Western Thrace was also subject to policies that led to similar circumstances. In comparison to the Greek Orthodox community of Istanbul, however, minorities in Western Thrace believe that socially unjust state policies continue to be found in Greece more so than in Turkey. As they argued, the economic crisis and the COVID-19 pandemic have only served to widen and deepen the socioeconomic gap between the minority and the majority, with ever-limited opportunities and resources available to minorities.

From Greek-Turkish Relations and Boundaries to Minority Memory Space

As boundaries between social groups gain in salience, due to one (negative) incident or period, the strength of the same boundary can diminish at other times depending on the situation. As one expert noted, with the emergence of a new *other* (the Kurdish minority) as a threat to national identity, the Turkish state has begun to perceive the Greek Orthodox of Istanbul as less of a threat. This underscores how boundary salience between the state and the Greek Orthodox minority has fluctuated over time. Crucially, most of the positive socioeconomic, cultural, and political developments between social groups emerge when the boundaries structuring their interactions lose their significance. For Istanbul's Greek Orthodox minority, given that so few of them remain in Turkey and the state no longer views them as a significant threat, they believe officials feel more comfortable about making progress on minority issues. More specifically, they view the reemergence of a nostalgic narrative about the Istanbul Greek Orthodox people as one of the *lost colors* of the Turkish nation as a reflection of the declining importance of majority-minority boundaries.

When boundaries change and states no longer perceive minorities as a threat, minorities' demands on the state are met more easily. This, in return, increases the minorities' agency and their visibility in society. This changing status also allows the minorities to question the honesty of the state's rhetoric and behavior toward them. As previously noted, tolerance and inclusivity are norms that states are expected to adhere to as a participating member of the modern state system where the respect for human rights is enshrined in various treaties and international conventions. However, the Istanbul Greek Orthodox minority, for instance, connects this rhetoric to the Ottoman tolerance of minorities that was built on expansive rights provided to non-Muslim *millets* in general. Though minorities argue that rhetoric on tolerance and inclusivity is necessary, when this rhetoric is not matched with substantive state policies that address minority issues specifically, there is little chance for minorities to become more equal in society. This lack of substantive change only serves to strengthen the boundaries between the minorities and the majority. Further, the Turkish state's emphasis on rhetoric also allows officials to give the impression internationally that they fully accept their minorities.

In Western Thrace, the Greek state's denial of the Turkish Muslim minority's ethnic identity is one of the major issues structuring state-minority relations. The boundaries between the state and the minorities become repeatedly salient as the respective parties engage in identity discussions. The more the minorities emphasize their identity demands, the more the state perceives them as a threat. From the Greek state's perspective, if the state accepts the Turkish Muslim minority's identity demands, it means accepting Turkey's de facto rule in Western Thrace. The minorities' identity demands have the effect of triggering historically built threat perceptions between Greece and Turkey, which results in a lack of honest policy change or state hesitation to meet the needs of the minorities. This has created a lose-lose situation for both parties whereby their relations are structured around stronger boundaries, a lack of trust, the reduced visibility of the minorities in Greek society, a diminishing sense of belongingness among the minorities in Greece, and an associated lack of attachment to their citizenship identity. This is despite the structural changes the Greek state introduced in the 1990s specific to the minorities. The minorities did not view most of these historic changes as either sufficient or genuine. The minorities even view more recent minority education policies that Greece introduced with suspicion. Minorities expect transformative changes in how the state handles their demands and needs given the state's membership in the European Union as well as their state's perception of itself as the home of democracy.

Even if Greece and Turkey's perceptions of their minorities are slightly different, common ground can be found regarding how both minorities experienced historical injustices and traumatic incidents. Official narratives in both countries acknowledge their negative past, agreeing that the minorities were the targets of unjust events and practices, but state officials hesitate to take any responsibility for that past. Rather, they engage in a blame game, suggesting the other party is at fault for past wrongdoings or the relative deprivation that minorities experience today. This blame game only serves to strengthen the social boundaries structuring majority-minority relations in both countries. When the state does not accept responsibility but seeks to make profound institutional policy changes, there is only limited room for healing and social reconciliation.

In addition to blaming the other side, the issue of generalizing injustice is also problematic because when guilt is generalized, the negative affect of the injustice is lessened, and the lack of responsibility is perceived as legitimate. Greek and Turkish official discourse generalizes past injustices, suggesting those incidents happened everywhere in the world. To some extent, it is true that there were (and continue to be) injustices throughout the world. However, genuine state leadership can only emerge when leaders acknowledge the past mistakes that occurred in their own territories and provide guarantees (through policy, changes in mentality, official narratives, and rhetoric) that the past will not be repeat itself.

For the minorities in Greece and Turkey, their minority memory space is where historically, categorically, and institutionally set social boundaries, which structure their relations with the state and the majorities, are negotiated daily. Minority memory work is, therefore, contested and reacts to the state's dominant memory forms. It is the minorities that hope their memory will create opportunity to make boundary changes. From a Foucauldian perspective, minorities' memory work challenges the dominant and hegemonic official construction of the past and becomes "contested territory, in which groups engaging in a political conflict promote competitive views of the past in order to gain control over the political center" (Misztal 2003). Minorities continue engaging in memory work; remembering and reminding others why they live the way they do in contemporary Greece and Turkey.

Is Boundary Change Observable? A Greek-Turkish Press Conference and Its Implications for Minorities

Symbolic boundaries have the potential to allow formerly conflicting parties to negotiate alternative ways of working together, how to perceive each other differently, and embark on a reconciliation process. In the narratives of the minorities, officials, and experts, there were hints that symbolic boundaries exist both within and across social boundaries. For example, youth minority members in Western Thrace mentioned boundaries between themselves and older generations in the minority community. They discussed how older community leaders do not take youth agency seriously. They also referred to the boundaries between themselves, Greek youth, and youth more globally to underscore the relative deprivation they experience in Western Thrace.

On the other side of the border, the Greek Orthodox minority of Istanbul mentioned the minority community's mixed identity and integration issues. They discussed the Greek Orthodox minority community's desire to open up their minority identity category to other minorities such as the Arab Orthodox community to preserve their numbers. Yet boundaries continue to exist between the two. However, instead of working on these symbolic boundaries, the community still experiences the consequences of stronger boundaries that stem from minority-majority categorization in Greece and Turkey. When considering how to embark on a reconciliation process, therefore, symbolic boundary issues can be areas to work on as alternatives to the historically and institutionally defined and quite rigid social boundaries.

In addition, minorities' expectation for a better future in their countries may increase when these neighboring countries begin to perceive each other as partners working toward a superordinate goal, a common interest, or a global or regional problem. One of the historical examples of this type of a work was Franco-German relations in the post–World War II period that brought the two together under the European Coal and Steel Community. Greece and Turkey have also managed to come together from time to time to solve their problems bilaterally (e.g., through exploratory talks beginning in the 2000s). However, the social boundaries between the two countries are so salient and strong that, even if they claim to come together for a dialogue in a constructive, open, and honest manner, these meetings are usually doomed to fail from the beginning.

Greece and Turkey started exploratory talks in 2002 on regional peace and stability but these talks were discontinued in 2016. After five years, they resumed talks in 2021 in Istanbul. After the sixty-first round of talks in January 2021, the Turkish president, Recep Tayyip Erdoğan, and the Turkish foreign minister, Mevlüt Çavuşoğlu, invited the Greek foreign minister, Nikos Dendias, to Turkey for a dialogue to find solutions to various bilateral and regional issues that have plagued their relations for years, including the militarization of the islands and islets in the Aegean Sea, the Eastern Mediterranean hydrocarbon and maritime boundary issues, the Cyprus negotiations, and refugee and minority issues (Antonopoulos 2021).

On April 15, 2021, the Greek foreign minister first met with President Erdoğan in Ankara, Turkey. Following this, both foreign ministers had bilateral meetings and met with the press. The press conference started with conciliatory remarks from the Turkish foreign minister. Çavuşoğlu mentioned the two countries' unique and historical neighborly relationship. By emphasizing Greece and Turkey's historical relations, the foreign minister underscored his state's desire for the two countries to engage in a bilateral dialogue to resolve their issues rather than with the interference of a third-party mediator, namely, the EU. He underlined Turkey's desire for constructive dialogue with Greece, concluding his speech with a positive story about his long-standing friendship with his Greek counterpart.

The real intent of the parties cannot be fully known. However, both their body language and the Turkish foreign minister's speech suggest the national boundaries between the two foreign ministers had lost salience. In that moment, the parties did not view each other as an enemy. The general atmosphere was positive and cordial. The Greek foreign minister spoke next and after a few conciliatory remarks, began to blame the Turkish side for the problems between the two countries. In an interview given by the Turkish foreign minister a couple of days following the incident, Çavuşoğlu noted:

> We discussed bilateral and regional issues with our Greek counterparts before the meeting. And right before the press conference, the Greek side told us they would not make any statements that would cause controversy and that they expected the same approach from us. I said to them that my conversation would be extremely constructive. I also said I would raise the issues we have disagreements over, but I would not use any blaming language and would highlight

> that the two countries need to solve these issues. . . . As I told them, I gave a very constructive speech but then we saw with dismay that the Greek side did not act honestly. . . . You make such a proposal and then derail the process. . . . It is not easy to advance relations when you have this attitude. . . . Although this happened, we are still hoping to continue our talks in a constructive manner.[9]

Among the claims and accusations that the Greek foreign minister levied at the Turkish side, one is particularly interesting given its connection to the minorities. In his opening remarks, the Turkish foreign minister referred to the minorities in Western Thrace as "Turkish minorities." The Greek foreign minister responded by referring to the Lausanne Treaty, noting that

> regarding the issue of the minority, of the Muslim minority, it is mentioned as such in the Lausanne Treaty, it is not us saying this. And, if I remember correctly, Turkey signed the Lausanne Treaty. This is the treaty. Whether Turkey likes it or not, the Lausanne Treaty is in force and will continue to be in force.[10]

The Greek foreign minister adopted confrontational language both here and throughout his speech, which contained similar threatening discourse. As he continued, the psychology of the Turkish side changed quickly. It was clearly understood that the national boundaries between the parties were growing in salience again.

When the Turkish foreign minister spoke for a second time at the press conference, the initial and cordial atmosphere had disappeared. It was replaced with negativity and posturing on both sides, as highlighted in their respective body languages and the content of the Turkish foreign minister's response. The Turkish foreign minister responded to all the accusations, reminding the Greek minister that

> in my speech, I did not use accusatory comments against Greece. We were hoping this first meeting would happen in a more positive atmosphere. However, Nicos Dendias made extremely unacceptable accusations against my country in his speech. . . . If you come here and speak like this, although we had mutually agreed to solve our problems between us, I have to answer you. . . . In Turkey, we accept the Greek Orthodox minority as Greek Orthodox. However, you say "no you are not Turkish, you are just Muslim" to the people who

> refer to themselves as Turks. This is neither humane nor acceptable under domestic law. . . . You try to give us a democracy lesson, but there are three ECHR [European Court of Human Rights] decisions about this issue and you do not allow these people to name themselves as Turks. So, who are they? Are they Greek Muslims? If they call themselves Turk, they are Turk. You need to approve this.[11]

Although the two ministers and their teams experienced the cycle of boundary change from less salient to more salient, less active to more active, the meeting's repercussions on the minorities are also noteworthy. After the meeting, I spoke to members of the Istanbul Greek Orthodox minority and asked them how they felt about what had happened. Their general view was neutral. They did not want to be involved in a political conversation or take sides because of the past traumas they had experienced. They did however highlight that the Greek foreign minister's speech appeared to have been delivered for the benefit of a Greek public audience or with the support of the EU and the US. Minority members did not like how issues that affected them directly were politicized. As one minority member noted,

> Both countries are dealing with a lot of problems right now. The major two are the pandemic and the economic crisis. While they need to focus on these, the issue is coming back to minorities again. I appreciate the Patriarchate's neutral approach. No parties should seek political advantage through minorities. I do not think there will be negative consequences for the Greek Orthodox minority because of this incident. We are not perceived as a threat anymore; there are only 2,000 people here.

Members of the minorities in both countries know about the historical incidents affecting their communities and other minorities, but they were not so aware of each other's feelings on contemporary issues or their daily struggles. Due to the social boundaries between the two minorities across a physical border, they know what the other side experiences only to some extent. As one Istanbul Greek Orthodox minority member stated,

> I do not know how the minority in Thrace felt about the ministers' comments, but I think we do not have the same status as the Western Thracian minorities. We are Greek Orthodox of Istanbul (*Rum*), meaning coming from Eastern Roma. In Western Thrace, they are

> not only Turkish; there are Roma, Pomak, and Turks. The Lausanne says they are Muslim minorities.

The Istanbul Greek Orthodox minority was silent on social media and mainstream media. There was no news about how the leaders of the minority community evaluated the meeting. On the other hand, minority media and Turkish Muslim minority leaders in Western Thrace disseminated news widely about the events (Erim 2021; Habipoglu 2021; Huseyin 2021). Community leaders were quite frustrated but not surprised by the Greek foreign minister's claims related to the denial of their Turkish ethnic identity. In every comment, the community leaders said it did not matter what the Greek foreign minister had said. They stressed that Greece was employing its usual denial politics to please its Greek (majority) constituency but whether the Greek state accepts it or not, "the Western Thracian minorities were Turkish in the past and will be Turkish forever" (Habipoglu 2021). It is clear national identity boundaries and minority-majority categorization between the Turkish minorities and the Greek state became more salient due to this incident.

Boundary change is, therefore, observable through both narratives and behavioral changes. When the root causes of conflicts are not addressed, any positive boundary changes are superficial and, in many cases, fleeting. However, boundaries can also change over time by gradually building relationships built on trust and fostering a reconciliation process. Working on historically and institutionally set national social boundary relationships such as in the case of Greece and Turkey, where complete reconciliation regarding past traumas is yet to be achieved and bilateral trust is superficial, any attempt to solve interstate issues may risk the parties becoming trapped in cycles of threat perception and blame games. However, focusing on achieving positive developments related to the minorities could help build the trust between the two countries that is necessary to work on more difficult issues. Working on alternative symbolic boundary issues (e.g., economic, social, and psychological issues relative to minority youth), working toward common regional goals (e.g., viewing the refugee issue as a regional problem instead of a bilateral issue), and prioritizing easier-to-solve issues (e.g., showing positive reciprocity in the areas of minority education, associational life, or religious issues) could start to build trust between the parties. This is essential to begin resolving more contentious contemporary issues constructively such as those related to maritime state sovereignty.

THREE

The Greek State and the Turkish Muslim Minority Memory

KADRIYE WAS SITTING in front of the window early in the morning, waiting until it was time to go to the tobacco harvest. Although she was tired, she couldn't sleep. She was thinking about her children's lives, about her husband, daughter-in-laws, son-in-laws, and others in her family. She was thinking about everybody except herself, her life, and her future. Her fragile thoughts moved to her minority community, to her people. She had always cared more for others throughout her life. This is what it means to be a minority woman in Western Thrace. Being a woman in the Turkish Muslim minority community means constantly struggling to earn a living, rotting away in the tobacco fields, and serving your husband and kids by cooking the best meals and making the most delicious börek [pastry]. You must do all of this to be considered a real woman.

Then, Kadriye remembered what happened a month ago. The conflict in Cyprus had just started but nobody really understood what was going on. All the neighbors were trying to understand what was happening from the Turkish language radio. She was not sure who reported it, but someone said the Greek police were listening to the Turkish radio. Then a few bad-tempered-looking [Greek] police officers raided the neighborhood. A small fight broke out and since her husband was right in the middle of the situation, they took him to the police station.

Kadriye remembered the horror of that night, and her thoughts about how she couldn't live without her husband, and how she couldn't explain the situation to her children if her husband never came back. She also remembered how her neighbors embraced her with their kind words and actions. They had tried to comfort her. They brought food, took care of the children, and never left her alone while she was dealing with this trauma.

These women were also the same as her, their hands were calloused from working in the fields, and as anxious as Kadriye was. They were also unsure about what would happen tomorrow. But until that time, they had made an unspoken promise to each other, to stand side by side, together, against all the problems that come from being a minority woman.

Then, the next day, Kadriye saw her husband at the entrance to their neighborhood. She remembered how happy she had been to see him and how in love she still was with her husband although she was always complaining about him on any normal day. Startled, she heard her husband's voice: "Good morning, my dearest wife. You are an early bird today!" She understood that it was time for the tobacco harvest. It was a new day and she bid farewell to her sorrowful thoughts.

—Kadriye's story, as told by her grandson, a Turkish Muslim minority youth member, Western Thrace, 2021

Kadriye's story is similar to the stories of other minority women who live a traditional village life (men usually work on the farm and women both work the farm and take care of the house and kids) and experience the intersectional disadvantages of being both a minority and a woman in Western Thrace. Yet minorities in Western Thrace are not a homogenous group. There are approximately 150,000 Muslims in Western Thrace where they mainly live in the region's three largest cities, Xanthi (İskeçe), Komotini (Gümülcine) and Alexandroupolis (Dedeağaç). Fewer than 5,000 Muslims live on the islands of Rhodes and Kos (Katsikas 2012, 445). More than 10,000 Muslims live elsewhere in Greece, mostly in Athens (Tsitselikis and Mavrommatis 2019, 7). The population also consists of three subgroups: ethnic Turks (around 50%), Pomaks (around 35%), and Roma people (15%). The Turkish language is used overwhelmingly by minorities. Tsitselikis and Mavrommatis highlight that the Greek state accepts Turkish as the language of the minority and all language and education-related rights of the minority are acknowledged only in Turkish (2019, 9). For instance, minority schools teach the Turkish language for both ethnically Turkish and ethnically and linguistically Slavic-speaking Muslims, or Pomaks (Dragonas and Frangoudaki 2006, 23).

The Turkish Muslim minority views themselves as locals of the land because of their centuries-long connection to this area. Historical accounts date the first appearance of a Turkish-speaking population in what is now known as Greece to around 1000 AD; records from the thirteenth century show that a sizable population of Turks existed when Turkish-speaking nomads and warriors arrived in the region, which at the time belonged to the Byzantine Empire. Since the fourteenth century, they were ruled by the Ottoman Empire, then by Bulgarian and French rule, and finally now they live under the rule of Greece.

Their existence developed a political significance when the land changed hands from the Ottoman Empire to Greece with the latter's independence. While they belonged to a dominant identity group in the empire, the very existence of Muslims within the new Greek state became an issue. After the 1919–22 Greco-Turkish War, the two new nation-states decided to rid themselves of their minority populations, only allowing a small portion of them to stay in their territories. Along with Istanbul's non-Muslim populations, which included Armenians, Jews, and Greek Orthodox communities, as well as the Greek Orthodox of the Imbros and Tenedos islands, the Muslim minority of Western Thrace, which included the Turks, the Pomaks, and the Roma, were exempt from the Population Exchange.

Ever since, the fate of the Greek Orthodox minority and the Turkish Muslim minority has been tied to the evolving interstate relations between Greece and Turkey. These relations are shaped by how both countries apply the principle of reciprocity to manage minority affairs. Since the Population Exchange, the Turkish Muslim minority has struggled to become an integral part of Greek society, facing social and institutional barriers. Based on interviews conducted in Greece, both the minorities and state authorities blame each other for this lack of integration while some also blame their respective sides directly, as examined in this chapter. Although there are contested views from time to time among the minority community, the Turkish Muslim minority view Greek state policy toward their community historically as largely negative because of how the state created a reality in which the minorities live under constant state scrutiny both locally and nationally.

In what follows, the Greek state's minority policies are discussed with a focus on the Turkish Muslim minority. Next, this chapter examines how the past has influenced the ways in which the Turkish Muslim minority maintain their identity while advocating for their rights. These historical accounts illustrate how the minority uses memory, particularly when they highlight how important remembering the past is to exist and to demand their needs and rights today as a minority. These narratives also reveal signs of unresolved historical traumas in the Turkish Muslim minority population, in addition to the generational transmission of the past. In their memory work, the minority community highlighted the interconnectedness between contextual changes and structural changes. This link illustrates the ups and downs in the state's minority policy in light of changes in Turkish-Greek relations, Greece's EU membership, economic crisis and depression periods, and similar events. Their historical narratives also displayed the *in-between* position of the minorities regarding their perceptions of the concepts of belongingness, loyalty, and citizenship.

Greece's Institutional Practices and the Turkish Muslim Minority

Minority Education

With the establishment of the Republic of Turkey in 1923, the country embarked on a process of modernizing education, which included supporting minority education. Greece followed this modernization process by printing schoolbooks using Latin scripts while also allowing the use of Arab scripts. This approach by the Greek Ministry of Education is perceived as the government providing support to modernists within the minority community (Aarbakke 2000, 133). In the early 1930s, bilingual primary schools (Greek and Turkish) attended only by students of ethnic Turkish origin reached almost 300 schools. This number was reduced to less than half as of 2018 (Huseyinoglu 2018; Tsitselikis and Mavrommatis 2019), 99 in 2022 (Gülnaz Özcan 2022), and 86 as of 2025.

Minority education in Western Thrace has always fallen short in terms of its quality due to the lack of a comprehensive minority education policy in Greece. During the dictatorship of General Ioannis Metaxas (1936–41) and the Greek Civil War (1946–49), the Turkish Muslim minority lived in a state of unpredictability regarding the education field because of the various issues in minority schools such as a lack of teachers and a lack of quality curriculum.

The 1951 Cultural Agreement (abolished by a new Protocol on Cultural Cooperation signed by Greece and Turkey in 2000) created some positive developments in both countries regarding the number of teachers, textbooks, curriculum, financial aid, and scholarships. Each country sought to appease the other by treating their own minorities better so their kin minorities would have access to better education. This positive approach to minority affairs, however, was not perceived as an extension of a comprehensive minority integration policy where minority development was a priority for either Greece or Turkey. As Vemund Aarbakke highlights,

> The Greek administration always supported the *Medrese* (religious schools) and it spent billions from the secret funds to keep it running. . . . the Greeks would let the Muslims practice their religion, but not become educated. . . . there have always been some dubious intentions behind the management of minority schools, and claims that many totally incompetent persons were given positions as teachers. (2000, 148–49)

Despite this perception, the Greek state took positive steps in relation to Turkish Muslim minority affairs. One of these changes was in the education law of 3065/1954 after which the state started referring to the minority as *Turkish* rather than *Muslim*. This law also provided financial support to minorities to build or repair schools and allowed Turkey to support these schools financially. Turkey wanted to educate minority children and schoolteachers from Western Thrace in Turkey, which Greece permitted. Both countries participated in teacher exchanges while minority community members received scholarships to study at Turkish teacher colleges each year (Aarbakke 2000, 134–45). However, the eruption of the Cyprus conflict in the mid-1950s[1] changed relations between the two countries dramatically and neither state hesitated to implement strict measures on minority education.

During the military junta regime in Greece between 1967 and 1974, Greek authorities implemented numerous discriminatory policies in the society, not excluding the minorities in Western Thrace. Turkey's deportation of Greek passport holders from Turkey in 1964 and its intervention in Cyprus further expanded the Greek state's negative treatment of minorities. Greece reciprocated the actions of Turkey by reducing the numbers of the Turkish Muslim minority in Greece with policies such as those that deprived the minorities of their citizenship as in the case of Article 19 of the Greek National Code of 1955. Konstantinos Tsitselikis highlights some of Greece's discriminatory actions in the field of education:

- Changing Turkish toponyms on minority teachers' diplomas who had studied in Turkey to their Greek variant, as a mirror practice in response to measures Turkish authorities applied to Greek Orthodox teachers (1964)

- Maintaining the same rate of use of the official language in the curriculum (1965)
- Obliging both Greece and Turkey to regulate the status of minority schools as having either private or public legal character, which would allow manipulation of the grade and quality of the educational autonomy of both minorities (1965)
- The mutual prohibition of Greek and Turkish textbooks by both governments and the redistribution of these on an entirely reciprocal basis (1966)
- Changing the name of minority schools from "Turkish" to "Muslim" (1968)
- Firing Muslim teachers from their posts in response to the dismissal of Greek Orthodox minority teachers in Turkey (1969)
- Both Greece and Turkey had to keep the same number of pupils who failed middle school entrance exams (1975). (2008, 84–85)

During the junta regime, the Greek state signed another cultural protocol that brought about some additional developments regarding Greek language instruction and teaching materials, but these policies were overshadowed by pressure from the state on minority schools. A recent report, *The Turkish Minority in Western Thrace: The Long Struggle for Rights and Recognition*, produced by the Minority Rights Group about Western Thrace's Muslim community, examines all of these periods and lists some of the issues in the field of minority education today (Verhás 2019), which include

- Uncertainty surrounding the educational autonomy of minority schools
- A lack of quality, well-designed, tailored textbooks for minority schools
- Issues regarding teaching staff such as a lack of competent teachers
- Textbook problems for the minority curriculum
- Effects of the Program of the Education of Muslim Children (PEM)

Although not active today, the opening of the Special Pedagogical Academy of Thessaloniki (EPATH) in 1968 was one of the most traumatic experiences for minorities. The Greek state opened this academy to educate aspiring teachers to teach the Turkish language to minority children. Rather than prevent teachers coming from Turkey under the quota policy to teach minority children, the Greek government established this teacher training institute, but the quality and qualifications of the graduates were lacking as minorities highlighted in their narratives. As minority families mentioned, the Greek state tried to indirectly control how minority children were educated by controlling how their future teachers were educated.

These teachers' salaries were paid by the Greek Ministry of Education and the candidates were chosen from Greece's mountainous regions from among originally Slavic-speaking Pomak people and mostly low-income Muslim minority families. These prospective teachers saw EPATH as a significant opportunity for their future and after five years of Islamic religious education (at *medrese*), they enrolled in EPATH, graduated with a degree but with little knowledge of the Turkish language they were meant to teach given that a majority of their classes were taught in Greek (Aarbakke 2000, 149–50). While attending EPATH, aspiring teachers were exposed to the Greek nationalist vision of education, which demanded these teachers' obedience to the Greek state, and, on the other hand, public pressure from the minority. As one prospective teacher noted,

> Over the course of time, you lose your language and religion under the influence of some occupying powers. You are Turkophone Muslims. In other words, you are originally Greeks. . . . Gentlemen! There are no Turks in Greece. If there is anyone among you who says he is a Turk, he can go to Ankara! . . . That is where the Turks are. Do not leave them here! (Aarbakke 2000, 151)

In a letter to the minority-led newspaper *Ileri*, one EPATH graduate said,

> I am a graduate of the Special Pedagogic Academy. But I have no intention to be appointed. Because here in Xanthi, it is a very delicate question: Some were called sellouts, some spies, and some heroes! What can I say? I have become confused and decided to be a laborer. (Aarbakke 2000, 153)

Another state policy that is central to the minorities' historical narratives is the policy that created obstacles for returning high school or university students from Turkey who found it incredibly challenging to receive a Greek equivalency diploma. If they attend colleges in Turkey, returning to Greece also creates additional trauma for the minority members because of the substantial amount of time it takes for Greek authorities to recognize degrees obtained in Turkey. They can sometimes require additional qualifications. It is known widely within the minority that the Inter-University Center for the Recognition of Foreign Degrees (DIKATSA) system created these obstacles for college graduates in the mid-1980s. The approval of their degrees obtained at Turkish universities became another battle for the minority community, which reached its peak in June 1987 when these students went on a hunger strike (Aarbakke 2000, 165).

In recent years, an increasing number of minority youth attends Greek colleges after the positive discrimination of the 0.5 percent quota brought for the minority youth in Greek college entrance exams. According to the Turkish Muslim minority,[2] the quota helped some of the children from the minority to attend university in Greece. Importantly, they also highlighted that most minority youth from rural areas still prefer to travel to Turkey to pursue higher education. According to these minority members, going to university does not mean that minority students will graduate or find employment easily. According to these interviewees, particularly among those who went to university,

- some succeeded and graduated (among these individuals some found a job while others did not)
- some dropped out for several reasons, including inadequate secondary education at minority schools prior to going to university or their inability to adapt. Among those that dropped out, some went to Turkey to further their education. Others did not continue their education after dropping out.
- some of them started their degree but found their chosen majors very difficult due to their inadequate secondary education. They decided to change to less difficult subjects.
- some of those students who traveled to Turkey to continue their higher education could not return to Greece to find work due to difficulties with degree accreditation issues in Greece.

This data corresponds with the findings of Askouni and Dragonas (2020):

> While the increase in the number of university entrants is an impressive development, individual trajectories vary. Only 37 percent of the admitted minority students managed to graduate within the mean graduation period of six years. Among the others, 25 percent only passed a few courses, while 18 percent seem to have been inactive. Twenty percent had discontinued their studies. Yet this figure may be deceptive since some students do not drop out but transfer

> elsewhere, often to a university closer to Thrace or to a higher education institution in Turkey. In sum, minority students' educational trajectory is rather skewed with only a little more than one out of three able to graduate on time. (252)

As the minorities highlight, affirmative action is a positive step, but the ability to go to a university does not ensure the condition of their lives after higher education will improve. Western Thrace remains the least educated part of Greece due to the legacy of these educational policies implemented throughout the 1980s and the early 1990s. The minorities' responses imply that affirmative action provides a great opportunity for minority youth but only if it exists in tandem with progress on the larger social issues regarding minority social inclusion, integration, adaptation to social life, and changing the majority's perceptions.

Askouni and Dragonas (2014) discuss the perceptions of minority youth regarding the opportunities brought about by the 0.5 percent quota. As they also mention in their work, their research does not aim to examine the impact of this opportunity on minority youth lives after higher education. There is a need for further research on quantity versus quality in minority education. The number of minority students attending Greek universities may not provide us with significant data on how this impacts the overall quality of minority education. The number of students also does not tell us if minority students develop significant job and life skills that prepare them to integrate into life in Greece. The 0.5 percent quota and its impact after graduation should be thought of holistically.

Minority education is not only about books, classrooms, and teachers. Minority education must also be concerned with educating society to change perceptions toward coexistence. Without intersecting discussions between the minority and the majority, "institutional biases and structural aspects of the discrimination" and "the stigma that the minority identity carries as being the 'enemy' within the country" (Mantouvalou 2009, 493) will continue.

Another initiative that facilitated the development of minority children's education was the Project for Reform in the Education of Muslim Children (PEM) in Western Thrace, which was implemented between 1997 and 2019. This EU-funded project tried to put aside past political issues and provide a systematic educational policy for the minorities in Western Thrace. The project aimed to introduce Greek language education, develop educational materials, work with the community, and provide teacher training for bilingual educational environments (Dragonas and

Frangoudaki 2006). As in any state-initiated minority project, the project implementers received criticism both from the minority and the majority. The PEM project was not initially supported by the minority community due to the minority's lack of trust in any state-initiated policy, but they eventually supported the project. On the other hand, the project's implementers received criticism from Greek nationalist media and religious authorities.

Although the project delivered some positive outcomes such as the development of minority school pupils' Greek language skills, a decrease in minority school dropout rates, and an increase in the rate of secondary school attendance (Verhás 2019), "the Greek government had drawn up a one-sided program," as the project's implementers admitted (Dragonas and Frangoudaki 2006, 35). The idea of a bilingual dual-literacy education was, in reality, an education delivered largely in Greek. Minority families who had been in need of good quality education for their children for decades were once again forced to adapt to a state-determined minority education system.

Another issue in the field of education that still affects the minority community is the lack of bilingual nurseries and preschools. According to Law No. 3518/2006, preschool education in Greece has been compulsory since 2007. The new law is not in line with international and bilateral agreements concerning the minority education system. All pupils with different linguistic, religious, and cultural backgrounds from across the country, as well as members of the Turkish minority of Western Thrace, are obliged to follow the compulsory preschool education, which is taught only in Greek. The new law on preschool education does not stipulate any special measures for minorities (Hüseyinoğlu 2013; Chairoula and Amptourachman 2010).

Therefore, as some of the minority youth who experienced the process themselves noted, children are taken from their environment and placed in another that is somewhat alien to them. Specifically, they feel isolated due to their lack of Greek language skills. Minority children exist in a Turkish-speaking social environment where they speak Turkish at home, they live in Turkish-dominated villages, and watch and listen to Turkish-speaking media. Their only experience with Greek, as a result, is their preschool education. They feel traumatized even years later when discussing their preschool experiences.

Last but not least, today, minority education in Thrace is also experiencing the contradictions of the liberal-communitarian divide, as Dragonas (2013) rightly highlights. Due to the lack of recognition of religious and linguistic differences as well as the lack of protection of these differences in the public sphere, Greece's approach to minority education is not a liberal one. With the prevalence of a monoculture (Greek Orthodox) in every realm of society and limited emphasis on multiculturalism, minority education remains primarily protected by the Treaty of Lausanne. In addition, bilingual minority schools have "two parallel monolingual curricula" (Dragonas 2013) that are not aligned with each other in terms of design, curricula, and teacher collaboration.

Population Policies

Article 19 of the Greek Citizenship Law (issue number 3370), which was in effect between 1959 and 1998, was a major discriminatory population policy of the Greek state in Western Thrace. According to the law, "A citizen of non-Greek origin leaving Greece without the intention of returning may be declared having lost Greek citizenship."[3] Through the application of this article in Greece, "this relatively young (1832–) state attempted to rid itself of a host of members of ethnic or 'politico-ideological' groups viewed by the state as dangerous to the country's wished-for homogeneity, or even its territorial integrity" (Sitaropoulos 2004, 205). More than 60,000 Turkish Muslim minority members lost their Greek citizenship and were forced to live as *heimatlos* (stateless people). The Greek state began applying this "overtly racially/ethnically discriminatory provision and the relevant state practice" (Sitaropoulos 2004, 206) in 1955 and continued it until 1998. This policy's main aim was to balance out the Turkish Muslim minority population in Thrace with respect to the Greek Orthodox minority in Istanbul (Anagnostou 2005, 338). According to expert estimates, nearly 50,000 Muslims in Thrace lost their citizenship (Anagnostou 2005; Sitaropoulos 2004). According to others (Anonymous 2018b; Grigoriadis 2008), this number is higher at around 60,000.

In many cases, members of the Turkish minority who had traveled to Turkey for summer vacation learned at customs that they had lost their citizenship in accordance with Article 19. As such, the implementation of Article 19 was similar to the 1964 deportations in Turkey, in that it was arbitrary. However, Article 19 differed in that it was enforced without prior notice. The policy was implemented "without consulting the interested individuals or families, who would often find out that they were no longer Greek citizens upon their re-entry to Greece" (Anagnostou 2005, 339).

As with other traumatic state policies in Greece and Turkey, this policy was the result of tensions in Cyprus. Turkey's military intervention in

Cyprus to protect its kin people, the Turkish Cypriots, against the Greek Cypriots in 1974 increased the implementation of the citizenship law dramatically in Greece. As Dia Anagnostou underscores, this law's implementation went against both Greece's internal laws and its commitments as a signatory to various international agreements. Neither Greece's readmission to the Council of Europe in 1975 nor Greece's EU process, nor Greece's transition to democracy through the new constitution after the military junta, helped ease the tension (Anagnostou 2005, 339).

The reason neither international actors nor internal laws could change ongoing discrimination against the Turkish Muslim minority in Thrace was directly related to the nature of why this policy was implemented. It emerged out of the power struggle, historical hatred, and political retaliation between Turkey and Greece. As Anagnostou notes, "The tenacity of Article 19 must be understood as an intrinsic expression of 'cultural idiom'" (2005, 16). The implementation of Article 19 in Greece and the 1964 deportation in Turkey were similar reflections of these two countries' mindsets. This mindset was shaped through each country's historical experiences and perceptions of the other, as a threat to their respective ethnic and religious national unity. These population policies created a space for political authorities to arbitrarily and non-empathetically deprive the needs of their minorities.

The adoption of Article 19 was not only a major source of deprivation for the minority but also of trauma as revealed through their own testimonies. While some became Turkish citizens, others became citizens of other European countries, or were forced to live as *heimatlos*. For the minorities, the Greek state applied this policy to reduce the Turkish Muslim minority population in Greece. The state abrogated the law in 1998 but it was not retroactive. Therefore, most of the Turkish Muslim minority who lost their Greek citizenship have not regained their status, leaving them deprived of their rights. As one minority member stated,

> You are going on summer vacation somewhere and when you come back, the officials do not allow you to enter your country. The Greek state told us: "Okay, now you are not a Greek citizen and you are not allowed to enter your house." Think about the trauma that these people experience at that moment when they are at the border with their families, kids, etc. (Minority association representative, interview, 2013, Komotini)

Another minority member spoke of the population policies in a historical context, arguing that

> Our relations were good until 1960. We lived side by side. Then the Cyprus incidents started, and nationalist feelings increased. The Greek government supported this increase in nationalist sentiment. The distance between Greeks and Turkish people increased with the Cyprus conflict. During the junta regime, this distance also increased. The junta brought the Vlachs [Karakaçanlar][4] and settled them in Western Thrace. They are like nomads. The state said, "You are Greek from now on!" The state extended bank credits to them. Then, the 1974 [Turkish] intervention in Cyprus happened . . . the policies of discrimination increased. (Retired teacher, interview, 2013, Komotini)

Beyond the reality of the loss of citizenship, for many within the minority community, the arbitrary deprivation of minority rights has become a natural part of their lives. The normalization of injustice has not only served to make the Turkish Muslim minority feel more deprived but has also kept the trauma of their experiences of injustice alive in their memories. As one academic figure argued,

> The Greek state's discrimination against the minority never stopped. The real aim of the citizenship policy was to force minorities to migrate to Turkey or elsewhere. It was to get them to leave one way or the other. Since 1923, they have made a significant effort to erase the minority population from Western Thrace. When the state could not achieve this, the Greek state arbitrarily applied Article 19 of the citizenship code, continuing its application for more than thirty years. It is so unfortunate that people could not come back to Greece and lost everything. (Interview, 2013, Komotini)

Religious Clergy Policies

The Greek state continues to strictly control the religious authorities who manage conflicts around family or inheritance issues within the minority community. Minority community members are free to choose the manner in which they seek to address conflicts and are not required to follow Islamic law to resolve these matters. According to the minorities, the Treaty of Athens (1913), the law of 2345/1920, and the Lausanne Treaty allowed Muslim minorities to elect muftis (religious clergy) in Komotini (Gümülcine) and Xanthi (İskeçe). In reality, they have not been elected, but rather appointed by the Greek state since 1985 when the muftis of Xanthi and Komotini died. Elites from within the minority began calling for elections, pointing to the Patriarch in Istanbul as an example (Hüseyinoğlu 2016, 33–34).

Consequently, the state appointed two muftis in accordance with the law, while the minority in Thrace elected its own muftis in a show-of-hands vote. As Samim Akgönül (2008) indicates, the main controversy concerned how the state recognized its appointed muftis as the legitimate authority. In addition to the Greek state controlling mufti elections, the community-elected muftis faced repeated prosecution. When I raised this issue with state officials in Greece, they referred to the Greek constitution, which legally permits the state to appoint judges. In addition, they referred to the role of the Patriarchate in Istanbul and how the Greek Orthodox minority pursues legal matters through civil law proceedings, rather than religious law. However, the Turkish Muslim minority in Western Thrace views the state's control over muftis as controversial. They argue that while the patriarch is chosen by the Holy Synod, the Turkish Muslim minority is prevented from choosing the muftis of Western Thrace.

As it currently stands, there are appointed muftis the state recognizes who are not recognized by the minority community, and there are elected muftis who are not recognized by the state but recognized by the minorities. The minority community views the state's application of this new law as yet another tool of control. As one minority community member argued,

> Honestly, the government does not trust, and actually cares little about, the minority's opinion about the issues directly related to the community. It says: "This is the law, I made it, and you will obey it." But this law, and so the appointed mufti, has no meaning to the minority. The mufti issue concerns the very needs of the minority; it is about who we are. That's why, based on Lausanne, we should be able to elect the religious authority. The appointed mufti has no legitimacy in the eyes of the minority. The reason the government insists on the new law is because they want to choose muftis who will assist the government to further control and suppress the minority. The current mufti behaves as the government wants, because the appointed leader is the state's man. (Religious authority, interview, 2013, Komotini)

In addition, the Greek parliament's adoption of law 4115/2013, known as the 240 Imam Law, now grants the state the authority to appoint 240 Islamic religious leaders to teach the Holy Koran in Greek throughout mosques and public schools in Western Thrace (Hüseyinoğlu 2017).

Although many within the Turkish Muslim minority view this policy as a new government mechanism to control them, there is a paradox some of them mentioned. Even if the minorities disobey the appointed imams rhetorically, they nevertheless need to work with these authorities who must rule on judicial matters. The minority community has a "fear of losing gains." They do not want to lose what they gained from former treaties, which means they resolve their judicial issues through these religious authorities but reject the appointed muftis publicly.

Another issue the minority community referred to was the preference some of the minority have regarding the use of the Greek (secular) legal system[5] to resolve issues such as divorce, child custody, or inheritance. Some within the minority community view this option positively, while others believe the new law is another intervention of the government to take away the religious rights of the minority community.

Property and Economic Issues

Members of the Turkish Muslim minority referred to the discrimination they faced in their historical narratives, particularly regarding land and property confiscations as well as restrictions they faced buying or selling property, which was only permitted among Greeks. As Dia Anagnostou and Anna Triandafyllidou highlight, these "unofficial but widespread administrative practices that flourished around the prefecture systematically prevented Muslims from acquiring property or performing even routine matters" (2006, 5).

Moreover, minority members highlighted their economic deprivation that worsened after the economic crisis in Greece with the COVID-19 pandemic. For the minorities, they feel this crisis has affected them twice as much as it has affected the majority. The lack of state subsidies to continue farming led to extreme economic problems for many minorities and their families given the overwhelmingly agrarian nature of the minority economy. The main agricultural crop the Turkish Muslim minority produce is tobacco. However, when Greece joined the EU, certain restrictions were placed on tobacco production because of policies and regulations at the EU level. The subsidy for tobacco was reduced significantly, which meant the minority population lost one of its main sources of income.

Due to these hardships, many families have been pushed to the brink of separation or divorce, while others have lost family members who are forced to leave in search of economic opportunities elsewhere. Depression and suicide have affected others unable to find work. According to the minorities, their communities were already in a precarious situation economically in comparison to the majority, but now it has hit rock bottom.

Minority's Memory Work

These policies have influenced the ways in which the Turkish Muslim minority remembers the past and who they are today. The memory work the minority engage in is one of the most basic tools that is continuously developed and contributes to their minority identity.

Minority Memory Is Existential

Remembering past discrimination is a political act for the Turkish Muslim minority because, as they argue, the Greek state is engaged in a strong but invisible effort to erase the minorities' memories. For them, this is evident in every Greek policy related to Turkish Muslim culture, heritage, and education. Intentionally remembering their past by keeping memories of state discrimination and the injustices against the minority alive have become acts of advocating for their rights. For minority community members, remembering the past is also a means through which to build a better tomorrow, despite any betterment of the minority lives through policy reforms seen as marginal. As one minority member stresses,

> We shouldn't be lulled into false pretenses when we see small policy changes. We must always be active in remembering and reminding everyone and the state what happened to us in the past. We should constantly tell the past to our children to keep them awake of their identity. To advocate for our rights, we should also remind the international arena and Greek policymakers about our past to make a better life for minorities here. If we stop remembering, we stop living as a minority and lose our identity. (Representative in a minority association, interview, 2013, Komotini)

Remembering is not only a means to advocate for a better life but also a major instrument used to sustain their minority identity. To analyze minority identity construction, it is important to understand how the minorities in Western Thrace construct these negative memories and how and why they transmit these memories intergenerationally.

For any social group, the historical incidents to remember, reconstruct, distort, and forgot can change for pragmatic reasons to serve the interests of group members in the present and the future (Ricoeur 2004; Nora and Kritzman 1996; Misztal 2003; Gellner 2008; Smith 1997). Turkish minorities follow the same path. Despite the presence of diverse and sometimes competing narratives, minorities in Western Thrace create their own memory space, focusing on the most dramatic and most devastating incidents they experienced in the past and transmitting these to newer generations to help them construct the meaning of their history as a minority.

While the Turkish Muslim minority's identity salience, personal involvement, and meaning making of the past are in low contrast to national Greek identity, it is just the opposite for the Turkish national identity. The minorities fear losing their identity and the socioeconomic and political gains they have received over time. Further, although the Turkish Muslim minority is not experiencing significant demographic erosion, as is the case with the Istanbul Greek Orthodox minority, they still believe their population is declining in numbers. As one minority member noted,

> We are a very reproductive community. We have large families with lots of children, especially in villages. If we had not been exposed to population policies and forced migration to Turkey and other places, we would be 500,000 people right now. (Health expert, interview, 2013, Komotini)

There is a degree of reality in this argument, but the narrative does not explain all of the reasons causing the minority's reduced numbers today. One of the reasons is that the minority gradually moved to the cities, becoming less agrarian, and followed the reproductive pattern of the majority, as is the case with all societies that move toward urbanization and modernity (Tsitselikis and Mavrommatis 2019). For the minority, their fewer numbers are related to the gradual state-led policies, including fewer subsidies and the expropriation of land. They highlight that the socioeconomic character of the minority began to change slowly and this prevented the minority from doing what they are good at. Another reason mentioned for why some have moved to urban areas was the state's decisions during the 2008–10 economic crisis. For these individuals, while they acknowledge that certain decisions affected the majority, the effect on the minorities was two or three times worse. That's why people who lost their jobs had to move to countries like Germany, the Netherlands, or elsewhere for seasonal work. These people usually left their families in the city. Therefore, for them, state policies during the 2008–10 economic crisis and, more recently, during and after COVID-19 indirectly forced many of them (from the minority) to leave their villages, their lives, and their minority schools. In sum, various factors, including modernity, urbanization, patterns of reproduction, and the disproportional impact of state policies on minorities, played a role in lessening the number of the minority today.

Therefore, for the Turkish Muslim minority in Western Thrace, dealing with the state's injustices can best be done by reminding younger generations and others interested in minority issues about what happened in the past. Retired teachers, former and current parliamentarians, the media, and others from within the minority all play a role in consciously transmitting the past to the present in Western Thrace. According to minority leaders, persistently remembering the past ensures that the Greek state avoids repeating its mistakes and prevents minorities from facing similar injustices. To reinforce the significance of their minority identity, they believe it is essential to remain connected to their past. For the minorities, therefore, history determines who they are in the present.

For minority members, teachers who graduated from higher education institutes in Turkey have been key actors in transforming the minority community in Western Thrace. Through the teachers' education, they have helped construct a new minority identity, increased awareness within the minority community, and defended the minority's rights. They remind their fellow minority community members about what happened in the past and explain how they can advocate for their rights in Greece and abroad. As described by retired teachers themselves, the major area of state discrimination against the minorities has always been education.

> The Greek state realized that the minorities were increasingly aware of their rights and of its identity because of the education Turkish teachers provided. The state also thought that Turkey was imposing its own nationalization policies on the minorities through the education system. Therefore, the Greek state had to be prevented one way or the other. (Retired teacher, interview, 2013, Komotini)

Minority media plays a central role in reminding the minority community about the past and in constructing the present. Minority media not only reminds its readers consistently about past incidents that disadvantaged their community but also helps build minority memory around these issues. There are several daily and weekly minority online newspapers (in Turkish and Greek) that publish news articles on minority news. These include *Gündem Gazetesi*, *Rodop Rüzgarı*, *Millet Gazetesi*, *Birlik Gazetesi*,

Trakyanın Sesi, and *Azınlıkça*. In addition to commemorating significant dates related to both historic traumas and glories[6] and promoting local events, festivals, and significant religious festivals, this media actively works to raise public awareness and concern regarding state policies affecting the minorities. They publish news about any positive and negative legal changes related to the minority community in addition to other current local, national, and international affairs. For instance, when the media discuss contemporary legal changes or government practices on issues affecting the minorities, the media first examines what this practice or change means and then reminds the broader community about how it relates to past injustices, finally reminding the community about their rights as enshrined in the Lausanne Treaty.

Most of the time, the past and the present are interwoven in the news. They always have news stories related to everyday problems affecting the minority, such as the issue of religious clergy (*imams*), the management of their cultural foundations, and education issues, which were discussed in detail earlier in this chapter. In general, the narrative running through minority media not only highlights that the state ignores the needs of the minorities but also that it is failing to uphold the Lausanne Treaty, particularly regarding the articles that lay out how the state should treat its minorities.

Many minority media and its journalists believe the minority communities must claim their rights constantly and raise their voices against all sorts of discrimination, even if the state does not want to listen. They believe there is no other option. In doing so, the media plays a similar role to the teachers by reminding the minority population about their rights enshrined in the Lausanne Treaty, reminding the state about its responsibilities to the minorities, raising concerns about the harassment minorities face in their daily lives, and constantly stressing the minority's cultural codes—that is, their Muslim Turkish identity.

While part of the minority community is currently working toward consolidating the past through historical memories, some issues or concerns emerge from the minority community itself. One of these relates to the identity issues that young generations in the minority community experience. Minority youth are not a monolithic group, which means that their individual absorption of the historical narratives and their attachment to minority identity are different based on their family, education, friendship, and similar socialization choices. Unsurprisingly, some of the minority youth seem to have integrated more into Greek culture through their exposure to the Greek education system, language, and media than those who have rigid positions about their minority identity. Those who were born after 1990 did not experience any of the traumatic historical incidents affecting their minority communities directly. Rather, their indirect experiences of these events are the result of historical narratives told by their parents, community members, and educators.

For instance, some of the youth members I spoke with seemed more integrated into Greek society based on their identity narratives. They highlighted that they and their parents preferred Greek schools, they had no issues with having Greek friends, and their families are liberal in terms of lifestyle choices. These youth do not feel inferior to Greek youth more broadly. They are relatively distant or less interested in minority affairs or negative past incidents. Some of them said they know little about what happened in the past, adding that their parents had not shared many details about their community's history.

Some of the other youth feels as if they exist in a state of *in-between*. They described how they felt neither Greek nor Turkish. On the other hand, there is one group of youth whose minority identity salience is strong. As they highlighted, they feel relatively inferior from time to time in Greek society. This group of youth defends the rights of the minority strongly and is relatively distant from their youth counterparts who do not have a salient minority identity. These youth also learn Greek to directly communicate with the state when needed. While their preferences about attending Greek schools and having Greek friends from the majority varies, their attachment to their Turkish Muslim identity is very high comparatively with regard to the first group.

According to this last group of minority youth, if they integrate fully into Greek society, which is what the state also wants, they will lose who they are. They feel that this is also another threat to the minority—one that comes from inside the community. As one minority member noted,

> The minority is an enemy of the minority sometimes. There are minority members who do not even question the real aims of the state, choosing instead to side with the state. They do not feel any resentment being like the Greeks. Their children go to Greek schools, their friends are Greek, and they appear more integrated into Greek life than the minority's life. (Minority former politician, interview, 2013, Komotini)

Obviously, minority education is a double-edged sword for the Turkish Muslim minority. Parents experience this *in-between* feeling; they do not want their children to lose their minority identity, but they also feel guilty for not providing their children with a better education either in Greece or elsewhere. Although the quality of education in minority schools is perceived by the minorities as very low due to the state's ignorance on the issue, some of them still insist on sending their children to these schools or to Turkey because of concerns over losing their minority identity. On the other hand, some families prefer to send their children to better quality schools within the Greek education system or abroad if they have the financial means.

Unmourned Traumas and Transgenerational Transmission

Any event that affects a social group traumatically becomes a central part of their historical narratives. More specifically, when these chosen traumas (Volkan 2004) affect a minority's (minority) identity (related to their status, needs, or rights), they highlight these events or time periods often in their narratives. Generally, minorities highlight negative events and time periods in conversations because they fear history repeating itself. For the Turkish Muslim minority in Western Thrace, remembering the discrimination they faced during certain periods is more significant than focusing on stand-alone events.

The Turkish Muslim minority did not experience exactly the same events similar to the September 1955 incidents or the 1964 deportations that Istanbul's Greek Orthodox minority faced. However, in their historical narratives, the Turkish Muslim minority constantly referred to the effects of Article 19 on citizenship loss and other discriminatory policies the Greek state implemented from 1955 until the 1990s. The major historical periods they referred to with the greatest frequency were the Greek-Turkish War (1919–22) and the Lausanne Treaty (1923), the Greek Civil War (1946–49), the Cyprus conflict (starting in the 1950s), the junta regime (1967–74), and the governments of Konstantinos Mitsotakis (1990–93), Konstantinos Karamanlis (2004–9), and George Papandreou (2009–11).

Members of the minority who experienced the junta period directly are still alive and serve as a sort of information hub whereby they reproduce and transmit information regarding past events through memories to younger generations. These memories act like a *social glue*, holding together minority members, keeping them together, and sustaining their identities over decades. Their memories, in the form of historical traumas, affect intergroup relations in contemporary Greek society. These traumas live on because they are embedded in the minorities' memories and can be easily found in their everyday narratives.

For the minority, the periods preceding the Cyprus conflict and following the crisis (before the 1960s and thereafter) describe two different pictures concerning their relations with the majority. As they describe, Greek people (both the minority and the majority) saw each other as equals until the 1960s. They had good neighborly relations, respected each other, and cohabited. Things changed with the emergence of the Cyprus conflict, which caused them to lose this friendship environment and social harmony to a greater extent.

During our discussions, minority members spoke about the military junta regime that ruled Greece from 1967 until 1974 and the injustices they experienced during and after that period, which they believe affected them the most. Older generations, in particular, spoke directly about state policies, the resulting injustices, and the discrimination the minorities suffered. Some younger minority members discussed this period in their community's history as if they had experienced the military regime's harsh treatment directly. Irrespective of their age, when the Turkish Muslims in Western Thrace spoke of past events, they not only discussed the same events, but the sequencing of the events in their memories was markedly similar, which underscores how often these memories are shared, told, and retold within the community. As such, they all reflect on past events in a similar way even if most of them did not experience these events firsthand, which speaks to the prominence and effect of transmitting narratives intergenerationally.

The transmission of historical narratives from one generation to the next is achieved through formal (school system) and informal educational (oral history, museums, and commemorations) processes. Minorities engage in this transmission of the past to the present to create, preserve, and secure their minority identity, particularly in reaction to state policies threatening to erase this identity. Remembering, for these minorities, is instrumental and existential. The minority memory-building process in which the past is instrumentally transmitted to the present functions to both create and preserve minority identity and legitimize the minority's position in reaction to the dominant identity and narratives. In line with Brubaker's (1996) triadic configuration of relations between the minority, the kin-state, and the nationalizing state, the Turkish Muslim minority has established networks of interaction with Turkey, with the Greek majority, and with their national state (Greece). This web of relations also extends to international actors such as the EU (Çakmak and Hüseyinoğlu 2020, 4–7). Therefore, past collective traumas are connected to the contemporary relations the minority has with all these other actors. The deprivation of minority needs through certain historical incidents and already set power relations between these actors are the minority's motivational factors, prompting them to remain attached to these collective traumas.

Deprivation of Needs

Today, a key component of the Turkish Muslim minority's memory work is the denial of their ethnic identity. One member of the minority discussed the importance of ethnic identity, describing ethnicity as a glue that holds the minority members together.

> There is no place where everybody likes each other. You can see people write antiminority views in minority newspapers, you can see people who say things against the elected mufti, you can defend different political views, we argue with each other very harshly during election periods. These are fine in the realm of democracy. However, the Turks vote for Turks. Our Turkishness is our reason to live here as a minority. (Minority former politician, interview, 2013, Komotini)

The Greek state's denial of this ethnic identity motivates them to defend their rights in Western Thrace and abroad. The issue of identity denial is associated with various psychosocial changes within the minority community. Among these, the most important is their fear of losing their identity's ethnic character. Interestingly, this fear motivates the minority to be more attached to their minority (ethnic) identity. However, the stronger the minorities' identity demands become, the more the state resists these demands. This creates a vicious circle of psychosocial changes on both sides. The state and the majority question the minority community's belongingness (and loyalty) to the state. They view the minority community as an out-group threat due to their perceived rejection of integration and for not "behaving" like Greeks. This threat perception generates a security dilemma whereby the state further deprives the minorities of their rights. In turn, the minority perceives this as a reflection of strained relations and historical grievances with the state. The minority community feels more deprived and inferior socially, and they become more attached to their minority identity rather than their citizenship identity. This vicious cycle increases mutual suspicion on both sides and deepens the lack of trust between the minority and the state and the minorities' frustration and hopelessness for future relations.

The Lausanne Treaty referred to the minority in Greece as *the Moslem minority*. However, this description only defines the contours of the minority's religious composition. The Muslims of Turkish origin feel Turkish ethnically and want to use this ethnic descriptor in their daily interactions. Notwithstanding the reality that Greek state policy toward the minorities is based on denying this demand, there have been times throughout Greek history when the state has recognized the minority's *Turkishness* officially and unofficially. Greece's accession to the European Union in 1981 and its subsequent process of Europeanization from the late 1990s were particularly influential.

During an interview, the then foreign minister, George Papandreou, highlighted the minority's ethnic character, noting "no one doubts that there are many Muslims of Turkish origin. Of course, the Lausanne Treaty mentions only Muslims. If no one contests the present borders, I could not care less if one calls himself a Muslim or a Turk, a Bulgarian or a Pomak" (Grigoriadis 2008, 30). The Turkish Muslim minority of Western Thrace has never made territorial claims (on the Greek state), but their basic human need to have the state recognize their (ethnic) identity has been constantly denied. Persistent historical issues, prejudice, and distrust between the Greek state and the minorities have only fueled the state's denial of the minorities' ethnic identity, which eventually took on another form with the imprisonment of two high-profile minority members for acting in a way that contradicted state policy.

Specifically, the Greek state imprisoned Dr. Sadık Ahmet and İbrahim Şerif for using the word *Turkish* during his electoral campaign to describe the Turkish Muslim minority in Western Thrace. Following the 1989 elections, Greek authorities imprisoned them for disturbing public order (Hüseyinoğlu 2022, 296; Gökçen 2010). When referring to these incidents, minority community members first mentioned the Thracian minority's nonviolent protest march against the state in response to Greek authorities dissolving their associations in 1988 and, second, the January 29, 1990 incidents that emerged after Dr. Ahmet's imprisonment for defending the minority community's Turkish identity.

After the aforementioned trial, groups of Greek extremists attacked minority members, looted their shops, and broke windows (Hüseyinoğlu 2023, 510–14). This incident also triggered a diplomatic crisis. Greece declared the Turkish consul general, Kemal Gür, as persona non grata, expelling him from Greece. In retaliation, the Turkish authorities expelled the Greek consul general in Istanbul, Mr. I. Klis. The memories of these incidents are active in the narratives of minorities in Western Thrace.

Some minority members draw comparisons between these incidents and what took place in Istanbul during the 1955 incidents. For some, the expulsion of the Turkish consul general in the 1990s (after the 1989 elections) was actually related to the 1955 incidents in Istanbul, as historical violence, rather than the events that took place in the 1989 and 1990s. As one minority member explained,

> The minority's status in Western Thrace is always dependent on Greek-Turkish relations. And the critical word here is revenge. States can seek revenge on others like humans: they apply whatever policy is necessary reciprocally to eliminate minorities from their territories. When the Greek state sees any discrimination against the Greek Orthodox minority in Istanbul, they find ways to take revenge on the minorities of Western Thrace through discriminatory policies. [Minority] associations closed in Western Thrace because the Greek state denies the minority's Turkishness. It is the accumulated revenge of several incidents that happened in Turkey, like 1964, and like Cyprus. (Academic, interview, 2013, Komotini)

In response to the societal tension following Dr. Sadık Ahmet's trial, the Greek government established a 3 percent barrier for minority political parties to achieve before they could run in general elections, which was a major loss for the minorities and for their community's political representation.

The more the Greek state denies the Turkish Muslim minority of Western Thrace of their rights based on their *Turkishness*, therefore, the more attached they become to their identity and defend the rights of the minority. It appears their minority identity salience is strongly correlated to this denial. A minority member echoed this sentiment, stating that

> the period between 1975 and 1990 became the most difficult one [for the minority], when discrimination reached a peak. There was only one reason why we faced these discriminations: our Turkishness. The January 29 protest march became the breaking point for the minority. It was nonviolent, but it was like a scream. It was like saying "enough!" For example, you ask why you failed the driving

> license exam and are told, "You are Turkish, that's why." (Journalist for a local minority newspaper, interview, 2013, Komotini)

The Greek state's denial of the minority's ethnic identity reached another height when the state dissolved three minority associations in 1986 through local courts and the Supreme Court due to the use of "Turkish" in their signboards (Human Rights Council 2018). These associations were the Turkish Union of Xanthi (İskeçe Türk Birliği, established in 1927), the Turkish Youth Union (Gümülcine Türk Gençler Birliği, established in 1928), and the Western Thrace Turkish Teachers Union (Batı Trakya Türk Öğretmenler Birliği, established in 1936). Today, these associations remain officially dissolved although there is a European Court of Human Rights (ECHR) decision in favor of the associations.[7] These spaces are significant places for minority members to gather for social and cultural activities. For the minority, the dissolution and refusal to register associations is perceived as a form of denying their identity.

Another area around which the Turkish Muslim minority conducts heavy memory work is the field of education. Returning to the issue of EPATH teachers, one minority member indicates that the EPATH policy was also part of a larger strategy that the Greek state wanted to implement.

> The injustices never end. In the field of education, in the past, school boards were allowed to choose the teachers who taught our kids, but then the state took this right away from us. Then, the state established EPATH. EPATH teachers were graduates of madrassas [religious schools] and they only received two years of education to teach in minority schools. This then increased to three years, but it was still not enough because there was a very fundamental problem. These minority members were taught mostly in Greek. So, when you get your education in Greek, how can you teach classes in Turkish? This was on purpose. The state wanted to control minority education and reduce the quality of minority children's education more and more. (Former teacher, interview, 2013, Komotini)

As previously mentioned, the Greek state changed the curriculum and restricted the use of the minority's own language. Over time, many courses once taught in Turkish were taught in Greek. The textbooks used in these school were also problematic given the restrictions the Greek state put on teaching materials coming from Turkey. As one former teacher noted,

> Well, there are so many stories to tell you about the education issue. For example, the textbook issue. Turkey sent textbooks, but they were kept at Greek customs for a long time. Nobody knew how long it would take us to receive the new books. Therefore, we had to copy the old books to teach the Turkish children. When we were teaching about the theories of going to the moon in classrooms, the first man had already gone to the moon! Officials were investigating all of the books that we were bringing from Turkey at the border. They were implementing a very strict form of censorship. I once brought some storybooks into Greece secretly. I knew if I were caught, I would have been arrested. But we were taking risks just for the sake of these children. Sometimes, if the Greek officials came to inspect the schools, the teachers would hurry to either tear up or burn the books. Do you see how hard it was to teach? Even today, school semesters start but the books are not sent to the schools because of several artificial reasons. The aim is to make minority education even worse, to deteriorate it further. (Retired teacher, interview, 2013, Komotini)

In the early to mid-1990s, when the Greek Ministry of Education prohibited textbooks from Turkey in favor of a Greek author, minority parents and teachers boycotted these new materials. This incident resulted in minority parents' and teachers' boycotting these materials (Verhás 2019, 18). Since 2000, new textbooks have been sent from Turkey to Greece, which is part of an agreement made between both countries following the boycott.

Another issue of minority education remembered by the minority relates to accreditation issues. When minority youth received their diplomas in Turkey, new graduates returned to Greece to work in their field of study but the state did not accept their diplomas. They were required to take new classes to receive their Greek accreditation. In addition, these students had to sit for new exams to work in their field, even after they have completed extra courses. According to the minorities, this policy was similar to others intended to worsen minority education and the minority's status socioeconomically (and politically). Among all these negative policies, the minorities mentioned what they view as an important development, which concerns the Greek government's policy of attaining a 0.5 percent admission quota for Muslim students to study at Greek universities.

One of the most repeated issues in conversations with minority members from older generations was their lack of education due to historical state policies. They repeatedly emphasized how negatively state officials and representatives, particularly civil servants, treated them, underscoring how difficult it was to communicate in Greek and interact with the state bureaucracy due to the discriminatory education policies targeting the Turkish Muslim minority. According to them, had they been as well educated as other Greek citizens, they could have defended and claimed their rights. As one minority member noted,

> In the past, when I went the public office for a license, it was so hard to communicate and most of the time the officials either ignored me or put extra obstacles in front of me since I was unable to speak Greek. I was not educated enough. I didn't know how to defend my rights. But my grandkids are not like the old generation. They speak Greek and trust themselves in society. That's why I go to public offices with my grandkids now. This is a much better feeling. The officials see that you speak Greek, and they take you seriously. (Community member, interview, 2013, Komotini)

Beyond the memory of the minority regarding the deprivation of their needs about ethnic identity and education, the minority also highlights their socioeconomic needs as economic deprivation and past discriminations about their property and housing issues. The minorities make comparisons between the present and the past to show their disadvantaged status in society relative to the majority. They argue that any national crisis affects them more severely due to their less powerful and more disadvantaged societal position. For instance, during the 2008 economic crisis, Greece, as a whole, was in trouble socioeconomically, but the minorities felt they were hit harder. For them, although some of the Greek majority may have entertained the possibility of moving abroad in search of better economic opportunities during that period, the minorities already felt deprived socioeconomically and had no option but to leave Greece to provide for their families. Relatedly, the minorities also discussed their experiences under the junta regime, noting that although the state was dysfunctional, which affected everyone in Greece, the minorities were more severely affected. As one minority member noted,

> We were already being treated badly by the government. The state was already ignoring us. But during the junta period, everything became worse. Minority education suffered more suppression. The quality of education was already poor, but it deteriorated further. (Retired teacher, interview, 2013, Komotini)

For the Turkish Muslim minority, the Greek state's discriminatory policies were unforgettable. Even today, the minority continues to feel that the state deprives them of some of their minority rights through discriminatory policies, which make their daily lives unbearable. As one young minority member noted,

> The minorities did not have the right to own property during these periods. They did not have the right to repair their existing properties either. My grandpa told me that one winter day he went to the roof to repair the leak and the police came to take him into custody. Can you believe that? Another thing, the Thracian minorities are highly agrarian. However, for a long time, they could not get driver's licenses to use tractors/caterpillars. They were allowed to take exams but they mostly failed [the driver's license] due to double standards and discrimination. If they were seen driving a tractor without a permit, they would be punished. So, how could they carry on farming the land, which was the only thing they knew how to do to make a living. (Youth member, interview, 2013, Komotini)

The minorities believe these types of state decisions were conscious because, for them, the state wanted to ignore the community's basic need for existence and recognition. For most minority members, the constant discrimination against them through a variety of policies was also a way through which the state could achieve a more ethnically and religiously homogenous country by forcing the minorities to migrate to Turkey or elsewhere. The more the minorities were pressured, the more likely they would be to leave.

Belongingness, Loyalty, and Citizenship

The discrimination and trauma the Turkish Muslim minority continue to experience has left many feeling detached from Greece and the majority. While both adaption and integration into Greek society have created various dilemmas for Western Thrace Turks, where they feel they belong and issues around belongingness are equally prominent within the community. Many minority members feel they belong to Western Thrace given it is the territory in which they have lived for centuries. However, their belongingness to the Greek nation is not only deeply connected to what they have in common with the rest of society (common historical narratives, language, ethnicity, customs, traditions, and national myths among other elements) but also how the Greek state has treated and continues to treat them.

Even if a few of the minority blamed Turkey's extreme nationalist agenda on the how the minority was treated between the 1960s and the 2000s, they still feel attached to Turkey due to its history, their ethnoreligious commonalities, and the way Turkey respects them. Some also argued that their feelings of belongingness to Greece could increase markedly if the state engages in serious and honest steps to improve its minority policies and change the discourse it uses against minorities. One minority member emphasized that

> if the Greek state increases the rights of minorities and tries to repair the wounds it opened in the minority's heart, the minority will change the way it sees the state. When you see the minority not as an enemy but part of Greek society, when you see us as a value rather than a burden you shoulder, we will begin to participate in social life and enhance the culture. (Minority association representative, interview, 2013, Komotini)

As another minority member suggested,

> There is a policy of suspicion toward the minority. In every society, there is prejudice against the minority, but Greek society has some stereotypes about Turkey. If you do not get rid of them, there cannot be reconciliation between the minorities and the Greek majority. A minority friend of mine went to university in Turkey and came back [to Greece] and had to go to the university to take extra courses to have her Turkish university diploma accredited in Greece. One day she met with a Greek student who learned that she is originally from Western Thrace and she started to yell at her that Turks are barbarians! Turks invaded Cyprus! Turks are this and that. My friend asked her if she had ever been in Turkey, if she had ever even met a Turkish person, if she had ever read a book written by a Turkish author, and asked: "What do you know about Turkey or Turks?" My friend told her that if she goes to Turkey, she will see how our cultures are similar, the food, the music, the way we think, etc. So this suspicion is based on a lack of information between two communities and is problematic. We need to know more about each other. (Academic, interview, 2013, Komotini)

The issue of belongingness, therefore, has both emotional and practical implications for the Turkish Muslim minority. When someone asks them where they are from, they do not say they are Greek. Rather, they say they are from Greece. Similar to the Greek Orthodox minority of Istanbul whose perceptions of their safety are very salient, most of the Turkish Muslim minority highlighted that they have "emergency houses" in Turkey and they are also ready to immigrate to Turkey at any moment if needed. Although the minority's fear of deportation is less now than it has been in the past, it is still present. Consequently, they want to feel they have a safe space in the event the state were to ever to deport or forcibly remove them from Greece. During our conversations, they noted that they began owning these homes during crisis periods, and particularly between 1974 and 1991, to escape Greece and find a safe haven in Turkey.

The minority usually connects the issue of belongingness to their perceptions of citizenship and loyalty. The topic of whether they see themselves as Greek citizens or not came up frequently in the many conversations I had with members of the Turkish Muslim minority, revealing how historical events, prejudice, and injustice have impacted how they feel about their status in Greek society. As one minority member noted,

> Today, I feel more comfortable about defending my rights in official places. In the past, minorities were more discriminated against and harassed in government offices in comparison to today. For instance, when minorities went to the municipality to obtain a document, the officials used to ignore them just because the minority members could not speak Greek. There was not even one translator in any of those official buildings to support minorities. However, today, as minorities have started to get a relatively better education and speak Greek, the perception and behavior of officials has also changed toward minorities. Now, they know that minorities can claim their rights by speaking with the officials like every other citizen. (Minority association administrator, interview, 2013, Komotini)

This demonstrates how, as the minority improves its integration into Greek society by learning the language and obtaining a better education, the state likewise modifies its perception of this minority by viewing them as citizens. However, there are still informal rules and redlines dictated by the state, as well as mental frames that condition minorities' meaning making of the past. As they explained, the minorities know where they stand in Greek society. Being visible in the society is appropriate sometimes but not everywhere and all the time. For example, one minority member described how

> in the past, job opportunities for minority members in official buildings were few, and so competitive. Today, there are at least a couple of minority members working in those offices. However, there are places that minorities cannot even dream of working, like in the higher ranks of the military and security forces. We join the army and complete our compulsory military service but when it comes to being an army general, we know that such a job is always just a dream that will never come true. These positions are Greek positions officially and are not available to minorities who are equal citizens under the constitution, but not in reality. Unofficially prohibiting minorities from working in the upper ranks of the military or the police force is against the Constitution's equal treatment of its citizens, but since there is no equality, there is no breaching of the law mentally. (Former politician, interview, 2013, Komotini)

The Turkish Muslim minority is torn between conserving their minority identity or adapting to Greek society, or both. For the state, choosing one must come at the expense of the other identity, as the minorities argued. Although the minority community is not monolithic, it is clear most minority members do not feel like they are equal citizens in Greece. The degree to which they feel they have integrated into Greek society is more ambiguous. For one minority youth member, even though she does perceive there is not any ongoing state discrimination against her community, that does not mean the majority and the minority are equal citizens. To be equal citizens, she noted, the quality of minority education must improve (Youth member, online interview, 2021, Komotini). Many minority youths and their parents have little hope that these changes will materialize in the near future, which has led those who have the necessary means to send their children to Turkey to receive an education. On the other hand, the data shows that the number of minority kids attending public elementary, middle, and tertiary schools increased today in comparison to the late 1990s due to several state policies (e.g., PEM, 0.5% quota).

During my conversations with members of the Turkish Muslim minority in Western Thrace, particularly related to discussions around belonging and belongingness, I felt these terms were very political for community members. Further, during our conversations, I had the impression I was in Turkey. They were highly interested in Turkish politics and life, yet with varying degrees of appreciation and criticism for the current government. In seeking to understand if their diverse political perspectives had created internal, intraminority tensions and how this diversity affects their feeling of belonging to Greece or Turkey, the minorities highlighted the lack of trust within their community. Although their community is typically viewed as monolithic from outside, it is highly diverse due to different political views and relations with different pressure groups. Leading minority figures were critical of other prominent minority leaders, as well as Greece and Turkey, depending on who was speaking. For instance, Dr. Ahmet is an important political figure within the minority community, but there are differing views about him and his actions. From my discussions with community members, it is clear most of the minority view Dr. Ahmet as a respectful figure, a prototype of the minority community. In particular, he has fought for the minority's rights. Conversely, for others, Dr. Ahmet worked on behalf of the Turkish Republic. They claim he tried to create an atmosphere that would frustrate the minority community and trigger an uprising against the Greek state. According to these few minority figures, he not only caused societal tension but also enabled the Greek state to postpone providing already gained rights to the minorities.

Therefore, while diverse opinions exist within the minority community on a range of topics, there is significant agreement on issues related to how the Greek state threatened and discriminated against the minority in the past. For the older generation who experienced these traumas directly, the vividness of their experiences penetrates their everyday narratives. Conversely, for younger generations, their narratives underscore the balancing act in which they find themselves between the negative narratives they receive from their families, neighbors, and as members of the minority community, on the one hand, and their need to adapt to Greek society, on the other. What they have learned from minority elders about their community's past is different from how they need to live in their daily lives. They live in cities and villages populated by both Greeks and ethnic Turks. To live a peaceful life, they respect the majority, and expect their respect in return. Younger generations place great emphasis on peaceful coexistence. They are eager to learn Greek, socialize with Greek friends, and even think about the possibility of marrying outside the Turkish Muslim minority, even if most of their families might oppose the idea. Therefore, positioning oneself according to the changing dynamics of a society creates an incredibly difficult situation for minority members, and particularly for those from younger generations.

For most conservatives and older generations, the minority community has its own internal minority. These minority group members blame some of their own for adopting Greek nicknames, for having close friendships with members of the Greek majority, and for forgetting their identity, as they integrate further into Greek society. For minority members critical of these actions, they view this behavior as being servile to the Greek majority and detrimental to the continuation of the Turkish Muslim identity, which may be lost as a result of these actions. More specifically, although the ability to speak Greek fluently is broadly accepted within the minority, adopting behaviors perceived to be Greek is not. Minorities who have a salient Turkish Muslim identity argue that they belong to the land more so than the Greek majority, since they have been living in their territories for 600 years whereas many of the Greeks who currently live in Greece migrated from Asia Minor.

For older generations and conservatives, the choice between adapting to Greece or conserving their minority identity is a decision to make. Minority media is also divided on this issue. While most minority newspapers define themselves as pro-minority, they view some others among them as pro-Greek. These two camps view national and minority identities as contradictory rather than complementary. Importantly, this dispute is a projection of the clash between minority members who think integration into Greek society is necessary and those who think such integration will lead to the community's cultural and historical erasure.

Beyond these contradictions between the minority who have different political views and different generations, for minorities, any fear the state may have about them is illogical because they have never revolted violently against the state, and instead have behaved obediently throughout Greek history. The concept of a security dilemma, developed by Herz (1950), is particularly relevant for its ability to explain how the Greek government behaves (and, for that matter, how the Turkish government acts toward its Greek Orthodox minority). As Herz (1950) argues, the reason individuals, social-political groupings, or nations demand more power is because of their need to be more secure against all threats whether they are real or perceived. They believe that to guarantee their ability to respond properly to an attack that seeks to destroy them, it is better to employ all measures through any means possible. However, this behavior results in unwelcome repercussions, including but not limited to ever-increasing suspicion of the *other* and distrust between the parties.

Contemporary minority-state relations in Greece are based on mutual suspicion and a lack of trust. These dynamics have deep historical and institutional roots that stem as far back as Greek-Turkish relations during the Ottoman Empire and the discriminatory measures the Greek state enacted on its minorities during the nation-building process. The state's lack of trust toward the minority has strengthened over time due to the minority's relations with its kin-state (Turkey). Some minority community members discussed Greek-Turkish interstate politics and how their bilateral relations affect them negatively. They highlight that both Greece and Turkey support their perceived allies among the minorities financially to strengthen their hand against the other. As one minority noted,

> For decades, the Greek state gave money to traditionalists in the minority to create alliances with them against the Turkish state. Turkey did the same and supported progressives in the minority community for a long time. Both states used minorities as a tool to divide the community into different camps. By treating the minorities like that, both countries found it easy to gather intelligence about the other country and be ready for its next moves. And unfortunately, the minorities who were already squeezed in between could only escape by internalizing this situation and choosing a side. (Journalist in a local minority newspaper, Interview, 2013, Komotini)

While a mutual lack of trust is an important problem in minority-state relations, members of the Turkish Muslim minority often stressed their community's loyalty to the state and their nonviolent nature in spite of all their hardships as well as the discrimination and harassment they have faced throughout history. At the peak of their frustration, they protested nonviolently. For them, their loyalty to the state and nonviolent attitudes are evidence that they have never planned to secede from Greece and unify with Turkey. As a result, the minorities question why the state has never affirmed their identity but rather viewed them as a threat. For many minority members, the state and a majority of Greeks view the minority community as inferior and the state is, therefore, guilty of treating its populations according to two different standards. As one individual emphasized,

> Minority community members were always good citizens; they paid their taxes, they did compulsory military service, they fought against Greece's enemies in wars, never used weapons against the state, and so on. However, the state saw them as worthless. Why? For a long time, the minorities were ignored and left to become invisible in Greek society. They existed [in society], about 150,000 people, with a huge historical, social, and cultural heritage, but they were also like a ghost. (Representative in a minority association, interview, 2013, Komotini)

In addition to the frustration associated with feeling invisible, the minorities believe Greek society is highly prejudiced against them even today. They had good relations in the past, but the deterioration of Greek-Turkish interstate relations and the effects of history directly affected minority-majority relations. These changing dynamics and the hardening social boundaries between the minority and the majority were at the forefront of the minds of minority members.

> There were good neighborly relations with the Greeks. I remember the days when my mom would go and drink a morning coffee with her Greek neighbor on the third floor. We were playing soccer together with Greek kids. But after the 1970s, everything changed. We were still playing soccer with kids but in different teams, and my mom was not going to have a coffee with her Greek neighbors. Today, only Turkish people live in our apartment building. (Academic, interview, 2013, Komotini)

Although this narrative contains some nostalgia, this individual was appreciating the relatively more mixed and humanized minority-majority relations of the past that were based on trusting neighborly relations in his memory act. For them, they are victims of identity denial but are also the ones who are trusted less. One minority member underscored the correlation between history and this lack of trust.

> It is difficult to prove our rightfulness in society, even in minor issues, because the prejudice and hostile attitude [of the majority] towards the minority is rooted deeply. What happened between the states and the minority created a feeling that the minority and the majority cannot trust each other. Minority stereotypes are so rigid. The state feeds these negative minority images through the speeches of some politicians, some of the media, and the education system. There is no constructive communication between members of society. Therefore, they do not know us, and we do not know them anymore. A lack of information brings a lack of trust. (Teacher, interview, 2013, Komotini)

Here this minority member refers to the rigidity of the perceptions of the majority toward the minority community and highlights the facilitating factors in the formation of this rigidity. According to her, the lack of meaningful contact deepens the distrust. Some of the minorities also underscored the totality of this distrust in their relations with the majority. According to them, this lack of trust transcends political boundaries. Both conservatives and liberals lack trust and are prejudiced toward the minority. The same minority member continued, noting that

> normally you would expect Greek liberals to behave differently about social injustices. Liberals are the ones who should be progressive about defending the rights of minorities, immigrants, women, youth, and the homeless, etc. But Greece's liberals are distant from the minorities. Greek liberals have always stood against state discrimination, human rights violations, and have been critical of Greek government policies, but they have always excluded minority issues from their agenda. They do not want to breach the state's redlines. How honest is this? (Teacher, interview, 2013, Komotini)

For the Turkish Muslim minority, there is a clear difference regarding how liberals in Turkey behave in comparison to their Greek counterparts. They claim Turkish liberals are not only active in defending the rights of all minorities in Turkey, including non-Muslim minorities, Kurds, Alevis, and many others, but they also have an influence on state policies affecting minorities. Conversely, they claim Greek liberals discriminate against the Turkish Muslim minority, and that championing the minority cause would threaten liberals' ability to make gains on their other political priorities. As the minorities described, the distrust between the majority and minority is so high that even liberals believe the minorities pose a potential threat to them.

Rigid Boundaries

Much of what has been discussed here underscores just how salient and resistant to change the social boundaries are that structure relations between the Greek majority and the Turkish Muslim minority. It is clear that the historical enmity that exists between Turkey and Greece has made these boundaries more rigid, but they have not been sufficient to create direct conflict between the majority and the minority in Western Thrace. As one minority member argues,

> Minority-majority relations are very superficial. You cannot find any Greek family who you can join to have a cup of coffee. You cannot tell your secrets. We have said we are the children of this territory

> and this country, we have said we have friendly relations with our neighbors. We do military service for this country. Otherwise, this country would be like Cyprus or Palestine. On the contrary, they injected enmity. When they stage a theater, the players who are performing the role of a Turk wore a fez [a red hat worn in the Ottoman Empire that is used to signify perceived backwardness] and saying Turks killed us like barbarians! In history textbooks, they wrote that the Turks stole Anatolia from us, they burned Smyrna (Izmir). These examples are not very widespread today but their views have not changed. They have always viewed us as inferior. These views have penetrated their genes. (Teacher, interview, 2013, Komotini)

It is important to note here that the Turkish Muslim minority argues that the social boundaries between themselves and the state were more permeable in the past in comparison to today. Although there were boundaries between minority and majority communities, these boundaries were still permeable, and they could be erased at the interpersonal level. However, the Cyprus conflict and the junta regime in Greece, which were historical turning points, strained their relations. Due to the state's negative treatment of the minority, the rigid boundaries between all sides were drawn and people who had good relations in the past started to view others as enemies. As one minority member in Xanthi described,

> Everything has changed over time. In the past, we trusted our Greek neighbors like we trust our family members. Today, both the majority and the minority prefer to live in ghettos. A Greek person who wants to rent an apartment, asks who lives in the apartment. If there is anybody from the "other" community, he won't rent the property. (Journalist in a local minority newspaper, interview, 2013, Komotini)

I went back to the minority community members and asked them if there has been any change in their relationships with the majority. Do they still feel like they live in ghettos? Do they still think the majority does not rent their places to the minority? They noted that there has been some progress on these issues. However, in one recent interview (2023), a minority community member noted that a majority-owned small shop closed, and a minority member wanted to rent the space for their business. The majority member, however, did not want to rent it to a minority. One cannot extrapolate from the scope of these occurrences to the entirety of minority-majority relations. However, one might easily make the case that the two still have societal barriers in place.

Along with the discussions about social boundaries, the issue of mixed marriages can be seen as one of the most intricate issues for the Turkish Muslim minority in Western Thrace. It is also an issue that brings to the fore a very real conundrum the minorities face regarding their minority identity, on one hand, and their integration into Greek society, on the other. The general tendency within the minority is to marry intracommunally for ethnic and religious reasons. However, increasing cases of integration into Greek majority society, particularly among the young generation, and their distance from many of the traumatic events their elders experienced directly, means this issue will continue to divide the minority community and, in some cases, families. Many minority members stressed how unacceptable mixed marriages were between the Turkish Muslim minority and members of the Greek majority. Specifically, they believe marrying with Greeks will steadily erode the minorities' culture and identity. On the other hand, a small number of minorities support the idea because, for them, connecting with people from outside the minority community is inescapable. They also believe that marrying people from other cultures is not a threat to their minority culture and identity. Irrespective of a minority member's own personal view, youth members are all too aware of how their community in general views marriages across identity lines.

> Mixed marriages are a taboo. If people from both communities want to get married to each other, they have to live in a remote place in Greece to escape the social pressure. This is where we are today. We are strangers. (Minority youth, interview, 2015, Komotini)

Another minority member also stressed the importance of in-group codes when it comes to the subject of mixed marriages.

> One of the biggest fears in the community is that the children who attend Greek schools may decide to marry Greeks. There are certain unwritten rules in the community that can be deconstructed and reconstructed over time, but the essence does not change. If you are going to live here, you obey our community's codes. (Former representative in a minority association, interview, 2013, Komotini)

Elsewhere, a community member who is more liberal and integrated into Greek culture explained that

> there is strong pressure in the community regarding mixed marriages. The minority community treats people who have mixed marriage very negatively. I totally understand the logic about loss

> of Turkish identity, but we should be moderate about our children. They were born here, even if their mothers and fathers are Turkish. It is natural for them to have both Turkish and Greek friends. I would love it if my child wanted to marry a Turkish person, but if one day he comes to me and says he is going to marry a Greek person, I will not exclude him. This is his opinion and I respect it. (Artist, 2016, Komotini)

Mixed marriages will continue to occupy the minority agenda in Western Thrace in the years to come given increasing generational divides and developments in information technology. Social media is, for example, one of avenues the minorities, and particularly youth members, use to access Greek society and the world more freely and easily. The effect of this new form of communication on the Turkish Muslim minority in Western Thrace remains to be seen.

Minority Youth: Social Injustice and Greece's Future

The Turkish minority's ethnic identity demands are right and legitimate. However, there has been a generational shift in minority perceptions regarding what is and should be a priority for the community. The concerns of minority youth today diverge from those of their parents and the Greek state. For a majority of the Turkish minority youth population, the issues of the past are not felt strongly among these minority members when compared to their parents and their community leaders, and they are often viewed as second order issues. For Turkish Muslim youth, there are more pressing, first order issues, such as the minorities' lack of development in various fields in contemporary Greece, which contradicts their national country's perception of itself and the future trajectory as one of Europe's leading democracies.

Turkish Muslim minority youth not only feel relatively deprived in comparison to Greek majority youth but they also feel relatively deprived in comparison to other youth globally. They think they deserve a better life in Greece. Today's rapid technological advancements and digitization may become a multiplier in the youth's perceived societal deprivation. They observe the majority Greek youth and others in the world through social media and other online mediums. They feel their minority status in Greece more viscerally when they see how few opportunities they have for no other reason than being part of a minority community. The deprivation they experience has a particularly notable and negative effect on minority youth. Cannabis use has spiked among males while antidepressant use among minority women, as health experts highlighted, is particularly high (online interview, Komotini 2021).

Johan Galtung (1969) refers to this treatment of a group of people in a state as structural violence. If a group of people are indirectly forced to live in a disadvantaged position politically, legally, economically, or culturally in comparison to the rest of a society, they suffer indirect violence resulting from social injustices built into the state system. The indirect violence that prevents the Turkish Muslim minority in Western Thrace from reaching their potential as individuals and as a community is evident. Western Thrace is one of the most economically underprivileged and least developed parts of Greece, with a large rural population who live in densely populated villages and work in the agricultural sector (Oran 1991). Based on per capita income and overall development, the region is at the low end of the EU scale (Anagnostou and Triandafyllidou 2006). Despite Greece's rapid EU integration process and an increased flow of EU development funds, which helped the country to flourish economically, Western Thrace's economic development remains limited. One of the most critical revenue streams for these minorities was tobacco production. However, low agricultural subsidies and the eventual loss of tobacco production deepened minorities' economic deprivation. As Anagnostou and Triandafyllidou (2006, 15) note, most of the funds were channeled by the state to the Christian-inhabited areas to the south rather than to the Muslim-inhabited areas of the north.

The Greek state's structural violence against the minorities is also evident in the field of education. As previously discussed, every youth minority member highlighted their lack of a good quality education in minority schools or their limited access to education due to language barriers. They argue that minority youth live with micro traumas every day due to education-related issues. For instance, they feel the state punishes them when they choose to attend a minority school. They know their minority peers who attend Greek schools receive a better education and they see this as a huge disadvantage. However, they do not want to be forced to attend a Greek majority school. They want the state to raise the education level in minority schools. Although choosing to attend a minority school may appear like a conscious decision on the part of these minority youth to receive a low-quality education, they also see it as necessary to support their community's existence.

Further, attending a Greek majority school is not a solution for the Turkish Muslim minority youth. Many youth who choose to attend Greek schools talked about the disadvantages that emerge because of language barriers. Although they see themselves relatively better off than those who attend minority schools, they discussed different hardships. For example, even if they attend Greek schools from kindergarten, they are still unable to attain the same level as their majority Greek counterparts due to inconsistencies between their school environment and their home and neighborhood environments. Their home environment and immediate surroundings are filled with Turkish Muslim people, they speak Turkish at home, watch Turkish TV, speak Turkish with friends, and attend events where Turkish is the dominant language. When they start school, their personal and academic lives are completely divided in terms of language and, to an extent, culture. This cannot only make it more difficult for Turkish Muslim minority children to achieve the same academic levels of Greek youth, but it can also create psychological issues for them related to feelings of being different, shame, and inadequacy.

For most Turkish Muslim youth, feelings of being a minority present themselves sooner rather than later in their lives. Reflecting on his experiences in preschool, one youth member spoke of how she was unable to communicate in Greek or understand what was happening in the classroom. Not only did none of her family members, neighbors, or friends speak Greek, Greece does not provide a bilingual (Greek-Turkish) preschool education. As she noted,

> At that point, I understood that I was different. The teacher was talking to me in a classroom full of thirty kids who were mostly Greek, but I felt like an alien. Feelings of being different and feelings of shame are strongly connected. That's probably the reason why many minority youth in Western Thrace are dealing with psychological issues because of these difficult feelings. (Youth member, online interview, 2020, Komotini)

She continued, adding

> you also feel shame because you don't know how to speak the language in your own country when you join the army for conscription. Many minority youth speak Greek for the first time in their lives when they begin their military service. Among all other things like racism and hierarchy, you realize that you cannot speak Greek. Again, you feel shame. (Youth member, online interview, 2020, Komotini)

One other disadvantage minority youth experience in the Greek education system relates to their treatment relative to other children, which can largely depend on the teacher they have. One youth minority member mentioned that there is still discrimination targeting minorities in some classrooms from both students and teachers (Youth member, online interview, 2021, Komotini). She recalled how her Muslim name and lack of so-called Greek features excluded her from presenting her work to the rest of the school. Rather, the class teacher chose her colleague who was from the Greek majority (Youth member, online interview, 2021, Komotini).

The Turkish Muslim minority also argues that Greek majority adolescents are not prepared to coexist with them in Greece. For example, one minority youth member argued that neither minority leaders nor the state attempt to prepare students who attend university where minority and majority youth from all over Greece meet for the first time (Youth member, online interview, 2020, Komotini). As youth minority members highlighted, their Greek peers are surprised to see there are still minorities living in Greece when they encounter Turkish Muslim minority students at the university. This lack of knowledge about the very existence of the Turkish Muslim minority of Western Thrace makes the community's youth feel invisible (Youth members, online interview, 2020, Komotini).

Conversely, the minority youth have always been aware of the majority's existence. As they begin interacting with the Greek majority more consistently, they can also experience additional hardships due to their new life in an environment that is culturally and religiously different. One conservative minority youth mentioned how she felt embarrassed about having to share bathrooms and shower blocks with male Greek students (Youth member, online interview, 2020, Komotini). Minority youth argue that their own communities and the state should work together to create cultural orientation experiences for students, irrespective of their background, who move from their home culture to the host culture for education and employment (Youth member, online interview, 2021, Komotini). Similarly, the majority's children should be better educated about diversity and inclusion to avoid learning much later in life that there are people of non-Greek origin living in Greece (Youth member, online interview, 2021, Komotini).

The structural violence that prevents Turkish Muslim minority youth from prospering socioeconomically does not only come from the state. They believe they are not permitted any space within the minority community itself. More specifically, they feel that most minority members, and particularly community leaders, neither listen to nor care about their ideas and problems. Nor do they believe they are allowed to be innovative. If a minority youth member wants to organize an event for a good cause, older community members question and, at times, censor the event. As a result, minority youth members shy away from joining community gatherings. Further, for them, other than a few people working in minority associations, they dislike the politics of the minority community. If the community organizes events, youth view them as superficial and unable to tackle any of the problems they increasingly face. They feel minority leaders are too far removed from the real problems that minority youth experience.

The State and the Turkish Muslim Minority

The minority policies adopted by the Greek state over time and their effects on the Turkish Muslim minority's historical memory and sense of identity have been assessed in the sections you have read so far. Although some minority members experienced these practices on an individual basis, others learned about the past through other social channels and intergenerational transmission. Minorities have provided us with hints through their memory work about how they define themselves now, despite the fact that not all of them are the same and occasionally disagree with or contradict one another. In the part that follows, the state's viewpoint on its own minority policy as well as the opinions of some specialists on the topic are examined.

The State and the Past

Greek state representatives referred to reforms Greece introduced regarding minority issues, highlighting the lack of honesty at the heart of past policy reforms, acknowledging the state's past mistakes. For them, the contextual changes Greece has experienced since the 1990s enabled the state to make and implement new laws and regulations to improve the sociocultural, economic, and political prospects for minorities. Greece became a member of the European Union in 1981, the Cold War ended decade later, and Greece signed and thereafter ratified various international treaties, which led to more international scrutiny from external actors regarding Greece's human rights practices and discriminatory policies. Due to outside pressure, in particular, Greece introduced several sociopolitical reforms. As one local government official noted,

> Honestly, everybody knew that these changes were not voluntary. On the surface, Greece wanted to be seen as positive in the eyes of international actors in terms of its attitude toward minorities. In this regard, minorities are provided some rights and freedoms in social, cultural, and economic areas. The Mitsotakis government, at the beginning of 1990s, met the demands of the minorities to some extent under the rules of "equality before law" and "equality in civil rights." But how much of these changes were targeted to make deeper changes in the status of minorities, I am not sure. (Local state representative, interview, Komotini, 2013)

Conversely, other state officials cited moments during which Greece and Turkey approached each other honestly and aided the other during humanitarian crises. Most of these officials noted how this situation changed their attitudes toward minorities and positively affected how the state engaged these communities. In 1999, Turkey and then Greece experienced a massive earthquake. These crises created an atmosphere in which both countries felt positive and acted humanely toward the other. As one official emphasized,

> Even if you were two enemies in the past, if you have a shared history and experiences, you cannot ignore each other during times of humanitarian crisis. The 1999 earthquakes were like this for Turkey and Greece. When the massive earthquake hit the Marmara region in Turkey, the first country that sent condolences to Turkey was Greece. The Greek people, NGOs, and local authorities did not hesitate for one minute to go to Turkey and help heal the wounds of the Turkish people. Greece sent rescue teams, humanitarian assistance, stayed with the people, and provided psychological support. And after some time, when Greece experienced an earthquake, Turkey did the same. Turkey and Greece do not have a pleasant history, but when it is about humanity, we can come together when we need to. (Local state representative, interview, Komotini, 2013)

Most officials also stressed that the term *human rights* is a new concept for Greece. Although the notion of human rights has gained ground practically in Greek life since the late 1990s, policymakers (nevertheless) apply the principle selectively, not universally. According to a Greek official,

> Greece has not implemented any radical changes in the status of minorities so far, not only because there is no strong political will for it, but also because the term "human rights" is relatively new in the Greek context. Therefore, the conditions of the minorities in Thrace are slightly different in comparison to the past, but the demands of minorities seem not to have been fully satisfied yet. (State representative, interview, Komotini, 2013)

The State and Historical Responsibility

Greek state officials were very much aligned with their Turkish counterparts in how they evaluated Greece's historic institutional practices. Some referred to the "earthquake diplomacy" as a good example of how a humanitarian crisis can change the way Greece and Turkey treat each other. A recent example of this situation was also seen in the 2023 earthquake in Turkey. After the earthquake, like many other countries in the world, Greece offered disaster relief support and helped the Turkish people. The two sides made statements that de-escalated the tensions between the two countries for a while due to the developments in the Eastern Mediterranean.

However, these moments of humanitarian support do not have a strong role in dramatically changing the way the actors perceive each other. During our discussion, Greek officials said that any progress made regarding the Turkish Muslim minority was always in the shadow of Turkey's larger desires to intervene in Greece's internal affairs and use the minorities as an instrument to that end. These Greek officials still believe Turkey is pursuing an interventionist agenda.

> There were times that Muslim minorities in Thrace faced difficulties caused by the state. However, we cannot blame Greece for everything. Turkey, throughout its history, was interventionist. We saw the clearest example in Cyprus. The Greek state always had this fear of "What if Turkey tries to intervene in the Western Thrace to merge it with Turkey?" Remember Yugoslavia. (State representative, interview, Komotini, 2013)

Official Greek narratives acknowledge the negative past and particularly Greece's discrimination against minorities. Yet, for these officials, it is Turkey who is ultimately responsible for these failings. They argue that the way Greece treated its minorities was a result of how Turkey treated its Greek Orthodox minority during the Cyprus conflicts, the 1955 incidents, and the 1964 deportations. The same official continued, noting that

> Turkey used every means to intervene in minority affairs in Greece through its kinship [with the minorities]. Greece never did the same in Western Thrace as Turkey did in Istanbul. We closely watched how Turkey treated the Greek Orthodox minority in Turkey, but never became involved in domestic affairs through our diplomats in Istanbul. We just tried to treat the Muslim minority similarly to Turkey's treatment of the Greek Orthodox minority in Istanbul. Therefore, if there are any injustices towards minorities, Turkey's behavior determined the way we would treat the minority here. (State representative, interview, Komotini, 2013)

Greek officials also highlighted the effect of history on the Greek parliament's contemporary decision-making processes regarding the Turkish Muslim minority community. During our discussions, they constantly referred to Turkey inciting Turkish Muslim minority leaders such as Dr. Sadık Ahmet against the Greek state. For these officials, Turkey's policy of interventionism reverberated negatively on the state and the Turkish Muslim minority in Western Thrace. According to one official whose perspective is not widely shared by Greek officials; the reason Greece continues to implement negative policies toward the Turkish Muslim minority is because of Turkey's continued interventionist policies. The minorities are viewed as the embodiment of Turkish interventionism. He added that

> the minority had the illusion that Turkey would one day come and save them. However, Greece will never allow this. For a long time, the Turkish consulate in Thrace wanted to prevent the minorities from integrating into Greece socially and politically. Even today, it plays a significant role in terms of determining who should be the leader in the minority community, who should enter the Greek parliament, what types of narratives and policies should be used in relations with the state, and so on. This interventionism unfortunately affects Greek officials negatively. If Turkey continues this interventionism, then the Greek state and the minority will experience problems forever because they will always see each other as "suspects." (Local state representative, interview, Komotini, 2013)

Greek officials who were asked about the ethnic identity demands of the Turkish Muslim minority in Western Thrace responded by underscoring that Greece's official policy is premised on the notion of a single, unified (national) identity. Minorities cannot hold multiple identities with this official narrative. As one official noted explained,

> While the Lausanne Treaty clearly defines minorities as "religious minorities," isn't it absurd for the minorities to stress a different identity as opposed to the state view? If one talks about loyalty to the state, how can he also identify himself as part of another country? If you defend that you are ethnically Turkish, you should be a citizen of Turkey because both Greece and Turkey are based on ethnic nationhood. In addition, minority community leaders who speak Turkish are trying to promote the idea that all Pomaks and Roma people are also Turkish ethnically. However, Pomaks and Roma people do not accept this. They have their own culture and language. (State representative, interview, Komotini, 2013)

As with Turkish representatives, Greek officials also highlighted their state's positive stance toward the minorities because of lessons learned from history. These past mistakes have motivated the Greek state to not only take an interest but also to take minority-related issues more seriously. The state tries to meet the demands of minorities as much as possible such as through the previously mentioned state-implemented 0.5 percent quota and allowing school textbooks to come directly from Turkey.

Some Greeks officials admit that work still needs to be done to change attitudes toward the minorities. Drawing on the higher education sector, one official argued that

> universities should also transform the way they see the minorities. To some extent, the state can find solutions to the issues related to elementary and secondary schools. But for higher education, universities themselves need to work harder and create an atmosphere to attract minority students. This way, the minority students will have the opportunity to get a higher education in their country and integrate into society more instead of going elsewhere. (Local state representative, interview, Komotini, 2013)

Referring to the economic crisis Greece had experienced, Greek officials highlighted the effect of the crisis on how many Greeks view the minority. These officials appear to acknowledge the underdeveloped and relatively deprived position of Western Thrace in Greece, but all of them generalize this situation, normalizing the lived reality of the Turkish Muslim minority. One official emphasized that

> the Greek economy is not doing well in general. I know Thrace is one of the least developed parts of the country, but honestly, everybody experiences similar economic problems in the country. The economic situation in Thrace was always like this. But other parts of the country have not experienced this much economic trouble. This is a new thing. (Local state representative, interview, Komotini, 2013)

The issue of elected and appointed muftis was also mentioned by some of the officials, but as a problem created by the minority. During our discussions, these officials implied that the government was trying to change things for the minority, but it was the minority's rigid and distrustful perception of the Greek government that was stalling these efforts. As one official argued,

> When the Greek state appointed muftis in Thrace, the ordinary [non-elite] minority members as well as community leaders reacted to that in order to delegitimize the government's decision and the muftis. They perceive that whatever the government does is for the malice of the minority. They voted and elected their own muftis by the raised-hand method and we had a mufti problem from that time on. Unfortunately, the minority is digging itself into a hole, not the government. Because of this two-headed mufti case, the minority itself is experiencing several legal problems in their own community. (State representative, interview, Komotini, 2013)

The State and the Turkish Muslim Minority Today

Greek officials defended several factors that affected state-minority relations after Greece gained EU membership and its subsequent Europeanization process (Grigoriadis 2008). One official noted that,

> now, interactions between the state and local authorities are much better compared to in the past. Especially after 1991, the state belatedly started to provide rights to the minorities that originated from

> the Lausanne Treaty. The EU grants and projects also supported positively the relationship between the local authorities and the community. In addition, Greece's democratization and Europeanization continue to constructively affect the way the state and the minorities communicate. (State representative, interview, Komotini, 2013)

Officials, experts, and the minority all emphasized that the 2010 economic crisis did not only affect the minorities, but that it impacted all of Greece. One Greek official noted, in a 2013 interview while the impact of the crisis was still strong,

> The minorities may think the state lessened its interest in minority rights and issues, but actually, the state is now channeling its energy toward economic survival on a national scale. So, after the crisis ends, new opportunities will emerge for both minorities and the majority. (State representative, interview, Komotini, 2013)

In terms of a stumbling block, preventing state-minority relations advancing, Greek officials highlight that the more the minorities stress their ethnic identity, the more reactionary the state becomes toward them. To overcome this issue, there is a need for more social and economic reforms. This could reduce the minority's need to focus on their ethnic identity, which is a source of conflict with the Greek state. One official stated that

> since the 1990s, the state changed its policy toward the minority. The positive changes are on the way, with some delay due to the economic crisis. We believe that the minorities will change the way they see their government with these positive steps. They will understand that insisting on the state's acceptance of the "Turkish" identity has nothing to do with their daily life problems. And the state will solve them as much as possible. (State representative, interview, Komotini, 2013)

Expert Views on the State and the Minority Relations

According to most experts I spoke with, the Turkish Muslim minority and the state use the same historical rhetoric. All actors—minorities and the state—use official narratives about "rights" and focus on the issues from their own perspective. The Turkish Muslim minority in Thrace focuses on the discrimination they have faced in the areas of education, identity, and religious issues. Conversely, the Greek state focuses on the Turkish government's interventionist actions in an effort to control the minorities in Thrace. For many experts, therefore, the future seems less than bright given the entrenched and somewhat stagnant stereotypes, negative images, rhetoric, and the general mindset of both the state and the minorities, which also structure bilateral relations between Turkey and Greece. One expert emphasized that

> when the human aspect of issues are tied to bilateral state relations and especially when these relations are based on historical enmity, even if there are periods of rapprochement between states, you cannot really care about human needs. Because when rapprochement ends, the interest in human needs ends. (Expert, online interview, Athens, 2020)

State representatives and minorities must work to transform the way they perceive and approach each other. Bilateral relations should not overshadow the real needs of people. People should not be afraid to construct bridges between themselves and the state. The minority community should allow alternative voices to be heard, permitting more democracy without fear of loss. There is strong social pressure within the minority community toward creating a homogenous (singular) identity, which restricts the minority's integration efforts in Greece.

Somewhat echoing the views of minorities and officials, these experts also mentioned the positive changes that occurred after 1991, as well as the effect of Greece's Europeanization process on state-minority relations. While there were positive policies and programs from 1991 onwards, experts also cited a lack of honesty in the legislative changes targeting the minorities. Accordingly, the state's starting point from which to introduce minority-related policy changes was wrong, as one expert explained:

> The state makes decisions with the mentality of "How can we control the minority more and how can we eliminate the minorities' dependency on Turkey?" First of all, even though the abrogation of Article 19 must be seen as a significant legal development, previous implementations of the article created the problem of a "stateless" people. The problem still continues. The law is not retroactive in character. Therefore, the abrogation of the law didn't allow the stateless people to regain their citizenship. The state thought that if

> it resurrected lost citizenships, it would imply that the state made a mistake in the past and now has to apologize to those people who lost their citizenship. Unfortunately, political interests come before the human dimension. (Expert, interview, Athens, 2013)

For positive change to occur, these experts stressed the need for the Greek state to match its claim to care more about the basic human needs of the minority than its own interest with tangible actions. The human suffering minorities experience needs to be understood and acknowledged. Otherwise, the issues hampering state-minority relations from advancing more positively may never be achieved.

Additionally, all the experts discussed the Greek state's policy, which established a national electoral threshold of 3 percent whereby any party with less than 3 percent of the vote cannot gain a seat(s) in the parliament. This policy was implemented following the election of an independent minority MP, Dr. Sadık Ahmet, in 1989 who, after being elected, pursued a Turkey-oriented agenda. By establishing a 3 percent threshold, no minority member could receive enough votes to become an independent MP directly. The new election system would force independent candidates to conduct politics within the framework of established Greek political parties. As these experts argue, the minorities perceive this policy as an obstacle to them achieving direct political minority representation in the Greek assembly. Further, they suggest the policy was a sort of security measure the Greece state implemented to defend against any attempted interventionism by Turkey. By making it more difficult for minority political figures to be elected who potentially had the political backing of Turkey, the Greek state sought to secure its own national authority in the Greek assembly. Through this policy change, the state again focused more on its own security needs rather than trying to understand the needs of minorities. As one expert succinctly explained,

> When you look at the election threshold issue from a political angle, the Greek state took an important step to stem Turkey's influence in Greek politics. As it is widely accepted by both minority members and Turkey, the independent MP, Sadık Ahmet, served as more of an MP of Turkey than as an MP of the Greek assembly. He took an extreme position against the state that eventually had a negative more than a positive effect on the minority. He was serving the interests of Turkey in Western Thrace more than [serving] the needs

> of the minority. Therefore, for the Greek state, it was important to stop him one way or the other, which would also stop Turkey's influence. The state did not actually focus on solving the issue of how the real needs of the minority's political representation in the assembly could be achieved, but they diverted their focus to protect national security. In a sense, the policy was created to stop Turkey's representation in the assembly. Therefore, the rivalry between the Greek and Turkish states created a disadvantageous situation for the minority itself. (Expert interview, Athens, 2013)

For the minority community, the most significant issue is to have a representative who is in a strong position in the parliament to defend the rights of minorities. Therefore, unless the election threshold does not lift, Greece may embrace a more multiculturalist vision and provide more seats to minority members to achieve a more equitable, diverse, and equal society.

Most experts also referred to the population policies the Greek state implemented in Thrace as dishonest. Academics and NGO representatives noted that the state consciously began settling Pontic Orthodox peoples of the Soviet Union in Thrace from the 1990s under the policies of Prime Minister Constantine Mitsotakis (Antoniou 2005). This has created tension between the existing Turkish Muslim minority and the Greek state because the minority understood this action as an attempt by the state to balance out the population of Muslim minorities in Thrace. Whether this was right or wrong, the Greek state should have sought to implement a more comprehensive governance strategy with the minority community to better manage this policy and explain to the minorities the reasons for this policy change, which had a direct effect on their lives.

> It is hard to say the Greek state could manage the policy of settling the Pontic Russians in Western Thrace well. It was a problematic process for both the Greek majority and the Muslim minority. The major aim was obviously to balance out the population of Muslim minorities in Thrace; however, the way the state conducts these types of policies is problematic. [It was] not only the Muslim minorities but also the Greek inhabitants of the region who were not happy about the integration of these newcomers because of the social problems attached [to their arrival], such as increasing crime rates, cultural clashes, etc. Therefore, the Greek state should include the people who are directly affected by policies in the policymaking

> process. Policies that come from the top create more problems than advantages for the people who were affected by them. More communication is always better. (Expert, online interview, Athens, 2020)

In summary, these experts stressed the significance of employing honest policies that are people-centered, which put the basic human needs of the minorities over the state's security interests, particularly if social harmony is the Greek state's ultimate goal. As these conversations with experts and state officials reveal, there is no consultation between the states and the minorities regarding reforms to existing laws and policies or when implementing new legislation that affects minorities. As one NGO representative mentioned,

> The mufti issue was also another policy that came from the top. The state, in order to increase its political influence on the minority in response to the perceived threat of Turkey, appointed muftis who have no legitimacy in the eyes of minority. Unfortunately, the mufti issue is another area of deadlock in the state and minority relations. But there could be better ways to make and implement these policies. Commissions that are composed of minority leaders, experts, and the state representatives could come together and make better policies that can then guarantee sustainability. (Expert, interview, Athens, 2013)

Therefore, experts consider the lack of governance to be a serious obstacle to creating better communication between the minorities and the state. As these experts note, this lack of communication largely originates from Greece not having internalized the concept of minority rights, its political culture, and the historical memories that have persisted and created negative perceptions on both sides. A lack of governance seems to have directly affected the way both the state and the minorities communicate and has resulted in a lack of empathy emanating from either side. Therefore, when one policy that affects the minority negatively emerges, the minority becomes frustrated and feels ignored. This also creates a negative image of the state in the eyes of the minorities.

Conclusion

The Turkish Muslim minority community has experienced a history full of periodic injustices and discrimination because of fluctuating relations between Turkey and Greece. As described by the minority, Greece's Europeanization process beginning in the 1990s saw the state's treatment of minorities through various policy changes improve significantly, but not entirely. One of the major issues facing the Turkish Muslim minority of Western Thrace is the low quality of (minority) education. Given that minorities mostly prefer to go to these schools, which have much lower standards in comparison to Greek (majority) schools, minorities do not have access to the same level of education as the Greek majority. Consequently, although the minority community appreciates certain state-initiated developments, they also expressed concern over the lack of honesty underpinning these policy changes and the lack of transformative change in the state's view of the minority community.

The minority community emphasized the significance of remembering the negative past to preserve their identity and the need to constantly focus on certain events to support this existential cause. As this chapter suggests, the minority believe that history determines who they are today. As such, remembering is a political act, which is a reaction to attempts by the Greek state to erase the minority memory space. The state consciously enacts certain political decisions to that end, such as suspending the Turkish minority associations where community members exchange historical narratives through storytelling, daily conversations, educational activities, and cultural events. Similarly, limitations in the areas of education and religion have motivated the minority to act against these limitations and ask for more of their rights. Remembering certain historical events persistently, therefore, helps the minority to remain attached to their past and to transmit their memory to the newer generations, which serves to strengthen their in-group bonds.

These acts of remembering the negative past and their persistence in remembering certain events are essential for the minority's existence. However, they also reveal the strong and deep social boundaries between the minorities and the majority in relation to the past. The effect of the Cyprus conflict on the Turkish Muslim minority, in addition to already existing in-group and out-group binary forms, enemy images, prejudices, and threat perceptions coming from the Ottoman past and nation-building processes in both countries, strengthens these boundaries. Consequently, there was a greater reduction in the already limited number of neighborly encounters and sharper criticism of mixed marriages within the minority. The minority accepts that the younger generation tends to adapt more readily to Greek society in comparison to the past, but the minority community's nationalist and traditionalist elements are highly concerned about the degeneration or loss of their Turkish Muslim identity through this adaptation process.

The minority is also highly preoccupied with their relations with the state. There are prominent blame games and scapegoating around the state's treatment of the minorities, while defending the idea of the minority's high and unquestionable loyalty to the state. According to the minority, the state's policies toward their community continue to lack honesty because state officials cannot overcome their distrust and the associated security dilemma relating to the minority (Former representative in a minority association, interview, 2020, Komotini). They appreciate the policy changes initiated since the 1990s, but they are highly concerned about why the state still distrusts their community despite their unwavering loyalty. Consequently, the state's denial of the minority's Turkish identity motivates the minorities to become more attached to their ethnic identity.

Finally, generally speaking, the minority still faces the undesirable choice between being a minority or a citizen of Greece, while also experiencing a feeling of belongingness to Turkey or Greece. All the minorities demand an expansion of individual and minority rights. In Greece, particularly, they demand more rights in the fields of education and freedom of association. They also recognize that most of these individual rights relate to their minority rights. However, their views about Greek citizenship or minority membership seem exclusionary, even though they demand both. Additionally, the Turkish Muslim minority in Western Thrace feels deeply attached to Turkey, but their attachment to Western Thrace (the territory) is unquestionable. Their overall desire is to live as equal citizens in Greece and to change how the state and the majority views them. As their narratives suggest, this requires transformative change in state policies. Lastly, the youth in Western Thrace diverge somewhat from their families about what their community should prioritize. For the majority of Turkish Muslim youth, it is essential to focus on their community's socioeconomic development and psychological issues rather than more historically defined political issues.

FOUR

The Turkish State and the Greek Orthodox Minority Memory

I WORK VERY ACTIVELY in one of the Greek Orthodox foundations. We do lots of work to keep the neighborhood culture alive. We organize cultural events, apply for EU grants, bring youth together, and discuss our traditions. Not everyone in the community has a similar interest in our work. We are in an era of technology and consumption. Some youth are not as interested in keeping the minority culture alive. However, we continue with our projects that bring together minorities. We got an EU grant and coordinated a project called Yanyana (The Encounter)[1] in which we brought together Greek Orthodox, Jewish, Armenian, and Assyrian communities. Young people realized they were not alone in their struggle of being a minority.

It is true the people who experienced past historical traumas raised us with anxious and timid psychology. They would caution us, saying: *Aman kızım, oraya gitmeyin, aman oğlum hakkınızı aramayın boşverin!* (Daughter, don't go there; Son, don't seek your rights, forget it!). In the past, there were policies like Vatandaş Türkçe Konuş! (Citizen, speak Turkish!). Because of this policy, minorities started to avoid using their own language in public. I remember stories of minority people lecturing their kids before leaving the house, telling them to shut their mouths and not speak Greek. This language policy probably continued for 10–15 years but its ramifications were huge. There was huge cultural erosion for our community and many people left Turkey.

> Today, we do not experience the same anxieties as previous generations because we live in a different time. In the past, there were wars. Things are different now. Even the way people fight with each other is different. It is more like economic wars, for instance. What can be done to the minority now? Violate our rights? For instance, [the state] is once again violating our right to hold elections in our foundations.[2] We elected people for a four-year term in 2011, but since then, our election rights were taken out of our hands and the same people have been in power for eight years. Some of these leaders either die or become very old while in power, and not having an election for a long time is an invisible obstacle that prevents our foundations meeting the minorities' needs.
>
> Things happened in the past, and we should not forget them, but we also cannot live with them. We should look to the future. We should ask ourselves: What can we do to raise our community up? When a member of the [Turkish] majority leaves Turkey, it's not a big deal. But when a member of the minority leaves a community of 3,000–3,500, the brain drain hits the hardest. We have a certain number of community deaths and births. Without transferring some of the population back to Turkey, this community cannot survive. We experience some reverse migration to Turkey from Greece or Europe in general. However, when these people come, they must deal with a lack of employment and education issues. This makes their adaptation harder. We currently have remedial solutions but no long-term community solutions. While we try to increase the number of Orthodox people, we also realize that some people who send their children to minority schools, for example, are not the same as the original Greek Orthodox community of Istanbul religiously or culturally. For instance, some Greek families who joined the Istanbul Greek Orthodox community don't baptize their children. In Greece, not everyone baptizes their children. There is a big question about whether these people should be counted as part of the Istanbul Greek Orthodox community or not. To me, religion is not definitive enough for identity in today's world.
>
> —Alexis, Istanbul Greek Orthodox minority, Istanbul, 2020

Alexis's desire to not be consumed by the past is a sentiment shared by many members of Istanbul's Greek Orthodox minority. Over the years, members of this dwindling minority community have not only sought to manage their declining population size, which is a source of great anxiety, but also to educate the Turkish majority about the reasons underpinning their community's dramatic erosion. The role the Istanbul Greek Orthodox community plays in Turkey's contemporary socioeconomic and political life has diminished gradually. The Turkish state prioritized laws and regulations to facilitate the construction of a new nation's identity based on ethnic *Turkishness* while reducing the existence of minorities in Turkey's socioeconomic, cultural, and political life.

As highlighted in the forthcoming discussion, these policies are central to the memory work the Greek Orthodox minority conduct. They conduct memory work about their past because, for them, their minority status and their marginal socioeconomic and political position in Turkish society stem from these nation-building policies. After the Turkish Republic was established, state policies aimed to replace non-Muslim minorities in the labor market and economy more generally with Muslim Turks under the framework of Turkification policies (Aktar 2000). For the policymakers, these policies were largely successful. Today, there are no more than a couple of Istanbul Greek Orthodox families involved in business and trade and there are only a handful of doctors and academics from the community (Erdem 2019).

In addition to these changes in the Istanbul Greek Orthodox community's role in contemporary Turkey, the presence of the minority as part of the cultural face of Istanbul has also changed. The Greek Orthodox architecture of Istanbul dates back to the Byzantine. While remnants of this architecture can be seen throughout Istanbul, the Istanbul Greek Orthodox community feels that almost all trace of their architecture and culture has disappeared. Relatedly, Turkish people with the necessary financial means buy properties that once belonged to Istanbul's Greek Orthodox families as they view living in these properties as a mark of prestige (Döner 2021). For the Greek Orthodox minority, however, the people who buy these properties do not ask what happened to the people who previously lived there (Döner 2021). Similarly, there are also cafes, bars, and restaurants that carry Greek Orthodox names such as Eleni Café and Meyhane Fotini despite being owned by non–Greek Orthodox people. Although this can be seen as the Greek influence on *meyhane* (tavern) culture, for some of the Greek Orthodox minority, naming these restaurants with Greek names is also perceived as the middle-class white-collar people's effort to integrate into "Istanbul" (Döner 2021).

This example underscores that Greek Orthodox culture, in Istanbul at least, continues to be important, remembered, and appreciated by many including the majority population. Although the minorities want to look to the future, as Alexis discussed at the beginning of this chapter, they still feel the need to live in the past and engage in memory work. For them, this memory work is important for three key reasons. First, they want to keep Greek Orthodox culture alive by discussing what Greek Orthodox culture was, the extent to which it has been lost, and why it has disappeared. Second, they want to teach their children about their identity, which is mostly achieved through transmitting memories to younger generations. Third, and perhaps most crucially for the Greek Orthodox minority community, they are afraid history might repeat itself. They want to protect themselves and advocate for their rights by remembering past wrongdoings. They want to increase awareness about the state's past mistakes to stop them from ever happening again.

This chapter consists of four sections, starting with a historical analysis of the Turkish government's minority policies with a special emphasis on Istanbul's Greek Orthodox community. Then I address the memory work conducted by members of Istanbul's Greek Orthodox community. In particular, this section focuses on how these earlier policies affected (and continue to affect) the minority. Their historical memories reveal the significant difficulties they face, including their demographic erosion and related issues as a consequence of past policies. In addition, this section examines the minority's discourse on concepts like belongingness, loyalty, and citizenship and concerns relating to the internal lack of democracy, rigid boundaries, and the visibility of the minority in Turkey today. I conclude with a discussion of the state's viewpoints on the previous policies, the state's position on them, and finally add the evaluations of experts.

Turkey's Institutional Practices and the Greek Orthodox Minority

Minority Education

Articles 37–45 of the Lausanne Treaty provided Turkey and Greece with a framework for how to treat their minorities. The treaty guaranteed autonomy to the minorities in decision-making regarding their children's education. Minorities were permitted to open, manage, and control their own schools at their own expense, and teach in a language of their choosing. In addition to these positive (minority) rights, Greece and Turkey had a responsibility to provide primary education to minority children in their own language. Notwithstanding the clearly stipulated guarantees enshrined in the treaty, both states have adhered to these articles intermittently. They were followed from the 1930s to the mid-1950s but then were largely ignored, most notably in the 1960s and 1970s.

The Lausanne Treaty was signed as the Ottoman Empire was transitioning to the modern Turkish Republic. As such, the treaty described the minorities as if they were still part of the Ottoman *millet* system rather than characterizing them based specifically on their linguistic or ethnic identity. During times of crises, Turkish and Greek political figures interpreted these articles narrowly, choosing to treat minorities as political entities, which resulted in cycles of negative reciprocity.

Debates over education have become one of the most controversial issues for minority communities. Historical narratives around education-related issues are reproduced constantly by community members and these narratives have become crucial elements of their memory space. The legacy of this policy area is so central to how minorities understand their past and present because of their lack of access to a comprehensive, tailored education system that has affected these communities profoundly irrespective of generation or age. Given the lasting and serious effects of Greece's and Turkey's educational institutional practices on their minorities, it is necessary to examine these policies in more depth.

Any analysis of Greek-Turkish bilateral relations, particularly concerning how they have treated their minorities for the past 100 years, reveals the lack of a comprehensive education policy that addresses the needs of the minorities. As a result, the quality of education in both Greece's and Turkey's minority schools is strikingly low. The school buildings are limited in number or in disrepair, they lack sufficient student numbers, which means many face closures, and there are numerous problems recruiting, paying, and retaining teaching staff. Textbooks and other educational materials either do not exist or are out of date.

While Greek and Turkish government officials want their minorities to adapt to this system, there is little minorities can do themselves to improve their children's limited education due to the power imbalance between them and the majority. The education sector, therefore, is the site of the most destructive power struggles between Greece and Turkey as well as between elites within the minority community. Those who have more power have a greater say in policies related to how minority children are educated. When this power is used to the disadvantage of minorities, these education policies affect minority children the most. Alexis Alexandris highlights some of the restrictive measures Turkey implemented related to education:

- By virtue of law 222 of 1961, the government placed all minority schools under the department of private schools, which meant these schools were no longer recognized as "communal schools" entitled to the minority clauses of the Lausanne Treaty.
- On March 27, 1964, a government protocol (no.410/16) prohibited Orthodox clerics from the grounds of Greek minority schools.
- Protocol no. 3885, dated September 15, 1964, banned morning prayer in Greek schools. Greek textbooks and encyclopedias were also strictly prohibited.
- In 1964, the Turkish state compelled Greek elementary and secondary schools to accept the appointment of Turkish assistant headmasters recruited by the Ministry of Education in contravention of the Lausanne Treaty's educational clauses (articles 40–41). While refusing to grant the necessary permission to repair dilapidated school buildings, the Turkish authorities withdrew state recognition from a number of elected school boards within the Greek community. (1992, 286–87)

As mentioned in previous chapters, the Greek Orthodox minority felt trapped between different political authorities and political decisions similar to the ones mentioned above. The trauma of existing in a state of *in-between* created uncertainty, insecurity, and a general lack of confidence among the minorities.

Members of Istanbul's Greek Orthodox minority noted that minority education in Turkey was significantly affected by the 1964 deportations. In 1964, there were around 60,000 Greek citizens living in the Republic of Turkey. However, the expulsion of Greek nationals triggered the departure of approximately 20,000 Greek-Orthodox minority members in a single year (Eligür 2020). As the population decreased dramatically, minority schools began to close one after the other. The legacy of the 1964 deportations can still be felt today, particularly in terms of the quality of minority education and the number of minority schools, teachers, and pupils.

Supporting these minority narratives, the *Minority Schools and Fundamental Problems in the Republic Period* report highlights several issues facing minority schools in Turkey today:

- A lack of public status (minority schools are treated as private schools,[3] so they lack significant state funding and these school encounter extra bureaucratic burdens)

- The role of the Turkish chief deputy head teacher (while the head teacher is a member of the Greek Orthodox minority, having a Turkish deputy causes a duality in management and a lack of trust in the school's overall management)
- Teacher training and recruitment (delays in meeting quotas or exchange teachers arriving from Greece)
- The Ministry of Education appointing and paying Turkish language and culture teachers (delays in appointing these teachers and limitations on the duration of their employment contracts)
- Supplying textbooks and other educational materials (delays in receiving books from Greece due to cumbersome bureaucratic procedures that result in curricular incompatibilities)
- Requirements that students be members of the same minority community and a Turkish citizen, which affects Greek Orthodox minority schools particularly due to low student numbers in this specific minority community. (Somel and Kaya 2013)

Population Policies and Property Issues

The policy of Varlık Vergisi (Capital Tax) is an example of a particularly harsh institutional practice that violated the Greek Orthodox minority's socioeconomic rights. In addition to the Turkish state collecting heavy taxes from the minorities, their properties were also *Turkified* in an indirect way, whereby minorities eventually lost their properties due to their inability to pay these taxes. Unable to pay, this paved the way for Turks to take over these properties. As the Turkish newspaper *Cumhuriyet* wrote,

> According to a more specific explanation which was whispered from ear to ear, or even at times voiced out loud, a second objective of the tax was to free the market from the control of the minorities and open it to the Turks. . . . Thus, our Jewish, Greek Orthodox, Catholic, and Gregorian people who were proud of being Turkish citizens had to sell off their property and wealth for nothing. (Alexandris 1992, 219–20)

The September 6–7, 1955 incidents in Istanbul serve as another example of how the state deprived the minority sociopsychologically and financially through property and land issues. These incidents were mainly intended to intimidate and instill fear among the Greek community, resulting in violence, destruction of property, and migration. There was speculation that the birth house of the Turkish Republic's founder, Mustafa Kemal Atatürk, had been bombed in Thessaloniki and anti-EOKA[4] protests were arranged in several cities, but mostly in Istanbul. These events occurred as tensions caused by the Cyprus conflict were rising in Turkey. The protests quickly spiraled out of control, turning violent in Istanbul's Beyoğlu district where minority properties and businesses were looted and destroyed. These events resulted in 11–15 casualties[5] and 200 reported rapes. As Alexandris documents, "The priest of the monastery of Balıklı, Chrysanthos Mantas, who was over ninety, was burnt alive, while the bishop of Pamphilos suffered fatal injuries" (1992, 256–57). In addition, "73 churches, 26 schools and 5 athletic clubs were destroyed . . . the two principal Greek cemeteries (Şişli and Kınalı) were desecrated" (Alexandris 1992, 259).

The Turkish government's response lacked authenticity. While expressing their deepest regret for what had occurred and promising to compensate those whose properties were damaged, not all the victims could receive full compensation, and some received token amounts that did little to aid recovery efforts. During our discussions, the minorities framed these events as "a warning" to them, which they also perceived as a symbolic message to their community of what could happen to them in the future. They also stressed that these incidents were not viewed as traumatic as the 1964 deportations, which had a long-term effect on the community.

The 1964 deportations were particularly traumatic because Greek citizens living in Istanbul had to leave Turkey with minimal time to prepare. They were forced to leave their properties and were only permitted to leave with 20kg of luggage and with $20. Most of these Greek citizens were married to members of Istanbul's Greek Orthodox minority, which meant the policy had a direct effect on the minority community.

Concerning property issues, Alexandris notes that "the fiscal authorities had already taken a series of measures intended to ensure that Greek nationals were deprived of all possibility of liquidation of their interests. . . . Property belonging to Greek nationals was seized by the fiscal authorities as a precautionary measure against possible default on taxes, the assessments being calculated at several times what would have been required in the past" (1992, 284). The 1964 deportation not only destroyed the lives of the minorities and caused them to lose their dignity but it also affected their well-being as they lost their homes, families, business, and other personal belongings.

Religious Clergy Policies

Religion by its very nature is a controversial topic. Freedom of religion is a belief guaranteed to the minorities in the Lausanne Treaty. Issues have emerged, however, around the amount of control religious authorities have on minorities and how this is balanced with respect for state authority. It is challenging to compare the cases of minorities in Turkey and Greece due to the imbalance between the power of the Greek Orthodox Patriarchate in Istanbul and Muslim religious authorities (muftis) in Western Thrace. The role of the former with regard to Eastern Orthodox Christians is much greater than the latter for Muslims in Western Thrace. Nevertheless, to examine the role of the state, power struggles, and negative reciprocity in the field of religion, some comparison is possible.

It should be noted that Greece and Turkey's perceptions of these religious authorities play a significant role in how authority over the religious sector has become the site of power struggles between the two countries. Turkey's position regarding the nature and the role of the Patriarchate in Istanbul is a distinctive one. Although the Turkish state largely views the Patriarchate as a foreign institution that will one day be eradicated from Turkey's territory, the state has also regarded this institution as a trump card that can be used against Greece if it moves against Thracian Muslims (Akgönül 2013; Macar 2008). As Elçin Macar succinctly notes, "Turkey has always rejected foreign suggestions that the Patriarchate is a Turkish institution, and thus, a matter of internal concern. In practice, Turkey has treated the Patriarchate as a Greek institution. . . . if it were an internal issue, how could it be a trump card against foreigners? How could a Turkish institution be considered to be within the framework of the reciprocity principle?" (2008, 144).

Throughout the history of Greek-Turkish relations, the Turkish state's perception of the Patriarchate has fluctuated based on whether these relations were characterized as tense or in a state of rapprochement. As both countries became NATO members in 1952, Turkey's stance toward the Patriarchate became more cordial. During this time, the Turkish state loosened restrictions on minority schools, the Halki Seminary (Greek Orthodox theological school) was once again allowed to receive students from Greece as well as other Christian countries, the state provided visa freedom between Greece and Turkey, and the state granted Greek Orthodox parliamentarians more political responsibilities (Alexandris 1992, 248–51).

When the conflict in Cyprus erupted in the mid-1950s, relations between the Turkish state and the Patriarchate became strained and increasingly worsened. For the state, the Cyprus issue, as well as the minorities in Istanbul and the Patriarchate, became one and the same issue that needed to be addressed. As Alexis Alexandris stresses, "The Turkish government regarded the problem of Cyprus and that of the minorities, as well as that of the Patriarchate, as part of the same question" (1992, 298). In the Greek Orthodox minority's historical narratives, one of the major grievances about their treatment at the hands of the state concerns how most of Turkish society perceived and still views Greek Cypriots and the Istanbul Greek Orthodox community as the same. Viewing these communities as one and the same, and treating their members in the same way, damaged minority-majority relations significantly in Turkish society.

The Turkish state as well as civil society began to put pressure on the Patriarchate during the Cyprus conflict, as the representative of the minority, to "take disciplinary measures against Greek prelates under his jurisdiction who had meddled in politics in connection with Cyprus" (Alexandris 1992, 253). Turkish media positioned itself alongside the state and against the Patriarchate by publishing news articles claiming the Patriarchate was involved in anti-Turkish activities (Alexandris 1992, 268). There was also a breakdown in communication between the state and the Patriarchate, as the state did not respond to the Patriarchate's attempts to obtain written information about the September 1955 violent incidents against the Greek Orthodox community (Alexandris 1992, 269).

In addition to the September 1955 incidents, tension between the state and the Patriarchate peaked again as the conflict in Cyprus intensified in 1964. The state placed extra restrictions on the Patriarchate, which was increasingly viewed as a threat and supporter of Greek Cypriots. For example, "From the academic year of 1963–4, only Turkish citizens were permitted to study at the Theological School of Halki, resulting in the deportation of Hellenic as well as all other foreign theology students" (Alexandris 1992, 299). Further, during the 1964 deportations, the state blamed members of the Holy Synod for "engaging in political, administrative, educational and social activities of a subversive nature, and the metropolitans were divested of their Turkish citizenship and asked to leave the country" (Alexandris 1992, 299).

Minority's Memory Work

The state's minority-related policies in Turkey have influenced the ways in which the Greek Orthodox minority community remembers the past and who they are today. Their memory work is one of the most basic tools that is continuously developed and contributes to their minority identity and to a defense of their collective rights.

Minority Memory Is Existential

The Greek Orthodox minority in Istanbul conducts memory work to deal with the everyday challenges they experience, which not only result from the trauma associated with their community's demographic erosion but also the mutual distrust that exists between them and the state. Remembering the past is important for the purpose of creating a shared memory for collective identity groups. As Anthony Smith (1991) argues, a shared memory creates a shared sense of continuity between the past and the present. For Olick and Robbins (1998), collective memory functions to keep the past active, which is necessary to form an identity in the present. Remembering a past incident is part of any memory formation process. As discussed previously, even if individuals have not been directly harmed in these past events, they remember through social learning and interactions with others in their identity groups. For most members of the minority community included in this book, remembering their (negative) historical past is challenging both psychologically and socially. Nevertheless, minorities engage in this remembering process consciously because it is also regarded as a mechanism through which to strengthen their (minority) group identity. More fundamentally, for minorities, there is a direct link between the need to remember and the very existence of their identity group. As such, even if past historical traumas are painful to remember, they must be remembered.

Feelings of injustice are vivid parts of the minority's lives in the present. Older generations are aware of the crucial role they play in transmitting memories to younger generations. Although Istanbul's Greek Orthodox community is experiencing demographic erosion, remembering the past is key to retaining its identity. As one Greek Orthodox minority member noted,

> We still remember and discuss what happened to our fathers, mothers, and neighbors in 1955, 1964, and during the Cyprus conflict in general. Sometimes our children show a lack of interest in the past. They sometimes feel that talking about past injustices is not healthy. However, they should not forget the past [they should remember the past] to remain attached to their identities. I still feel anxious, as a minority, and I want my children to take care of themselves all the time. I even tell them not to be so "visible" in society because I

> am afraid they might be treated as I was treated in the past. (Writer, interview, 2015, Istanbul)

Members of the Greek Orthodox community also indicated that remembering the past allows them to know who they are and where they live, which is essential given existing problems with how history education is taught in Turkish schools and how the media frames minorities. Even if there have been some positive developments such as the inclusion of minorities in images used in Turkish history textbooks, there is much more work to be done. Liberal Turkish media largely romanticizes the Istanbul Greek Orthodox minority, portraying them as a near-extinct social group that must be protected. Conversely, conservative media is more threatening, employing hate speech against minorities and portraying the Greek Orthodox minority as a national threat. According to the Istanbul Greek Orthodox minority, part of the media works to preserve negative images and stereotypes regarding their community. In the words of one member of the community,

> I scrutinize newspapers every day. Certain newspapers and columnists always target minorities. They use specific discourse persistently, which contains hate, revenge, stereotypes, and other negativities about the Greek Orthodox minority as well as others. I find these writings and send corrections or complaints. I do this every day. It is my job. But I still know that these stereotypes are entrenched in society and hard to transform. (Journalist, interview, 2013, Istanbul)

Feelings of both hope and hopelessness about the future are woven throughout in the narratives of the Greek Orthodox minority community. These mixed feelings also manifest in how they behave in their daily lives. While they complain about the persistent negative images of their communities in history education, the media, and in the discourses of some state officials, the minorities themselves also work to transmit negative memories to younger generations to preserve their identity and protect themselves.

Unmourned Traumas and Transgenerational Transmission

Unmourned traumas are alive until the perpetrators and the victims or the victim's family decides to deal with the past and reconcile their relationship. Otherwise, the wounds of these traumas, whether personal or societal, remain open. We typically observe the transmission of these traumas to younger generations through various means but mostly through stories, written and visual media, and education. One minority member tells the story of the September 6–7, 1955 incidents as a form of transmitted historical trauma and quotes his granddad:

> They smashed into our house and destroyed everything inside, but the only thing that truly upset me that day was this: we were forced out of our own home and lined up on the street like happy kids. They kept throwing our belongings from our closets on the second floor to the street while they wanted me to wave the Turkish flag in front of my wife, son, and daughters. I would have sacrificed my life to ensure that the flag was safe. My allegiance to this nation has previously been tested numerous times. . . . So that no harm could come to the flag, I had already spent four years in the military. (Actor, interview, 2023, Istanbul)

Then, the minority member added: "This is the biggest wound in me. It should be known! I didn't experience the September 6–7 incidents. My grandparents experienced and told me about that terrifying night. Nowhere in the world should it ever happen again" (Actor, interview, 2023, Istanbul).

Societal traumas are difficult to overcome unless there is a safe space to discuss them and there are policies that directly support reconciliation. When referring to the past, most of the Greek Orthodox minority emphasize specific historical episodes. In doing this consistently, these events have become memory markers and unmourned historical traumas for the community. Many of the stories told to me by the Greek Orthodox minority who remembered the past in connection to their own identities were full of negative incidents. Simultaneously, however, they also looked at the past nostalgically, using such phrases as *eskiler güzeldi be çocuğum* (the past was good my dearest), while also noting *ah be yavrum, çok çektik biz* (O my dearest, we experienced a lot).

Some of the most prominent memory markers for Istanbul's Greek Orthodox minority include Turkification policies such as the Wealth Tax or Capital Tax, the September 1955 incidents, the 1964 deportations of Istanbul's Greek citizens, and the Cyprus conflict. They cited these tragic historical episodes as integral to understanding who they are today. During our conversations, the minority community remembered these events through the lens of what happened to them directly and what happened to their relatives and members of their community. Since most of the minority community members I spoke with were old enough to remember those days (they were either children or teenagers during these tragic events), their witnessing of these events and narratives revealed how and why the historical tragedies a group of people experience is memorialized in a persistent way. During my conversations with youth from the Greek Orthodox minority, they demonstrated how memories of the same incidents have been transmitted from generation to generation, although they refrain from talking about them in the same way as their parents.

Turning to the Wealth Tax (1942)[6] as an example, the Greek Orthodox minority members remember this episode, reflecting on how the Turkish state sought to erase minorities, particularly the Jewish minorities from Turkey's economic life. Some of the Greek Orthodox minority focused on how unjust the implementation of the policy was against the minorities.

> According to the officials at that time, this tax would be collected only from the people who had illegitimate economic gains during World War II. However, shortly after, we understood that the policy's aim was to erase the whole minority community from economic life. The economy had to be "Turkified" too, as with everything else. We were punished and pushed aside in society. We had to become less visible in every part of society in the following years just to be safe and untouched. (Retired teacher, interview, 2013, Istanbul)

Minority members argue they were exposed to arbitrary tax rates on their properties and were made to pay much higher tax rates than Turks. During our extended and repeated conversations, the feeling of injustice felt by the Greek Orthodox minority was quite salient. They felt grief and despair when they talked about the consequences of this policy on their community.

> Consider two children in a house; one is adopted, and one is your child by birth. At the dinner table, you say, "The adopted will eat less and clean the table and the other one will eat more and play after." This may not completely explain, but we, as a minority community, would understand after some other incidents, too, that we were that adopted child and would be punished all the time. I'm too old to remember and talk about this, but why we deserved this treatment, I still do not know. (Minority foundation representative, interview, 2013, Istanbul)

Members of the Greek Orthodox minority community also compared the 1955 incidents[7] and the 1964 deportations[8] in terms of which episode caused more damage to their community physically, economically, and psychologically. For the minorities, although the state aimed to eliminate the entire Greek Orthodox community from Istanbul with the 1964 deportations, the policy only demanded the explicit deportation of Greek citizens living in Istanbul. Nevertheless, given the deep familial ties between Greek citizens and the Istanbul Greek Orthodox community, this policy affected both Greek citizens and their Greek Orthodox family members. As one minority community member remembered,

> The termination of the Ankara Agreement and the deportation of Greek citizens in 1964 not only focused on the Greek citizens. The policy was focused on the families of Greek citizens who were generally from Greek Orthodox minority. Greek citizens had been living in Istanbul for a long time. What happens when you live somewhere for a long time? You start to build a new life there. They did the same thing. Greek citizens married members of the Greek Orthodox minority, they had families and kids. So, what the state planned was not only to expel Greek citizens with this policy but also to expel the Greek Orthodox minority who were married and had children with Greek citizens. Therefore, the state wanted to cleanse the minority population, too. When the state asked a Greek citizen who was already married to a minority member to leave Turkey, how could he leave his family behind? He could not. Therefore, both Greek citizens and their minority family members had to leave together, leave everything behind, and go somewhere else with only 20 kg of baggage. (Journalist, interview, 2014, Istanbul)

In comparison to the 1964 deportations, the Istanbul Greek Orthodox minority viewed the 1955 incidents as a warning for the community. They argued that the 1955 incidents were a "cinematographic" event in which the stores belonging to minorities in Istanbul's Istiklal Street (in Beyoğlu district) were looted, windows were broken, and the minorities were threatened verbally. Consequently, some of the Greek Orthodox minority decided to move from Istanbul's European side to the Anatolian side, but this migration was voluntary and within the city. Recalling these events, one minority membered noted that

> it was a message to the minorities living in Turkey to be careful and be as invisible as possible. They [the majority] wanted us to see that Turkey belonged to them. The 1964 deportations, on the other hand, were more than a message. That was real violence. The state did not kill us, but [it] did more than this. It took our memories from us. We had to leave the territories where we were born, we became insecure, we left our neighbors, our plants on our patios, our animals, and our homes. How much of your life, how many of your memories, could fit in 20kg of luggage? (Academic, interview, 2014, Istanbul)

According to the minorities, the real motivation behind the events of 1955 and 1964 was the conflict between Greek and Turkish Cypriots on the island of Cyprus. The minorities believe that the Turkish state and the broader public were punishing the Greek Orthodox minority in Turkey for what was happening to Turkish Cypriots. The most important aspect emerging from their memories of this period is their denial of any connection the Turkish majority established between them (Istanbul's Greek Orthodox community) and Cyprus's Greek Cypriot community. As such, they felt the state viewed their minority community and Greek Cypriots as one and the same, which resulted in the state's negative treatment of minorities in Istanbul. Whenever Greek Cypriots mistreated Turkish Cypriots, Istanbul's Greek Orthodox minority faced retaliation from Turks in Turkey, which also included a series of state policies that had negative repercussions on the minorities.

> We are not the same community as Greek Cypriots. There are similarities in our traditions and religion, however we are two different communities historically and territorially. However, even though these differences were well-known by everyone during that time (by the state, the public, and Turkish media), there was an atmosphere in which everybody started to believe that Greek Cypriots were equal to Istanbul's Greek-Orthodox community. The media and members of the press, in particular, worked to consolidate this idea that Istanbul's Greek Orthodox people were the same as Greek Cypriots. [In doing so], they encouraged the Turkish majority to be against us. To punish the wrongdoings Greek Cypriots in Cyprus perpetrated against Turkish Cypriots, we were targeted. We became the scapegoats . . . the 1955 and 1964 incidents happened. We were treated badly, and we were forced to leave our homes, and we had to

> lose our memories. That's why there are only a few thousand Greek Orthodox people left today in Turkey, as opposed to being more than a hundred thousand. (Former minority foundation representative, interview, 2016, Istanbul)

In criticizing the past, members of the Istanbul Greek Orthodox minority also analyzed who did what to them and why. They focused on themes of injustice, scapegoating, blame, memories, and a fear of disappearing or becoming lost. The bridge between the past and present, for them, is built by their memories of the past and by transmitting these to younger generations through historical narratives.

Demographic Loss

Istanbul's Greek Orthodox minority perceives itself as having been an integral part of Istanbul's cultural development, particularly during the Ottoman Empire and the early Turkish Republic. The Greek Orthodox minority, therefore, perceives themselves as locals, not as guests in Turkey. Despite being in the minority, they feel they are co-owners of the city of Istanbul with the majority. According to them, their contribution to Istanbul's culture is bigger than their numbers today. Much like the Turkish Muslim minority in Western Thrace, they note repeatedly, "We have been living here for centuries." The Istanbul Greek Orthodox community has always been proud of being Istanbulian (from the cosmopolitan city of Istanbul) and of their roots that date back to the Roman Empire.

While the Greek Orthodox minority feels proud about their centuries-long attachment to Istanbul, they also acknowledge that the minority is on the brink of being lost due to their demographic erosion. The Greek Orthodox community and scholars use various figures to describe how many of the Greek Orthodox minority still live in Istanbul. One of the reasons for this variety is that no recent census data exists on the number of Istanbul's Greek Orthodox minority. Nevertheless, broad estimates suggest between 2,000–3,000 (Kara 2009) to approximately 5,000 (Gavroglou 2012) people.[9] The age of the community is alarming with approximately 60 percent of the community aged between sixty and seventy years old (Çapan 2019). Therefore, demographic loss is also a key component of the Greek Orthodox minority's memory work. The issue of continued demographic loss is the contemporary manifestation of trauma for the Istanbul Greek Orthodox minority. This loss not only stems from an aging community but more importantly it stems from the policies implemented by the

Turkish state in the past such as the 1955 incidents and the 1964 population deportations. It is this loss and the fear of being lost as a community that motivates the minority today to conduct memory work around these incidents.

The demographic loss at the heart of the Istanbul Greek Orthodox minority is most felt in minority schools. As community members highlighted, there are limited groups of people who can send their children to minority schools in Istanbul. These are Greek-speaking traditional Istanbul Greek Orthodox minority families, Arab Orthodox community members who have migrated to Istanbul from Antakya, Iskenderun, and Mersin since the 1980s,[10] families of those who have married across identity lines (mixed marriages), and Greek citizens who live in Turkey. These schools face the constant threat of closure due to the gradual decrease of the minority community. Today, there are only five minority schools in Istanbul including one on the largest of the Princes' Islands (also known as the Büyükada) in Istanbul's Adalar district and the minority school in Imbros (Gökçeada) with an average of 281 students in total across all of these schools (Çapan 2019). As one minority member mentioned,

> Especially after 1964, the Greek Orthodox minority population decreased significantly. When there are not enough children to send to the minority schools, the schools faced closures. Currently, there are only a few active schools, and they have few students. There is one preschool, three elementary schools, and three middle-lyceum. To combat the declining numbers of students attending minority schools, the minority community decided to change its policy of only accepting the children of the Istanbul Greek Orthodox minority families. Today, the only formal requirement to become a student at the minority school is to be a member of the Orthodox religion. (Teacher, interview, 2013, Istanbul)

The most explicit example of trauma the Greek Orthodox minority experienced related to education can be observed through the testimonies of teachers working in minority schools. One teacher emphasized that working with so few children—in some cases only 4–5 students—is not only incredibly dramatic but also challenging due to the cultural diversity of these children. Some of these children speak Greek, while others are unable to communicate in this language. Likewise, some children speak Turkish, while their classmates cannot. Consequently, teachers not only experience difficulties in communicating with students but they also feel anxious over the small student numbers. Walking into their classrooms every day reminds them of historic state policies that targeted the minority and have led to the community's drastic reduction in size (Teacher, online interview, 2020, Istanbul).

What unites these minority children of different cultural backgrounds, and their minority community more generally, is their Christian Orthodoxy. As alluded to above, what divides them is their language. The Greek spoken by Istanbul's Greek Orthodox minority differs from the Greek spoken in Greece. Further, members of the Arab Orthodox community speak Arabic as a community. Notwithstanding these differences, Istanbul's Greek Orthodox minority has sought to stem their demographic erosion and preserve the Orthodox identity by integrating the Antakya Arab Orthodox community into the Greek Orthodox community through the Patriarchate, the minority education system, and by giving them key positions in the management of minority foundations.

While the issue of demographic loss is the major concern for the minority, for some within the Greek Orthodox community, allowing other Orthodox communities to integrate into the mainstream Greek Orthodox community has created identity-related concerns, that is, about preserving the "purity" of the Greek Orthodox identity. For others, the integration of other Orthodox communities has increased minority numbers and will help to preserve the Orthodox identity. As one Greek Orthodox minority community member succinctly noted,

> So now the Greek Orthodox community is behaving pragmatically and accepting everyone into the community, even though they do not share the same cultural, historical, and social past with the Istanbul Greek Orthodox community. The children of the Antakya Arab Orthodox community do not speak Greek. The children of people in mixed marriages (with Turkish-speaking people) also generally do not speak Greek because in their daily lives and in their families, they mostly speak Turkish due to its practicality. Therefore, the importance and usage of Greek have declined in general. So, how are these children going to learn their history if they do not speak Greek? These children also experience difficulties integrating into the schools when they do not speak Greek. Their educational development moves slower. Most importantly, when they do not speak Greek, how will they talk about the past, the memories of their families and so on? We are increasing in number maybe, but we are losing our identity. (Retired teacher, interview, 2013, Istanbul)

For some within Istanbul's Greek Orthodox minority, and particularly those who consider the Greek Orthodox to be Istanbul's original minority and the primary actors in minority affairs, they are concerned about the role of non-Greek Orthodox in the community's affairs. Their discontent was palpable in their narratives about non-Greek Orthodox minority members in key decision-making positions in the minority community. For instance, they questioned whether only Greek-speaking minorities could identify as part of the Greek Orthodox minority, or whether members of the Antakya Orthodox community can really be included. Another issue is that in recent years some Greeks have begun relocating to Turkey due to work and educational opportunities. In doing so, they have also begun to integrate themselves into Istanbul's Greek Orthodox culture by joining events and attending minority schools and churches. Although they speak Greek, they are not fully part of the Istanbul Greek Orthodox minority community due to their own historical experiences, which differs from the history of Turkey's minorities.

Conversations with youth members of Istanbul's Greek Orthodox community revealed that they are open to the integration of other Orthodox minorities into the community. However, they also mention that the Patriarchate and leaders of Istanbul's Greek Orthodox community provide privileges, including more economic support and more tolerance in schools to the Arab Orthodox community. Some youth members are even frustrated with these privileges, noting that "if the community provided us with the same privileges they provide to the Antakya Orthodox community youth, we would be even more developed" (Youth member, online interview, 2021, Istanbul).

Some of them also argue that the narratives their Arab Orthodox friends use toward them are irritating. One minority youth member mentioned how disappointing it is to hear jokes from their Arab Orthodox friends about the Istanbul Greek Orthodox community's so-called desire to exclude other Orthodox minorities (Youth member, online interview, 2020, Istanbul). For instance, one youth member noted that Greek Orthodox youth "speak in Greek when we are together, but when an Arab Orthodox friend joins us, we try to be mindful and change to Turkish because we think our friend would want to feel included" (Youth member, online interview, 2021, Istanbul). As this young person revealed, the intention is often misunderstood, however, and their Arab Orthodox friends can view this as a form of marginalization. These youth members also mention that even if the Orthodox culture is what brings them together and they have friends from the Arab Orthodox community, there are moments when both community members feel at odds due to their lack of a common language (Youth member, online interview, 2021, Istanbul).

Beyond these internal identity-related concerns, the minority also questions the perspective of the majority about the demographic loss of the minority today. Despite their acknowledgment of their significance for the city's history and culture, one of the most bothersome narratives for the Istanbul Greek Orthodox community is the narrative of *the lost colors of Istanbul.* Although they acknowledge that their numbers are dwindling, when the majority Turkish population refers to their minority community as one of the lost colors of Istanbul, they find it an incomplete narrative. The Greek Orthodox minority neither disputes that their community is rich and diverse culturally nor that their numbers have declined dramatically.[11] However, they argue that it is essential for the Turkish majority population to question more consciously *why* this colorful part of Turkish culture has been lost or, at the very least, actively attempt to learn more about the remaining Greek Orthodox culture rather than lamenting its absence. The Istanbul Greek Orthodox community wants neither their existence nor their past experiences reduced to nostalgic, rose-tinted songs as quoted below:

> İstiklal Caddesi eskiden böyle değildi. Burada hep şık Rum Hanımefendi ve Beyefendiler vardı. Dükkanlar hep onlarındı. Hiç unutamam köşedeki Rum pastanesini. Hele o Rumca şarkılar!
>
> (İstiklal street was not like this in the past. There were very fashionable Greek Orthodox women and men walking on the street where the stores were owned by them. I cannot forget the patisserie at the corner. Especially, these Greek songs . . . !)

Although this narrative contains a form of positive recognition of minority culture and its centrality to Istanbul's culture, as well as an awareness of the minority community as cosmopolitan, modern, and educated, for minorities, this nostalgic narrative nevertheless partially obscures the very real issues facing the minority community. Istanbul's Greek Orthodox minority, therefore, demands that the state and members of the Turkish majority take more concrete and conscious steps to elevate Greek Orthodox culture, specifically in Istanbul, but also more generally throughout Turkey. As mentioned at this chapter's outset, there are projects that not only bring Istanbul's Greek Orthodox community members together but also that bring the Greek Orthodox community together with other non-

Muslim minority groups, namely Jewish and Armenian minority members. Through these projects, minorities from these different religious communities meet and learn about each other while highlighting for the majority that non-Muslim communities continue to live in Turkey who are culturally different but proud Turkish citizens.

Belongingness, Loyalty, and Citizenship

> One day, the state would honor my efforts with a prize. The day before the awards presentation, a representative of the state called me. "I'm really sorry, but I must ask you a question," he said. Then, he added: "Please don't get me wrong." He appeared to be exceedingly anxious. I wondered what sort of problem would have him so concerned. Then, in an ashamed tone, he inquired, "Are you Turkish?" I snapped back by saying "What do you mean, are you Turkish? I've been employed by state theaters for more than ten years." "You are right," he answered, "but I'm not asking, the bureaucracy is asking." I understood him because my name is not Turkish. I never considered altering my name because I am an Istanbul-born Greek Orthodox. I understood him. He was asking if I am a Turkish citizen. He didn't want to make a mistake. I am Turkish and believe in the nation-state system. In the law, it says, "Everyone bound to the Turkish state through the bond of citizenship is a Turk." This is not an ethnic, but a civic description to me. (Actor, online interview, 2023)

This story belongs to a minority member, but he describes himself as "Turkish. I am above and beyond of my minority identity with the works I have been doing in Turkey." In a way, he thinks his citizenship identity is his superordinate identity. However, this does not mean that he sees his identity as exclusionary. He notes that he has not attended Sunday prayers for more than six years and he does not like tea/barbeque parties of the minority churches. However, he adds that he was invited to an event recently by one of the minority churches and he had shivers while singing the songs and realized how much he missed the feeling of being part of the church. Proudly, he adds, "Even my Turkish wife was surprised how could I sing all the church songs."

The Greek Orthodox minority in Istanbul view their identities and the interpretations they gave to historical events involving their group in different ways. It is clear that because identity is such a fluid concept, it is difficult to fit into a mold, especially when traumas and historical experiences have an impact on the process of identity formation. As with the Turkish Muslim minority of Western Thrace in Greece, Istanbul's Greek Orthodox minority is not monolithic as a group. They are from various political, social, and economic backgrounds. Their narratives about how they create meaning about the past also contain differences from time to time. Therefore, as observed in the above case, minority identity salience and the degree of attachment minorities have to their minority community vary based on the time and the context.

Therefore, the Greek Orthodox community's belongingness to the land and especially to Istanbul was unquestionable. The salience of their minority and citizenship identities, however, was relatively dynamic. During the interviews I have conducted in Istanbul, I felt that although the minority community is concerned about their demographic erosion, their foundations, and minority education, they are also concerned with issues that affect the whole of Turkey. While rare, some of those I spoke to noted that they were not "interested in the minority-related issues." Rather, they were more preoccupied with human rights, poverty, and refugee issues in Turkey.

They explain the fluctuating salience of their minority and citizen identities as related to not only the importance of their Turkish citizenship identity but also the effect of external developments, which serve to increase the salience of their minority identity. According to Istanbul's Greek Orthodox minority, their minority and citizenship identities are relatively exclusive. Although they do not explain this as a clear binary, from time to time they think their minority identity comes above their citizenship identity. As an example, when bilateral relations between Greece and Turkey sour, the minority position themselves accordingly. They become more inward and focused on their minority identity because they fear their existing place in society is at stake. Consequently, their minority identity increases in salience. When the Turkish media attack their identity, their minority identity once again becomes more salient. At that moment, their minority identity takes priority over their Turkish citizen identity.

On the other hand, they define their citizen identity as being part of Turkish society, feeling like a relatively equal part of the country, and being interested in the same sociopolitical and economic issues that are relevant to any Turkish citizen irrespective of their association with a minority community. Their citizen identity becomes more salient in moments when they feel like any other citizen. More specifically, when their needs and rights are met, they feel satisfied as a minority and feel comfortable enough to focus on their nonminority identity and non-minority-related issues. This renders their minority identity less salient. As one youth member of the minority noted,

> I appreciate what the current government does. The changes in the Foundations Law and the return of expropriated estates back to the minority are huge achievements. It means that minorities are in a better situation in terms of collective rights. But what about the rights of Kurds, the rights of women, the rights of youth in general, the rights of LGBT, and so on? I'm a minority member but this is just one part of me. I also feel I need to defend the rights of others in society. The government is dragging its feet over democratizing in general. (Artist, interview, 2013, Istanbul)

Another individual from the community echoed these sentiments, noting that

> I see that I am not the only minority in this society. We are very few in number, so the state changed its perception regarding us and does not see us as a threat anymore which is very positive for the community. However, there are others in society who are treated very negatively. When I feel like an equal citizen in society, I begin to think about other discrimination and feel right to raise my voice against them. (Youth member, online interview, 2020, Istanbul)

Importantly, this does not mean that those whose citizenship identity is more salient care less about minority issues. Rather, they are more outward-looking, aware of the struggles of others, and of universal human rights and values. For example, when there is a protest around an issue that is important to them, they do not hesitate to join. Among the Greek Orthodox community, young people whose citizenship identity is more salient seem more open toward their dual identity (citizen and minority identity) than members of the older generation.

Nevertheless, despite their attachment to their land, their city, and their citizenship identity, there still exists an overarching lack of mutual trust between the Istanbul Greek Orthodox minority and the state, which is deeply embedded. Consequently, this lack of trust means that for those within the minority whose citizen identity is salient, it is never consistently so.

From the minority's perspective, there is no reason for the state to distrust the minority or to conduct constant loyalty checks. Members of Istanbul's Greek Orthodox community argue that the community's belongingness to Turkey is nonnegotiable. For them, attachment to a territory brings with it attachment to a country. Turkey is where they, as well as their grandparents, were born. The Greek Orthodox minority maintains a deep attachment and feeling of belongingness to Turkey despite feeling that they are not treated as equal citizens, holding on to past resentment toward the state because of how they were treated, and the continued anxiety they experience in the present. As one member of the Istanbul Greek Orthodox minority community argued,

> If you were to ask all the members of the minority in Turkey where they wanted to be buried when they die, they would all respond with: "Turkey, I was born here, I was raised here, and my family is here. All my memories are related to this territory. If I die here, how can I think about moving to a different territory to be buried? My country is here." If there is an earthquake in Athens (Greece) and Izmit (Turkey), the Greek Orthodox minority feel primarily worried about [their relatives], the ones in Turkey before the ones in Athens. Because even if we have friends and relatives in Athens, Turkey is our home. And you think about your home first. If your child and her friend were in an accident, who do you think about first? First, you think of your child and then the other. (Minority foundation representative, interview, 2013, Istanbul)

Istanbul's Greek Orthodox minority constantly questions why their loyalty to the state continues to be in doubt. They believe the state and the majority perceive them as traitors, outsiders, and the enemy. They think these frames and forms of othering relate to their history with the state as well as contextual issues such as conflicts between Greece and Turkey. More specifically, the Greek Orthodox minority underscore that when the Cyprus conflict erupted, and Greek Cypriots treated Turkish Cypriots negatively, the state used the Greek Orthodox minorities as a scapegoat irrespective of the difference between the minorities and Greek Cypriots. According to Greek Orthodox minority members, negative historical narratives or mental frames about their community should change because they are simply not true.

According to the Greek Orthodox minority, the state's treatment of them is connected to Greece-Turkey bilateral relations and how relations between these two countries have changed over time in response to local, regional, and global events. Both Istanbul's Greek Orthodox minorities and the state view their relations to be more open and constructive than in previous decades. They believe this change largely stems from Turkey's EU candidacy process and an associated positive approach to minority affairs. Since 2002, the governing AKP (Justice and Development Party) has adopted notions of tolerance and multiculturalism, which has benefited minorities somewhat. Although Turkey moved away from the EU process around 2005, the state returned more than a thousand previously seized minority properties to minority foundations[12] and provided compensation for some others as of 2022 (Oktay 2022). Minorities also perceive their participation in parliament as significant. Since the beginning of the Republic, various minority members have become parliamentarians in the Turkish assembly. Some who became representatives have supported different governments, while others have complained about state injustices against the minority.[13] Lastly, the state's decision to delay the elections in the foundations has always been a point of contentions among Istanbul's Greek Orthodox minority. However, following the implementation of new electoral guidelines (after ten years of delay), elections were held in 2022 (Directorate General of Foundations 2022).

Despite the state's rhetorical commitments and some of its policies benefiting them, the Greek Orthodox minority mostly remains suspicious of the government's current position on minority affairs. While the minority acknowledges that the state has made some structural changes in the past, they argue that any rhetorical commitments must be complemented with tangible and constructive structural changes. Despite the state's discourse on multiculturalism, there has been little structural change in terms of how minorities are perceived or their socioeconomic or political status. The minority also argues that the internal motivation for democratization within Turkey should take precedence over any democratization brought through an external process (that is, the EU process). As one minority member highlighted,

> Whenever the state [Turkey] was frustrated with other nations or communities outside, they sought revenge inside [domestically], which was directed toward us. Now, since Cyprus is not a big deal and the minority is very small, there is no minority threat at all. The current government is working very closely with minorities and changing laws relating to the minority for our benefit. Very positive and [yet] very late. (Minority foundation representative, interview, 2015, Istanbul)

Another member of Istanbul's Greek Orthodox community shared a similar opinion, emphasizing the trust deficit that exists between the minority and the state.

> Since history contains many negative memories, the positive developments achieved by the current government are, of course, appreciated but viewed with suspicion and caution. The minority community seems to be paranoid in the sense that even when there is a positive picture in front of us, we still feel anxious and fearful about the steps [the government] has taken. This is not healthy, but this is how we are, at least, the older generation. So, the new government expresses "tolerance" to the minority. What is tolerance? Who shows tolerance? The government today shows tolerance, but what about the next government? You never know if contextual changes will affect the minorities' lives negatively again or not. This ambiguous situation has made us paranoid for decades. (Retired teacher, interview, 2013, Istanbul)

In one-on-one interviews, especially the minorities whose memories of past injustices are vivid, these individuals showed more sensitivity to the gradual souring of Greek-Turkish relations that has occurred since 2015 over the refugee crisis, sovereignty in the Mediterranean Sea, increasing armament, and issues related to NATO and the EU. In line with these issues, the Greek Orthodox minority feels more tense when geopolitical crises emerge that involve the two countries. In such moments, minority members noted that they try to become as invisible as possible. This manifests in their active disengagement from any form of commentary or action that may provoke the government or the Turkish majority during times of interstate crisis. The Greek Orthodox minority fears that if an incident were to occur today between the two countries in the Mediterranean, they could be swept away from Turkey. This fear stems directly from the historical traumas they experienced in the past. When tensions flare between Greece and Turkey, memories of the 1955 and 1964 incidents become more salient for the minorities who fear they could once again become the political target of the state and the majority. Istanbul's Greek Orthodox minority feel they deserve to live without fear irrespective of the shifting geopolitical dynamics between Turkey and Greece.

Their narratives of fear are also connected to the narrative of showing *tolerance* toward minorities. In social psychology, tolerance is often discussed as "being nonjudgmental, open, and valuing diversity, or it is considered a generalized positive attitude toward out-groups" (Verkuyten and Yogeeswaran 2017). Even if tolerance refers to positive attitudes, treatment, and ways of behaving toward others in a pluralistic society, Istanbul's Greek Orthodox minority views the term negatively in the context of minority-state relations. For them, the tolerating actor (the state) typically has more power than the actor who is tolerated (the minorities).

This negative view was emphasized throughout my conversations with the Istanbul Greek Orthodox minority. They highlighted the discomfort they felt when their Turkish majority friends acted as their saviors. According to the minorities, their Turkish friends feel the need to defend their minority friends when they are exposed to clear verbal attacks related to their identity. Even if the minorities feel their friends do so sincerely, this behavior nevertheless conveys to the minorities that they are viewed as weak and lacking in their own agency. They view this behavior as an overt manifestation of the subconscious internalization of strict minority and majority categorization, whereby the minority is less powerful or, in some cases, inferior. As one member of the Istanbul Greek Orthodox minority succinctly argued,

> It is such an interesting feeling that you experience when your friends behave like you are creatures to be defended against others all the time. Even they sometimes use the phrase "siz de insansınız" [you are human too!] to prove that they do not think negatively about the minorities. I am not sure if there is a need to stress that I am human, too. Maybe it would be better if they would say "There is no difference between you and me in this country. We are both part of it." (Business owner, interview, 2014, Istanbul)

In a similar vein, another community member noted that

> when we go out with my Turkish friends, my friends always feel the need to keep me out of conflicts. They do it instinctively. They advise me not to speak and avoid any trouble for my benefit. And this is what I do not want to accept. (Minority foundation representative, interview, 2013, Istanbul)

During our conversations, it became clear that members of Istanbul's Greek Orthodox minority were irritated by these demonstrations of saviorism by some of the majority, believing this behavior reinforces existing power relations and the differentiation of people categorically. For the minority, if the parties were equal, nobody would need to be saved and tolerated. However, in-group and out-group relations are structured around historical traumas and sociopsychological boundaries, as in the case of the Istanbul Greek Orthodox minority and the Turkish majority. The minorities view the actions of their Turkish majority friends as unnecessary and, at times, humiliating. Further, for the minorities, these actions only serve as a reminder of the power imbalance that continues to exist in Turkish society.

In such cases, the savior party employs tolerance subconsciously, which causes the boundaries between the two parties to become stronger. The less powerful party becomes aware of this because the relationship happens on the boundary zone (majority-minority). As such, a high percentage of the minorities said they were uncomfortable with narratives of tolerance and wanted a relationship with the majority based on mutual understanding and power.

In addition to feelings of irritation regarding tolerance narratives, Istanbul's Greek Orthodox minority community also argued that the state used them to signal its progressive stance toward minorities for the benefit of external stakeholders. According to the minority, even if some politicians are honest about implementing policies to improve their lives in Turkey, they think these policies have been created to appease the international community and especially the EU and the US. Consequently, the Greek Orthodox minority view the behavior of the state with much suspicion.

> The government overadvertises when it appoints a minority member to an official position. They want to say that the state respects minorities and has made some policy changes. Turkey is more pluralist, inclusive, and tolerant today. But why advertise it so much? Is not it normal to appoint a minority member to an official position? Is there a law that says minority members cannot work in official positions? There is not, but the state acts as if it is granting [us] a favor. The EU demands and Turkey achieves and shows it. It is like we are material to be displayed in Turkey's front window. (Business owner, interview, 2014, Istanbul)

Rigid Boundaries and Visibility-Invisibility

To understand changes in the social boundaries between the minorities and the majority, it is necessary to examine their interactions in the social boundary zone. As Tilly argues (2005, 137), our social interactions with the world around us are based on the formation, transformation, activation, and suppression of social boundaries. The conditions around which these boundaries are formed and transformed, including the time period, the place, and the varied modes of interaction, influence the relationship between identity groups. Interactions between the majority and members of the Istanbul Greek Orthodox minority have shifted over time. Periods of conflict, such as the Cyprus conflict and the incidents of 1955 and 1964, negatively impacted these interactions within society. These majority-minority dynamics have continued to evolve in contemporary times.

As the Greek Orthodox minorities explained, group identities are usually not salient in everyday conversations between the Greek Orthodox minority and their Turkish friends. During these conversations, they do not talk about past traumas, which largely means social boundaries between them are unimportant. In every conversation, however, there is a potential for discussions to turn toward history. In such cases, minority and majority identities can become salient. Some of the minorities noted that an ordinary conversation about the past, particularly one related to the Greek Orthodox minority's identity, can turn into a heated debate and group identities can become salient. It should be noted that the Greek Orthodox minority's integration into Turkish culture is very strong in comparison to the Turkish minority in Western Thrace who speak relatively little Greek. Istanbul's Greek Orthodox community speaks Turkish well and is immersed in Turkish culture. Therefore, the Greek Orthodox minority recognizes the relativity of the social boundaries (which is based on context, conversations, and relationships) between them and the Turkish majority. Even if every interaction between the minority and the majority is unique, these interactions still influence minorities.

According to members of the Greek Orthodox minority group, these social boundaries or invisible barriers have been built over time through state policies, how history has been taught in schools, and general negative discourse about minorities transmitted by the media. Another minority member referred to the boundaries and how they were formed, arguing that

> when I was conducting my compulsory military service, one officer became obsessed with my minority identity. Every day he was asking me to go to his room and asking me to tell him how Turks defeated the Greeks in the Greco-Turkish War. I stayed in "attention" mode in front of him and repeated the story to him every damn day! A person who experiences this becomes nationalist to keep his/her

> identity. I do not claim that being a nationalist is something special or good. All of my friends are Muslim Turks. But I cannot be candid with them. They open their heart to me. But I'm still afraid about whether they are going to do something negative to my family or me. And I am fifty-five years old. I still have these feelings. But my kids are not like me. Their communication is great with the majority, with their Turk friends. They are visible and are not afraid of being visible. They are at the top of the classes in school and do not hesitate to take these roles/duties. They are more courageous and fearless. (Former minority foundation representative, interview, 2015, Istanbul)

Although minority group members highlight similarities between their everyday relationships with members of the majority and those with other minority members, they emphasize that they are still aware of redlines they cannot cross even with their closest friends from the majority. According to them, there is always some sort of psychological barrier, which is invisible but reflects their relationship in one way or the other with members of the majority. As one member of the minority community argued,

> The most concrete example of this situation emerges when the conversation between me and my best Turkish friend comes to certain topics like the Greco-Turkish War, loyalty to the state, nationalism, belongingness, and so on. At one point in the discussion, I feel like my words are listened to very carefully. So, you can sometimes feel questioned even in conversations with your best friends. I feel like I shouldn't cross these redlines, but, instead, be moderate in my ideas. (Business owner, interview, 2014, Istanbul)

It is clear from the minorities' own narratives that these invisible social boundaries, which are deeply embedded on all sides of the boundary, seem impermeable, even if members of the minority argue they are willing to dissolve these boundaries. Further, as the minorities noted, their fear of confrontation (not to breach any redlines) means the boundaries are unmovable.

As one of the minority members mentioned, "It does not make sense and there is no need to talk about history in daily life" (Teacher, interview, 2013, Istanbul). However, one way or the other, when discussing sensitive issues, people begin to generalize, see the other as part of a homogenous group, and view themselves as superior and more legitimate than the other.

When this occurs, collective axiology and boundary mechanisms start to function automatically during these kinds of conversations. The two variables comprising collective axiology—the degree of collective generality and the degree of axiological balance—create shifts in interpersonal relations between a member of the majority and a member of the minority (Rothbart and Korostelina 2006; Korostelina 2014). The higher the collective generality, the more an out-group is seen as unitary and homogenous, demonstrating fixed patterns of behavior, and committed to rigid beliefs and values, wherever those in the out-group may live in the world (Rothbart and Korostelina 2006; Korostelina 2014).

Irrespective of the depth of friendship between those involved, when people begin to broach sensitive issues during a conversation, the collective generality of the majority group member increases, and the other individual is viewed as the same as other group members. The qualities of their friendship are erased suddenly. Discussing past incidents, therefore, can easily alter relations between people who experienced past incidents or are living with memories of the past. In addition, the degree of axiological balance relates to a parallelism of sorts between both positive and negative characteristics within groups. In the case of minority and majority relations, when both or one of the parties have a high axiological balance, the more constructive the parties become in their relationship. Conversely, when a majority member has a low axiological balance, they feel superior to the minority and can determine that the minority member is to blame for past events. During discussions that touch on sensitive issues, the axiological balance can change the direction of the conversation and result in conflict.

Members of Istanbul's Greek Orthodox minority community also emphasized the "othering" process adopted by the Turkish majority. According to the minority, the state and media worked together to attribute negative values to the minorities and create a common enemy by blurring identity lines between Greek Cypriots and Istanbul's Greek Orthodox minority. According to the minorities, the main goal of the state was to seek revenge on them for how Greek Cypriots treated Turkish Cypriots. Therefore, while the state erased the boundaries between Greek Cypriots and Istanbul's Greek Orthodox minorities to argue they were the same people, Istanbul's Greek Orthodox were defending their uniqueness and highlighting their differences from Greek Cypriots. Tilly (2005) refers to this latter process as boundary inscription, which is the opposite of erasure. The minorities' narratives of their victimization due to the Cyprus conflict seek to delegitimize the state's position on this issue, to strengthen the minority's position, and to justify minority in-group identity.

Boundaries are also significant to explain the visibility and invisibility of the Greek Orthodox minority in the society. In comparison to past decades, minority community members in Turkey say they generally feel more visible in contemporary society even if they acknowledge that the degree to which they are visible is heavily dependent on the political dynamics between Turkey and Greece. Structural changes, such as legislative adjustments regarding the return of expropriated properties to minorities,[14] were viewed as significant developments for the minority community. When the Turkish state has taken similarly positive steps, Istanbul's Greek Orthodox community feels more comfortable conducting its activities overtly. Their perception of the boundaries between them and the majority dissolve in a way. They become more active in cultural and social life by organizing exhibitions, festivals, and concerts and celebrating traditions on important days and engaging in public events more freely. They have also launched minority publications that have attracted society-wide attention throughout Turkey. The Association for the Support of Greek Community Foundations plays a vital role in these activities, as one of the most prestigious minority organizations that is respected by the government.

Christmastime is particularly important to Istanbul's Greek Orthodox minority. For the community, it is a time to come together with relatives, share stories and meals together, sing, and dance. Importantly, the Greek Orthodox do not feel they need to partake in Christmas-related festivities discreetly. As one member of the Greek Orthodox minority member emphasized during Christmas in 2012,

> For the past couple of years, we have celebrated Christmas in front of the Turkish public by singing Christmas songs and distributing small goodies to the public on Beyoğlu Street. It is important for us to be visible and celebrate our holiday with the Turkish people. This way, they know us, our culture, and our holidays better. The more we know each other, the more we will trust each other. (Teacher, interview, 2013, Istanbul)

Emphasizing the increasing cultural visibility of the Greek Orthodox minority in Istanbul, another member of the community noted that,

> recently, minorities have become more active in Istanbul's cultural life. Exhibitions, cultural day celebrations, conferences, new publications . . . for example, a new publishing house, Istos Publications, has opened which is a great achievement for both the minority and

> Turkey as a whole. Yes, there is a very positive nostalgia about the Greek Orthodox people among the majority, but we need more than this nostalgic view of the minority. Through the publications of Istos, both the minority and the majority will know each other better. Minority publication life was interrupted for decades. Now, we have an opportunity to revive our cultural life through different types of publications about history, culture, and the life of minorities. (Journalist, interview, 2013, Istanbul)

When the Istanbul Greek Orthodox minority makes attempts to close the information gap between themselves and the Turkish majority, some of the Greek Orthodox minority believe they will become more citizen-like and less minority-like. That means that the more the majority comes to know them, the more the minority will be able to participate in issues related to public affairs as equal citizens. This process of knowing each other also helps decrease the salience of the boundaries between the minority and the majority. Some minority members mentioned that the minorities were less visible in the past due to tensions between Greece and Turkey, but they do not currently feel afraid to be recognized. This is allowing the minority community to become more proactive in society. According to the Greek Orthodox minority, there is an increasing interest among the majority population to learn more about minorities and their experiences. Just as an example, the Turkish people formed queues at the door of the Phanar Greek Orthodox High School for the Christmas bazaar in December 2022 (Mantaş 2022). They waited hours and paid a fee to get into the school that opens its doors to the public once only at Christmastime.

The demand coming from the majority to learn the minority culture, history, architecture, and similar, in particular, motivates the Istanbul Greek Orthodox minority to work to overcome the historical traumas of their past and look to the future with more hope.

> I have media interviews, or I attend conferences and seminars. I am a very liberal person due to my education abroad. Young people, especially, want to learn more about who the minority community is, what we do, where we come from, why we are here, etc. The more they ask and the more they learn about the minority's history, the more normal their perceptions become. I am hopeful about the future because if young people gain more authority, they could begin to change something. The new generation will be very pluralistic and liberal. (Former minority foundation representative, interview, 2013, Istanbul)

Despite feeling more visible in Turkish society and continuing to demand more visibility, the Greek Orthodox minority is acutely aware of the lines that continue to exist that they must not cross. These are related to situations or moments when social boundaries become rigid again. For instance, not being visible in political or military spheres. Although members of the minority are comfortable with their overt presence in Istanbul's social and cultural life, members of the Greek Orthodox community argue that they prefer not to apply for government posts since they assume these positions are "existentially" closed to them. Social boundaries essentially transform into institutional limits that are impermeable. These minority members had never imagined working in foreign affairs, being a military pilot, or becoming prime minister. Even if they imagined such things happening, they said they have not in our conversations. Memories of being barred from certain sectors in accordance with laws enacted to exclude them continue to affect their decisions about just how visible to be, and particularly in which areas of public life.

> I was a biology student at Istanbul University at the beginning of the '60s. I wish I could have chosen another job because I never liked biology and did not do anything related to biology afterwards. But, you knew you were not allowed to do certain jobs at that time. So, I did not question it. Minority members already knew their place in Turkish society. It hasn't changed much today. The minorities cannot work in foreign affairs, the military, judiciary etc. The laws allow it but, in practice, it does not work. (Former representative in a minority foundation, interview, 2015, Istanbul)

Another member of the Greek Orthodox minority echoed this sentiment.

> My wife is Turkish, and my brother-in-law did his military service. He was a lieutenant in the army. One weekend, he came to visit us and I remember I wore his military outfit because I always wanted to work in the military. It is a psychological hardship to desire to do something but not be allowed to do it. I was a successful student. But there are things more important than being successful, like your identity. (Business owner, interview, 2015, Istanbul)

Another member of the minority reflected on why she had entered a particular profession.

> I am the child of teachers. My mom and dad were teachers, my uncle, my aunt, everybody were teachers. I never wanted to be a teacher. I

> was among the first 300 successful people in the national university entrance exam. Think about it. I could choose any department/job I wanted. But I became a teacher. In this country, under the conditions of the state of that time, it was the safest for me. (Teacher, interview, 2013, Istanbul)

Internal Lack of Democracy

The internal negotiation process underpinning broader questions of who the minority is does not only consist of discussions around who should be included in the minority. Rather, members of Istanbul's Greek Orthodox community are also concerned with what they perceive to be a lack of democracy within their community. During our conversations, some members of the Greek Orthodox minority discussed the lack of transparency and inclusive governance around decision-making within the community as well as instances of in-group discrimination against others within Istanbul's larger Orthodox community such as the Arab Orthodox minority community. According to those minority members, older and conservative minority members hold the power in decision-making, they are the ones who disseminate ideas to the rest of the community, and they have close ties to the Patriarchate. More liberal and progressive minority members, in particular, complain about the way these powerholders behave. Those who are less religious, more progressive politically, or who are against the uneven power dynamics within the minority community feel pressured by others. Some youth from the Greek Orthodox minority, for example, discussed how these power holders interfere in their lives, particularly regarding their own personal decision-making. One minority community member noted that she

> had felt like a "minority in the minority" many times. The minority community is conservative and like a small family. And members of the community intervene into your life like a father and mother intervenes in the lives of their kids. For example, I am an atheist, and that is not well perceived in the minority community, which is based on a religious identity. I tried to explain this to others in the community but my individuality was rejected. I said I did not want to accept their demands like a teenager argues with his/her family. They also questioned why I was [in a relationship] with a Turkish person. They ask me questions about whether I am going to marry him, if I am going to have a baby, etc. (Minority foundation representative, interview, 2013, Istanbul)

The financial (mis)management, internal decision-making, and general lack of transparency in how minority foundations are run are also sources of internal tension. Rumors about how these foundations are run have proliferated and generated a significant lack of trust among community members. As a result, calls are increasing for more transparency and the need for the management of these foundations to be decided by free and fair elections based on fixed leadership terms.

> There haven't been any elections in [our] foundations for a long time. In 2006, the minority foundations conducted free and fair elections that were a great democratic development for the future of our minority community. In the past, there were certain people who held on to their seats and never wanted to leave their position. They were taking advantage of being in certain positions. They had a symbiotic relationship with the state; both the state and these people were happy, but not the community. The Ottoman mentality is over now. A younger generation is coming with demands for more democracy, transparency, and accountability. But we still need more time for things to become more completely democratic. (Minority foundation representative, interview, 2013, Istanbul)

Another member of the Greek Orthodox minority focused on this lack of transparency, noting that

> there are a couple of foundations like the Balıklı Greek Hospital Foundation (Balıklı Rum Hastanesi Vakfı) that do not want to conduct elections and have not declared the foundation's income for more than twenty years. Balıklı, for example, is a very rich foundation and nobody in the community knows how the income is used. These foundations belong to the community, not to the people who manage them. Nothing about these foundations is transparent. They start to manage the foundations, never conduct elections, and never leave their positions. The minority community has concerns about these foundations and does not appreciate the leaders of these institutions because they are obstacles to a more transparent and accountable community. (Minority foundation representative, interview, 2016, Istanbul)

How elections (or the lack thereof) are held in minority foundations is a significant contemporary issue facing the Greek Orthodox minority. Elections are important for the minority community's internal transparency and democracy, and to develop better ties with the state. The Law of Foundations that entered into effect in 1936 permitted all non-Muslim minority foundations to conduct free and fair elections under the jurisdiction of the General Directorate of Foundations. Yet the Greek Orthodox minority only held elections in 1969–70 and in 1991 (Anonymous 2020). The Turkish state made changes to the Foundations Law (5737) following their EU candidacy process and democratization after 2004, which allowed minority foundations to hold board elections. After the 2006 elections, there were elections again in 2008. The last elections held in minority foundations were in 2013 with more expected to be held four years later. However, the government suspended any further elections, which caused significant issues with the governance of these foundations given that many of the elected officials were elderly.[15] Although there is a strong desire for more transparency, accountability, and internal democracy within the minority community, election delays are a major obstacle to achieving these goals, which has only served to reduce trust between the minorities and the state. As the head of the Association for the Support of Greek Community Foundations, Toros Alcan, noted,

> If we are part of this society, if we are citizens of the Turkish Republic, our discontent needs to be solved and it needs to be met. We do not want this issue to bother us more. We want to focus on different issues. This social trauma needs to end. (Cited in Anonymous 2020)

The State and the Greek Orthodox Minority

The sections you have read so far have evaluated some of the major minority policies the Turkish state has implemented over time, in addition to the effect on Istanbul's Greek Orthodox minority's historical memory and identity. Due to the aging of the minority, most of the minority members interviewed personally experienced the impact of these past minority-related policies. The younger participants had learned about the past through other social channels including generational transmission. Even though they are not all the same and occasionally disagree with or contradict one another, their stories and memory work provide insights into how they describe themselves now. The state's perspective on its own minority policies, as well as the perspectives of various experts on the subject, is examined in the next section.

The State and the Past

The main theme emerging from all my discussions with state officials was one of the need for the past to stay in the past. For these officials, although both states made mistakes in the past, their government's contemporary approaches to managing their minorities is one that is positive. Turkish officials stressed that the current situation for minorities in Turkey has been improving under the AKP government since 2002.

> It can clearly be seen that the minority is not the same minority of the past. With the AKP government, you can see visible changes in the minorities' lives. The government gave back expropriated properties, the government renovates important historical-religious sites, the minorities have more freedom to organize events, exhibitions, festivals, etc., to reintroduce the Greek Orthodox minority's important religious dates, literary figures, Greek music, food, etc. They arrange cultural activities and invite Turkish people to them, and there is a very positive exchange of information and interactions between the two cultures. (State representative, interview, Ankara, 2013)

Although Turkey's position has dramatically shifted in terms of its EU agenda, most Turkish officials I spoke to acknowledged that Turkey's EU candidacy process, as well as the Copenhagen criteria, have motivated the state to take positive steps toward improving the status of minorities in Istanbul. As these officials noted, the current government's political will is also exceptionally important and it is based on notions of multiculturalism and tolerance like that of the Ottoman Empire's rulers toward its *millet* (ethnies). One official stressed that

> the EU process motivated every candidate country to make structural changes like those happening in Turkey. Nobody could say the reverse, I guess. But what is more important is the political will of the AKP government to change their views about minorities. (State representative, interview, Ankara, 2013)

As another Turkish official noted,

> If Turkey didn't have political will to make policies, Turkey's EU process wouldn't change much, honestly. From the Ottoman Empire until today, Turkey became the land of a variety of nations and this land welcomed them all. Today, the government believes in the importance of an alliance of civilizations and sees minorities as colors of Turkish society. They are our heritage and we keep them safe. (State representative, interview, Ankara, 2013)

The State and Historical Responsibility

Another major theme that emerged in discussions with state representatives in both countries was that Greece and Turkey have a confusing and pragmatic view of the past. In Turkey, while most officials referred to the Ottoman Empire as a role model for how to treat minorities, taking responsibility for past injustices enacted during the Republican era is not considered necessary. Most of these officials acknowledged past state injustices toward minorities but also stressed that the government should feel no responsibility for what occurred in the past. As these officials noted, the state mismanaged its relations with the minorities and the minorities experienced some wrongdoings. Officials even noted that the state had responded vengefully toward the minorities when its Turkish Cypriot kin was treated negatively by others, as in the case of the Cyprus conflict. As one official explained,

> What happened to the minorities during the 1955 incidents and 1964 migrations were related to the crisis in Cyprus and the mistreatment of Turkish Cypriots by the Greek Cypriots. The mistreatment of Turkish Cypriots created feelings of revenge at home. And unfortunately, this revenge and hatred were directed toward the Greek Orthodox minority in Turkey. (State representative, interview, Ankara, 2013)

For another official,

> the incidents in Cyprus definitely affected state-minority relations. I cannot say that this specific event in Turkey happened because of how Turkish Cypriots were treated by the Greek Cypriots, but there was discontent in Turkish society during that time. (State representative, interview, Ankara, 2013)

Another important point regarding the state's view of the past relates to overgeneralizing the discrimination minorities experienced. Despite acknowledging that minorities were the targets of discrimination that created difficulties for these communities as well as accepting that past actions against minorities were wrong, these officials argue that such "incidents were happening everywhere in the world." They refrain from discussing how these incidents might have affected the minorities psychologically and their daily lived experiences in the past as well as the legacy of this historic discrimination. It was evident from these discussions that the current government feels no direct connection to or any responsibility for what happened to the minorities in the past. Rather, their tendency is toward normalizing or overgeneralizing the violence minorities experienced. As one argued,

> Yes, some injustices might have happened in the past toward minorities, but it should be mentioned that these types of incidents happen everywhere in the world. It is not a Turkey-specific case. (State representative, interview, Ankara, 2013)

When injustice is normalized, there is no need to correlate the past to the present, especially if it concerns negative historic actions. As Turkish officials noted, this does not mean lessons are not learned, but rather that there is no direct link between the past and the present. As one official suggested,

> Now, we cannot argue that the current government's positive perspective toward minorities (e.g., making some legal changes) is because of what happened in the past. Actually, the state learned to be more objective toward minorities. The current government has a totally new perspective toward minorities and whatever it is doing now is about its own policy decisions. (State representative, interview, Ankara, 2013)

Assuming no responsibility for historic injustices committed by the state was coupled with a view that any contemporary injustice minorities experience is attributable only to individuals rather than the state. Further, for these officials, such injustices are sporadic incidents rather than indicative of a systemic problem. Turkish officials noted that the current government only seeks to meet the present needs of the minorities. As these officials argued, in contemporary Turkey, minorities are treated as equal citizens. As one official indicated,

> Let's say we make a legal change but one of the administrators in one institution does not implement what we wanted, and minority members are mistreated or face injustices. This does not mean that this wrongdoing is committed by the system. It is the wrongdoing of this individual, not of the government. We treat our citizens equally. (State representative, interview, Ankara, 2013)

The State and the Minority Today

In addition to how the state views the past, state representatives also discussed contemporary state-minority interactions. Turkish officials argued that the state's attitude toward the minorities was not different from one minority to another, which they viewed as a reason to be proud. For these officials, the state treats every minority community in Turkey (from Greek Orthodox Christians to Armenian Apostolic Orthodox Christians and Jewish communities) with equal distance. Further, these officials argue that dialogue between these minorities and the state is much more open than compared to the past, which allows minorities to have more power to make decisions related to minority affairs. According to one official,

> The Turkish state approaches each minority member with equal distance. We do not favor one more than the other or discriminate against any minority member. The communication between the government and the leaders of the Greek Orthodox minority community is much better. They can even call us and discuss problems over the phone. Moreover, we ask them for their opinions on legal changes, and they come with some ideas or problems from the community. We work together in close cooperation to solve these problems. Additionally, the minorities can elect their minority foundation boards in a democratic way, which is a new and very positive change. Now, the minority organizations can have a better governance system and freedom in the decisions that are directly related to their community. (State representative, interview, Ankara, 2013)

The way officials approach the issue of reciprocity was the direct opposite of how the minorities perceive the state's behavior regarding this principle. Every Turkish official argued that the state does not believe in or support the so-called policy of "reciprocity." As one official mentioned,

> The only policy of the state is to listen to the problems of the minority community and make necessary changes to solve those problems. In international law, the policy of reciprocity can be applied to foreigners, not to citizens. Therefore, while the state approaches its citizens equally, how can it implement this policy to minorities that would normally be applied to foreigners? The minorities are an integral and valued part of this country, and they cannot be the subject of reciprocity at any time. (State representative, interview, Ankara, 2013)

Another official acknowledged the role of negative reciprocity by admitting that

> reciprocity was a negative policy that, for a long time, one way or the other, usurped the rights of the minorities in both countries. Rights cannot relate to reciprocity. The AKP government is conducting work to open this Halki Seminary since the first session of the government, and we will open it.[16] (State representative, interview, Ankara, 2013)

Building on these comments, one official stressed the need for positive steps from both countries:

> The principle of reciprocity [to manage] minority affairs is the wrong one. As the prime minister said, Turkey does not look at minority affairs from an absolute reciprocal perspective. Both Greece and Turkey should take positive steps to improve the status of the minorities in both countries. In that sense, if we open Halki Seminary, Greece should also take a positive step and open the mosque in Athens[17] or Thessaloniki or should take positive steps on the mufti issue. (State representative, interview, Ankara, 2013)

Expert Views on the State and the Minority Relations

The opinions of experts who have worked on minority-related issues for decades were vital to researching the attitudes of the Greek Orthodox minority and state officials regarding the past and present. For these experts, situational and governmental changes have gradually shifted how the state and the majority view the minority. Minorities and minority affairs were viewed increasingly as legitimate in Turkish society. Minorities' rising demands for expanded needs and rights coincided with this legitimacy, or at least recognition, of minorities. The rights minorities seek and the ones the state is willing to grant, however, are at odds. As one expert explained,

> The state clearly means collective rights, not individual rights when the issue comes to offering rights to minorities. When the state means rights, it means religious rights, which originated from the Lausanne Treaty. It is like a redline. In line with that, the political, social, and economic rights of minorities are not regarded as collective rights. However, minorities are also like other citizens in society and have several identities at the same time; they are leftist, rightist, women, men, young, old, and so on. With the increasing legitimacy of minorities in society, the demand for more rights, both collective and individual, emerged. But the state is clear about which types of rights they offer to minorities. Therefore, the state focuses on the collective nature of the community and offers collective rights, which are related to the entirety of the community. (Expert, interview, Istanbul, 2013)

In line with this discussion, minorities also demand recognition as individual agents in their respective societies. However, the way they are perceived by the state and the Turkish majority is not the same as how they perceive themselves. As one expert stressed,

> The more society uses the word "minority," the less this society normalizes. If society proudly hails the appointment of an Armenian-origin Turkish citizen [as a] diplomat to OSCE [Organization for Security and Co-operation in Europe] as a sign of tolerance, we need to understand that minorities are still oppressed. (Expert, interview, Istanbul, 2015)

These experts also discussed the future of the Patriarchate's authority in the minority community, which they argued continues to be the most important institution in the Greek Orthodox community. However, while some among the minority experience a tension between feeling more attached to their Turkish citizenship than to their Greek Orthodox minority identity, which leads them to demand more individual rights than collective rights, the question of what will happen to the Patriarchate's authority continues to be a central issue within the community. As one NGO representative explained,

> The Greek Orthodox minority community in Turkey should also have some discussions [among themselves] about their internal issues. There are wide array of challenges facing the minority community today and those problems are mostly not related to religious issues; therefore, talking about the authority of the Patriarchate and its problems becomes irrelevant. So, will the authority of the Patriarchate decline? Will the Patriarchate play the role of a nostalgic entity in the future? How will this new role be perceived by the Patriarchate itself? These are some of the questions that must be answered by the minorities themselves. (Expert, interview, Istanbul, 2014)

In line with this, these experts highlight that demands for more democratic progress in Turkey comes from the minorities themselves who seek more democracy within their own community. According to some of these experts, there is a lack of transparency and democracy in the foundations the minority community has created. The same people occupy leadership positions for years. Further, the issue of minority representation is a paradoxical one. As the minorities become more visible in Turkish society and experience more attachment to their Turkish citizenship identity, this increased agency has raised questions about their need for specific minority representation. For years, minorities were perceived as living on the margins of Turkish society and in need of representation. These experts argue that the only contemporary representation the minorities should focus on is political representation in the Turkish Grand National Assembly. More specifically, as one academic argued,

> In order for the minority community's citizenship to mature, the minorities must focus more on national representation, not minority representation. However, until that time, both representations must be held and supported. (Expert, interview, Istanbul, 2013)

Similarly to the views of the minorities themselves, these experts also argue that no other historical incident had a greater effect on the Greek Orthodox minority than the 1964 deportations. Being uprooted and sent to a foreign territory created deep-seated trauma within the minority community. As previously described, mixing a population is easy; it is not traumatic. The hardest thing is unmixing them. Greek citizens in Turkey married others in Turkey, which was not problematic. However, the Turkish state ordering those Greek citizens to leave the country created significant issues given the state's attempt to unmix those with Greek citizenship from others, and particularly the minorities.

Beyond Memory Work: Reconciliation in Minority-State and Bilateral Relations

The historical incidents, which are social traumas and integral to Istanbul's Greek Orthodox minority's narratives, remain vivid parts of their memories. The erosion of the minority population due to past events, as well as the profound lack of trust structuring state-minority relations, motivate their memory work. More specifically, they conduct memory work by remembering negative past incidents for several reasons, including to protect themselves, to advocate for their rights, to teach their children about their shared minority identity, and to elevate their culture. These unmourned traumas are revitalized every time the minority and the state interact, or stories of the past are discussed due to the lack of a comprehensive reconciliation process.

One of the biggest obstacles between the Greek Orthodox minority and reconciling with the past is the lack of trust underpinning their relationship with the state and the Turkish majority more broadly. At the same time, however, it is also necessary to build trust in Turkey's bilateral relations with Greece. This is not a linear process but rather two interconnected processes of trust building that need to happen simultaneously. Addressing these processes simultaneously is important because of how Greece and Turkey use the principle of reciprocity enshrined in the Lausanne Treaty. Although this principle was, in theory, meant to protect minorities, it became an instrument both states used to triumph over the other in various disputes. As such, they neglected and, in many cases, simply ignored the needs and rights of their minorities.

Moving beyond this 100 years of negative peace toward more positive relations may still be achieved by fostering the necessary political will to usher in changes structurally and in terms of narrative. Systemic change would facilitate a transformation in the negative structures (laws, policies, and their implementation) currently underpinning state-minority relations. Narrative changes would entail addressing enemy images, prejudices, boundaries, and othering processes.

There is no recipe to deal with all these issues. However, there is a need for a safe space for dialogue in both countries that is currently lacking. In a safe space, minorities, state representatives, and majority community members would have an opportunity to engage in a dialogue around future reconciliation. In this environment, they would have the opportunity to discuss why there is no transparent dialogue about past events. The fear of being blamed, judged, and punished, particularly related to discussing minority affairs, is real. Relatedly, the minorities would have the opportunity to be heard and trusted. They feel they belong to Turkey and are proud to be part of this territory and country.

It is also important that the minority community conduct intraminority dialogues regarding their lack of democracy and their internal vision for the community given the limited transparency on several issues from the management of minority foundations to the integration of the Arab Orthodox minority community. These processes all demand strong political will and change both within the minority community and in state-minority relations.

Conclusion

Restructuring the Memory Space

A storm caught us, blew into the sea
Our reunion, oh my love, postponed to the day after we die
Our reunion, oh my love, postponed to the day after we die
New coffee pot, new coffee pot was boiling, does not boil anymore
My coy lover was talking with me, but does not talk anymore
New coffee pot, new coffee pot boils on the stove
We have bayonet at our belt (oh my love) our martini rifle in our arms
I became old while serving my time in prison
My hazel eyes are about to close waiting for you

Bir Fırtına Tuttu Bizi Deryaya Kardı
O bizim kavuşmalarımız a yarim mahşere kaldı
O bizim kavuşmalarımız a yarim ahirete kaldı
Yeni cezve yeni cezve kaynar kaynamaz oldu
O benim nazlı yarimin dilleri söyler söylemez oldu
Yeni cezve yeni cezve kaynıyor ocakta
Kasatura belimizde (a yarim) martınımız kucakta
Mapsanede yata yata her yanlarım çürüdü
Yollarına baka baka a yarim ela gözler süzüldü
—"Bir Fırtına Tuttu Bizi" (A Storm Caught Us),
Turkish folk song from Thessaloniki, Greece

This Turkish folk song, "A Storm Caught Us,"[1] (also known as the Thessaloniki song), was written as a poem by Sabri Ağa, a member of the Turkish Muslim minority of Western Thrace. Sabri fell in love with Angelika, a Greek girl. Forbidden to marry by Angelika's family, the lovers decide to escape but are captured by her parents and Sabri is sent to prison. While in prison, he writes this poem mourning their separation. When he was finally released, the Population Exchange between Greece and Turkey had already started and he was forced to leave Greece, but with this love story as part of his memory.

The effects of the Population Exchange were manifold on the people who were part of the process. As in the case of Sabri, the people who migrated from one place to another left their loved ones behind. These memories have passed from generation to generation, influencing Greeks and Turks on either side of the Aegean Sea. These memories and the state policies enacted during this time of nation-building in both countries created the identities of those who were exchanged and those who were left behind (the minorities). As their identities formed, the boundaries crystallized between the minorities and the majority populations as well as between the state and the minorities. This process did not occur overnight, but rather over decades. Acknowledging the fact that every individual and every society around the world has their unique characteristics and experiences, the question to answer here is the following: Is it possible to transform negative historical memories to create a more resilient, empowered, and developed society?

To transform minority memory, as this book suggests, it is necessary to have sustained dialogue, critical reflection, and deliberate actions by all the relevant actors to reconfigure the future of the minorities. An essential part of this is to create the space in which there can be dialogue around minority memory and the national memory of a given country. Minority memory space is a contested zone, particularly when minorities' needs continue to be unmet, and they exist in a state of relative deprivation. Despite their desire to focus on their communities' respective futures, Istanbul's Greek Orthodox minority and the Turkish Muslim minority of Western Thrace continue to both live with and in the past. As shown throughout the previous chapters, remembering their state's past injustices and discrimination against their identity groups not only anchors their memory work but also strengthens the social boundaries between them and their states as well as the majority population.

For these minorities, remembering historical traumas is neither an easy process nor it is undertaken lightly. Yet it is inescapable and can, at times, be an empowering process. For both minorities, they feel they have no better means through which to demand their rights and advocate for their governments to meet their basic needs. Further, through their memory work, they legitimize their needs and rights. Minorities engage in this memory work heavily when there is a political or contextual window of opportunity domestically, regionally, or internationally that enables them to raise their voices. Through their memory work, they remind political authorities and the majority that they were treated unfairly in the past and there is a need for justice and accountability today.

However, the minorities' memory work can also put them in a more disadvantageous position socially. The more they engage in memory work, the more they remind the state about past injustices, and the more minorities remind their national states about past discriminatory policies and structural violence, the more the social boundaries separating the state and the minorities strengthen and become rigid. In this environment, states can increasingly question a minority's national loyalty. There is evidence of the lack of loyalty discourse used toward minorities as in the case of minority parliamentarians in Greece (Taşkın 2017, 2014) and in minority narratives about the past.

Notwithstanding the legitimacy of the minorities' demands, advocating for their rights is less challenging than securing their rights. John Paul Lederach asks "is building peace an art or a skill?" In response, he suggests that "building constructive social change in settings of deeply rooted conflict requires both" (2005, 9). To embark on a reconciliation process, relevant parties need skills to both change how community members perceive each other and initiate intercommunal healing. In addition, reconciliation is a process during which communities must begin to reimagine a shared future that begins to satisfy all sides socioeconomically and politically. When formerly conflicting parties decide to reimagine their relationships, it may take them decades to work toward peace and justice.

The minorities' historical traumas of the past in Greece and Turkey may heal when both countries allow democratic space for dialogue to repair the broken relationships between the state and the minorities as well as between the two countries at an interstate level. Being open to active and honest listening processes regarding the needs of the other party is one of the most significant ways to rehumanize enemy images. Yet this process is susceptible to disruption from daily political events and changing interests. The following recommendations propose complementary structural and psychosocial change processes. In doing so, these recommendations are based on an acknowledgment that they are vulnerable to contextual and political changes at the local, national, regional, and international levels.

Authentic Encounters versus the Fiction

Bilateral relations between Greece and Turkey are structured around a thick layer of boundaries resulting from categorization, a lack of trust, threat perceptions, fear, and negative images. From time to time, this thick layer is peeled back, and the parties begin to view each other positively (to a degree) interpersonally and at the interstate level. This occurs especially when there is a political or contextual change, or both, as was the case with the EU process in Turkey and Greece, when conflicting parties decouple conflict issues from social identity groups such as in the aftermath of natural disasters such as the 1999 and 2023 earthquakes, or for geostrategic cooperation as seen in the recent normalization efforts (Yeşiltaş 2023).

One other way to rehumanize the other party is through more intergroup and interpersonal contact. In his comparative study of three Turkish writers'[2] works of fiction versus their memoirs, Hercules Millas reveals a particular reality:

> In their fiction almost all Greek characters were negative personalities, i.e., expansionists, cruel, dishonest, cowards, sadists, corrupt, etc. Greek women were mostly prostitutes. But in their memoirs, whenever they presented the Greeks that they had actually met in their lives, then Greeks were almost all positive personalities, i.e., honest, pleasant, helpful, etc.[3]

During my discussions with minority members, this differentiation between fictitious and negative versus real and positive was evident, particularly in the narratives of minority youth. In both Greece and Turkey, youth discussed the reality of minority communities living next to majority populations in many neighborhoods, shopping in each other's stores, eating in the same restaurants, listening to the same or similar music, and entertaining similarly. Their everyday encounters in these shared spaces help to somewhat dissolve the boundaries between minority members and the majority. They do not see each other as fictitious and negative. Some minority youth in both Greece and Turkey discussed their friendships with other youth from the majority. However, they also added that although they are friends, their larger group identities (their national, ethnic, and religious identities) fluctuate in salience. Consequently, when these group identities become more salient, friends view each other through the categories of minority and majority. Here, one of the most significant factors that can change the dynamics of boundaries is more structured dialogue and awareness among in-group members as well as in-group and out-group members about the existence of different perceptions and narratives of the past. If the parties in conversation have the skills to listen and understand the other party's needs, this conversation has the potential to be transformative. Among the youth, at least, there is huge potential to create this safe dialogue space.

Boundaries and Relationship-Building

Boundaries and social categorization between the minorities and the state, as well as between majority and minority populations, are salient particularly in Greece, while limited in Turkey due to dwindling numbers of the minority. To minimize these boundaries and categories, there is a strong need for cross-boundary initiatives. These would help increase trust and reduce prejudice, and initiate deep reconciliation. Researching, predicting, and preventing potential violent conflicts, examining relationship-building initiatives between various actors at different levels in society, as well as being more inclusive in terms of the actors involved in dialogue opportunities between Greece and Turkey, could be beneficial for any future interstate reconciliation attempts between these countries and their respective minorities.

Korostelina discusses identity-based early warning systems as a way to predict and reduce conflicts in nation-states (Korostelina 2007a). As Korostelina highlights, how ethnic minorities are viewed within a nation is a major issue to discuss when examining the potential for conflict. It is essential to understand "whether minorities are oppressed by the majority, or whether they have opportunities for maintaining their ethnic culture" (234). According to Korostelina, if a national identity is defined ethnically and the needs of other ethnic groups (ethnic minorities) are deprived, there is a potential for intergroup conflict between the minority and ethnic majority. Conversely, if a national identity is defined around the concept of multiculturalism, this system can reduce conflict. In such cases, ethnic minorities have access to "guaranteed resources to maintain their culture and communities such as an opportunity to receive education in their language, and their cultural heritage as part of the national heritage" (234).

The narratives of the Turkish Muslim minority in Western Thrace reveal that one of the major root causes of tension between their communities and the Greek state is the state's denial of their ethnic Turkish identity. Although they emphasize their loyalty to the state and their opposition to any violent conflict, it is still important to consider their relations within the framework of an identity-based early warning system. Factors such as the level of intergroup prejudice, real or perceived out-group threat, in-group support, real or perceived relative deprivation, and security dilemma (Korostelina 2007a, 223–38) should be evaluated to predict and prevent conflict between the minority and the majority.

As discussed earlier, these factors are historically embedded in Greek-Turkish relations as well as state-minority relations in both countries. Any future attempt to understand, predict, and prevent violent conflict behavior between these actors should consider how these factors interact. These two countries became relatively more multicultural in terms of their population today. However, it is hard to say that they have multiculturalist laws and policy frameworks. Their road to a multiculturalist future that respects all ethnic, religious, linguistic, and other identity groups and guarantees their rights before the law seems a difficult yet not impossible task due to the nature of their nation-building past. This multiculturalist vision is a process that necessitates a sustained and comprehensive national dialogue regarding the role of all the identity groups in these countries and how diverse, inclusive, and equitable the state will be about these groups. This vision has the potential to allow various cultural identities to flourish and to facilitate the democratic development of both nations and their neighborly relations.

Researching, predicting, and preventing future conflicts through an early warning approach would also benefit both states and their respective minorities. This process could be strengthened by initiating structural dialogue processes among the actors who have a stake in minority issues, which only partially exists in the Greek and Turkish contexts. Due to historical institutional practices and strong boundaries, as discussed in earlier chapters, meaningful contact between actors in the Greek-Turkish context is currently either limited or scattered. Consequently, although there are political, economic, and social initiatives in progress, it is not clear how these initiatives contribute to prejudice reduction or reducing threat perceptions among actors.

The contact theory emphasizes that under favorable conditions, interaction between members of different groups helps reduce prejudice (Allport 1958; Pettigrew 1998; Pettigrew and Tropp 2011). Mohammed Abu-Nimer also emphasizes the application of modified contact theory in minority-state relations. According to him, some of the tools within this approach could include "face-to-face encounters, focus on the relationship, need for extensive analysis, the concern and focus on individuals, identification of the base most appropriate for intervention, and the recognition of good in everyone" (1999, 20). This approach works toward reducing the parties' hostile attitudes and perceptions of the "other," reducing stereotypes and fears, as well as facilitating trust and confidence among adversarial parties (20). Due to historical hostilities and their effect on minority memory and identity formation, relationship-building initiatives among various actors at different levels of society is essential.

As part of a comprehensive process to reconstruct perceptions among actors, it would also be beneficial to expand the variety of actors involved in these attempts. John Paul Lederach develops a level of action triangle that describes how various actors and initiatives can be implemented for sustainable peace (1997). According to this model, there is a need for coordination between high-level talks (Track I), midlevel trainings and problem-solving workshops (Track II), and grassroots prejudice reduction and other psychosocial initiatives (Track III). Crucially, middle-level actors should be able to reach out to the grassroots and top-level actors to create synergy.

Putting aside the shortcomings, one of the greatest examples of a state-to-state relationship-building initiative between Greece and Turkey is the exploratory talks that leaders of both countries have initiated over the years. As discussed earlier, the initiative was started by the then foreign ministers of Turkey and Greece, İsmail Cem and George Papandreou, in the early 2000s. During the writing of this book, both sides participated in the sixty-second round of talks. These talks can be understood from two perspectives. First, as a conflict management tool with the aim of bringing state-level actors together to discuss and, if possible, avoid preventable conflicts. Second, these talks can be viewed as a transformative relationship-building process.

Another example of collaboration between Greece and Turkey is the Greek and Turkish Forum, which functions as a Track 1.5 form of diplomacy involving leading businessmen, respected senior academics and journalists, and distinguished former politicians and diplomats in a dialogue process about the ongoing issues between the two countries. This forum was established in late 1997 and then expanded in 2006 with the addition of Greek Cypriot and Turkish Cypriot chapters. Besides its benefit of bringing various influential actors together from both sides for an exchange of ideas and mutual understanding, this type of sustained communication is a great way of keeping the two sides engaged with each other on key topics. The forum has the potential to become a peace infrastructure (Lederach 1997), for instance, if it can become more inclusive by containing grassroots representatives from minorities when they discuss minority-related issues.

Needs-Based and Bottom-Up Approaches

The populations affected directly or indirectly by historic violent and nonviolent incidents can develop collective traumas. When this trauma is not addressed, it can become intergenerational, passing from generation to generation as an emotional and psychological burden. Istanbul's Greek Orthodox minority and Western Thrace's Turkish Muslim minority are two such collectives that experience living with open emotional and psychological wounds and traumas, which they transmit to younger generations. These minorities are also resilient and conduct memory work as a means through which to advocate for their needs and demand their national governments respect their rights. Their struggle to have their basic needs met by Greece and Turkey, respectively, has been ongoing for decades. However, when emotional wounds remain unhealed, the outcome of this struggle is not efficient. Their struggles to have their basic needs met by Greece and Turkey are long-standing and ongoing processes that have been largely ineffective.

It should be noted that both minority groups are distinct from each other in terms of their characteristics, their problems, and their prospective futures. The declining number of Greek Orthodox minority members in Istanbul limits their needs and rights struggle to a few issues related to their minority identity such as demanding regular elections in their foundations, finding students for minority schools to prevent them from closing, and not being able to educate clergy in Turkey. On the other hand, the Turkish Muslim minority in Western Thrace still has a future in Greece even though they deal with a wide range of issues from education to religious issues, from foundations to their ethnic identity demands. Therefore, the way to approach both minority issues will necessitate different approaches. Prior to addressing more tangible issues related to their unmet basic needs such as their religious and education rights, minorities first want their states and the majorities to acknowledge and understand the sources of their emotional and psychological collective trauma. Without centering a needs-based approach and psychosocial support in minority trauma healing, their struggle to have their states meet their basic needs will continue to be ineffective.

Below are two conversations I had with minority youth members from the Istanbul Greek Orthodox minority and the Turkish Muslim minority in Western Thrace, which underscore the learned hopelessness and powerlessness felt within the minority community even among younger generations who did not experience direct violence.

AUTHOR: What are you interested in doing? Are there any topics you are passionate about?

MINORITY YOUTH #1: I am very into quantum science and space.

AUTHOR: Do you plan to study that at university?

MINORITY YOUTH #1: No, I am going to be an English teacher.

AUTHOR: That's great! Why not do something related to quantum science?

MINORITY YOUTH #1: You cannot study what you are interested in when you graduate from a minority school. I will probably go to Turkey for university. (Turkish Muslim minority youth member, online interview, Komotini, 2021)

AUTHOR: Did you go to a minority high school? Are you at university now?

MINORITY YOUTH #2: Yes, a minority high school. For me, I have never been a good student. I couldn't get into university.

AUTHOR: Why, what happened?

MINORITY YOUTH #2: My whole education life was disrupted. We [family] were all over throughout my childhood. My dad [Istanbul Greek Orthodox minority] wanted to move to Greece because he could not do business here in Istanbul and then my mom [Turkish Muslim] wanted to come back to Istanbul. After a couple of years in Greece, my siblings and my mom, we came back, and my dad stayed in Greece. They also got divorced afterward. I didn't have a chance to focus on my studies. I applied for a scholarship that the Greek government provides for students from minority high schools. But I also didn't get that. (Istanbul's Greek Orthodox minority youth member, online interview, Istanbul, 2021)

During our conversations, it was evident that the historical burden of the past weighed heavily on them. These young people, like many others in their communities, feel haunted by the past despite being more open to change and learning about the world. This has affected them and their ability to realize their potential to become successful and healthy individuals who help develop their societies. Although the younger generations of both minority communities did not experience past traumas directly, as their parents did, they were born into and have lived with the narratives of their communities' past due to their socialization (family, school, or community). They have internalized their deprivation and experienced everyday challenges resulting from Greece's and Turkey's historic actions.

Their hopelessness not only comes from history but also from the realpolitik between Greece and Turkey. The clashing interests of the two countries over various bilateral and regional issues, as discussed throughout this book, have influenced minorities in an indirect way. The negative application of the reciprocity policy can be viewed in the poor quality of the education minority children receive in contemporary minority schools and the state's lack of interest in working with minority leaders to develop a comprehensive minority education system.

Considering history and realpolitik as factors that determine how minorities construct meaning out of their everyday challenges is evidently a top-down perspective. On the contrary, any future intervention or initiative that is relevant to the minorities' needs and rights needs to originate from the minorities themselves. Approaches that only examine minority issues from the perspective of realpolitik will only produce short-term progress. When an auxiliary factor or trigger emerges between the two states, relations regress, which often results in the minorities' experiencing various harms, and relations between Greek and Turkish societies also worsen.

Therefore, there is a need to complement top-down approaches with more bottom-up initiatives where stakeholders in minority issues, including state representatives, minority leaders, civil society representatives, and experts on minority issues, among others, come together and listen to the minorities' everyday stories, including their challenges. As mentioned earlier, how these initiatives look will be different for both minorities due to the issues they deal with and the priorities they have. As shown throughout this book, there is a missing link between state-to-state interactions and state-to-minority interactions, as well as between macro-level minority issues in economic, social, religious, and political affairs and their micro-level impact on the daily lives of minorities. It is essential to gather the parties together to listen to the effects various policies have had on the everyday lives of minority families. Future initiatives must consider these stories in any further policymaking. Linking top-down and bottom-up approaches creates the necessary synergy among stakeholders on a variety of issues, which means a reconciliatory environment can be achieved gradually through this collaborative process as well as through acknowledging past injustices. This is necessary to begin repairing the damage done by these policies. As Joseph V. Montville suggests, "Ways have to be found to help adversaries face the historic burdens on their relationship, to help them present their historic grievances but also, especially, acknowledge the wrongs they have inflicted on the other side" (2006, 368).

Delinking Structural Changes from Historical Frames: Syncing Minority and National Policies in Education

Various factors have affected minority-related policymaking and implementation in both Greece and Turkey. Some of the most significant factors include the changing context (domestic developments and geopolitical priorities), political will, and the historical memory of each state. As discussed throughout this book, there have been times in Greek and Turkish history when the Greek Orthodox minority and the Turkish Muslim minority experienced positive developments regarding their socioeconomic and political life. These developments were brought about due to the changing domestic and regional context as well as the available political will to support this more positive environment. During these times, the historical memories and images held by the minorities and the majorities about the other were put aside and the focus was more on positive change. Peace and justice are, therefore, not impossible to achieve in the Greek and Turkish context. However, there is one dynamic that continues to influence the relations in both countries: the future of Cyprus.

The status quo between Greek and Turkish Cypriots continues to affect how Greece and Turkey treat their minorities. In the past, both countries employed the principle of reciprocity negatively, as a means through which to seek revenge on the other side or to pressure the other to make certain policy changes. Based on the political climate between the two countries, there is potential for this mechanism to be used in the future in the same or similar way. The Cyprus conflict triggered various internal conflicts between Greece and Turkey and their minorities, which could reoccur. The conflict deepened preexisting boundaries that had been created historically, categorically, and institutionally between these two states and their minorities. While the past effect of the Cyprus conflict cannot be undone, a solution that satisfies both sides of the island could facilitate an improvement in Turkish-Greek relations as well as between these countries and their minorities. When the biggest obstacle to structural change is the negative past—whether concerning minorities or state-to-state relations—reconciliation becomes possible by delinking turbulent history from these relationships. This requires reframing structural change not as conditioned by past grievances, but as steps toward democratic progress.

Further, there is a positive correlation between structural changes and healing historical traumas. By way of example, minority members viewed Turkey's steps toward minority foundations and property issues from the 2000s relatively positively whereas the Turkish Muslim minority viewed Greece loosening restrictions on them from the 1990s in a similar positive way. Both minority communities appreciated these developments, and they continually refer to these changes in their narratives. At the same time, however, they also found these developments to be somewhat disingenuous attempts by the states to improve minorities' lives. This stems from the lack of trust that continues to structure state-minority relations. These structural changes were neither coupled with sociopsychological processes nor viewed as permanent. Rather, the minorities feel these policies were only implemented to appease external actors, which, for the minorities, means they could be rescinded and undone at any moment.

One of this book's central arguments is that the states' motivation underpinning minority-related policy changes should be internally motivated processes rather than driven by external motivations. As discussed earlier, this can be achieved by adopting complementary top-down and bottom-up needs-based approaches. When governments make policies, they need to be reconciliatory. They should bring the leaders of the minority community to the table, listen to them, and include their perspectives in policymaking. When this is achieved, the historical past is less likely to be an obstacle to constructive policy changes and the minorities will be more likely to perceive the rhetoric states adopt as more genuine and not artificial.

Given the significant trust deficit between the states and their minority communities, achieving this internally driven process will not be easy but trust-building mechanisms should be developed in state-minority relations. This book does not neglect the significance of existing initiatives focused on fostering peaceful relations but suggests complementing these initiatives with more sociopsychological processes. The motivation to implement enduring change in minority-state relations as well as in interstate relations between Greece and Turkey needs to come from inside, from both policymakers and the people. When motivated by external sources, the demand for peace fades when relations sour with external actors. Therefore, the people of Greece and Turkey are the ones who need to address the wounds of the past and discuss how to move forward. Otherwise, any peaceful intervention may result in superficial and temporary change.

One policy area that has significant potential to transform minority-state relations in Turkey and Greece is minority education. As discussed previously, minority youth in both countries perceive their positions in society as hopeless. Both the historical past and tensions due to realpolitik between the two countries are major reasons why these students see no future in their societies. They witness every day how the world is changing, yet they feel left behind and relatively deprived in comparison to the youth from the majority. For minority youth to develop a neutral attitude about the past and current relations between the two countries, they need to be hopeful again about their future. They are ready for this attitudinal change, but they see no possibility in the current environment. Therefore, the states need an internally driven and comprehensive minority education plan for minority youth that would allow them to contribute to their societies. Developing these young people by providing them with a better education would facilitate the eventual and overall development of Greece and Turkey. The lessons learned from fostering better minority education policies may also provide a good example for the two states to develop other policy areas.

However, the field of education can also be a challenging policy area to address given the nationalist narratives that surround this sector in both countries. Therefore, as minority education becomes more comprehensive, each national education system should also consider including subjects around changing attitudes and narratives about the image of the internal as well as external other. This could include critical thinking, reflective practice, increasing empathy, prejudice reduction, and conflict resolution classes among others.

Anna Frangoudaki and Thalia Dragonas argue that the Greek nationalist project created an ethnocentric Greek national narrative that manifests most acutely in the education system, and particularly in history classes. They suggest that this project has not permitted Greece to address contemporary societal concerns (2018, 35–36). Given that these narratives are present in textbooks, embedded in teachers' attitudes, in literature, and in everyday discourse, the problem only deepens. As Dragonas and Frangoudaki further suggest, when past traumas are not dealt with, Greece will continue moving between feeling superior and inferior to other nations such as Turkey and other European countries. This situation is also applicable to the Turkish case. Merging a comprehensive and more developed (minority) education policy with a national education policy that contains transformative subjects, which address perceptions about the "other," may create positive outcomes for both countries internally and bilaterally.

These developments in the overall education system with all its components (teaching philosophy, teacher training, textbooks, school buildings, management, and funding structures among other issue areas) should be restructured as peace education. New pedagogical approaches that recognize the historical, sociopsychological, and cultural realities at the local level can be researched, developed, and implemented for positive peace.

Although these recommendations may appear easier said than done, Hercules Millas also points to the complexities of changing perceptions about the "other" in an environment where history is the national identity identifier:

> Transcending national prejudices and developing a "neutral" attitude vis-à-vis the Other is a complex process that is related to national identity and all the founding myths of each nation. Actually, the whole enterprise is usually presented as an effort where, on the one hand, the Other would be stripped of its negative characteristics, and on the other, "our" national identity and "our" related myths would be preserved. This sounds like a contradiction, an oxymoron. The negative Other is a constituent of national identity. The revision of the historical Other presupposes a revision of "our" history. (2004, 58)

To contribute to these ideas and, as this book suggests, inclusive memory work that focuses on the existence of others' stories may help create space for relationship-building between the state and the minorities, between the minorities and the majorities, and between the minorities themselves. There are many other minority stories like those mentioned throughout this book. These stories can be recorded or written in textbooks and used in classrooms as part of a national education policy. Majority and minority students from each national state, as well as a mix of students from both Turkey and Greece, could be brought together through projects to hear each other's story. This would allow them to understand how history has not only influenced their own lives, and how they create meaning about who they are, but also the lives of others. Further, these stories could be used in history classes to initiate difficult conversations on a variety of subjects related to the past. As it currently stands, teachers can often hesitate, shying away from engaging in such discussions about past incidents between Greece and Turkey or in their own countries. History course assignments could integrate some of these ideas and ask students to imagine a common future based on what they heard in the stories. Teacher trainings about how to discuss difficult subjects about the past could also integrate these stories.

Youth in general are adapting to contemporary global developments through their access to information technology and different forms of communication. They are not only aware of all the changes the world is experiencing but they also compare themselves to youth elsewhere. Greece's and Turkey's neglect of minority youth's real needs will only exacerbate their lack of basic human needs and rights. The future of relations between Greece and Turkey will be designed by these young people whether they are from the majority or the minority. An investment in complementary minority and national education policies would be a significant step toward positive peace between Greece and Turkey, which may also facilitate negotiations on a range of other challenging issues related to the minorities as well as bilateral geopolitical interests.

Finally, the main obstacle to progress, particularly as it relates to the everyday lives of the minorities, is the complicated nature of Greek-Turkish relations. If the political will were to emerge, the context would be right, and the two states could reevaluate their minority issues in a comprehensive and constructive way. In doing so, there is a possibility that the minorities would not only be heard, but they would also feel more integrated into their societies.

Appendix

Interview Questions

Minorities

Q.1. What are the significant historical events in your ethnic-religious community's past? Why do you think that they are important?

Q.2. What historic events still have an important impact on Greek/Turkish minority-majority relations in your host country and how do they impact these relations?

Q.3. How are these events discussed in your community, in mass media, history education? Where else do you think they are represented and how?

Q.4. How do you see yourself as a minority group member? Or do you feel yourself as an equal citizen?

Q.5. When do you feel yourself as a minority most? In which kind of situations?

Q.6. What are the major policies related to Greek/Turkish minorities? How have those policies at various levels affected you?

Q.7. How would you describe your interaction with the rest of the society? With the members of the majority group?

Q.8. How would you describe your interaction with your home country?

Policymakers/Implementers in Host Country

Q.1. What do you think about the current situation of Greek/Turkish minorities in your country?

Q.2. What are some of the policies that were designed to assist Greek/Turkish minorities?

Q.3. Which historical events do you think may have influenced or impacted the policies implemented about Greek/Turkish minorities?

Q.4. What historic events still have an important impact on minority-majority relations in the host country and how do they impact these relations?

Q.5. How would you describe your interaction with the minority members? Do you have regular communication between yourself and the Greek/Turkish minority group members?

Q.6. How would you describe your interaction with the home country of the Greek/Turkish minorities regarding the status of minorities?

Majority

Q.1. What is your view of those who are in minority status (Greeks/Turks) in your country?

Q.2. Which historical incidents do you think affected the status of Greek/Turkish minorities?

Q.3. What historic events still have an important impact on minority-majority relations in the host country and how do they impact these relations?

Q.4. How are these events discussed in your community, in the mass media, in history education? Where else do you think they are represented and how?

Q.5. How do you evaluate the current policy implementations of your government on minorities?

Q.6. How would you describe your interaction with the Turkish/Greek community?

Policymakers/Implementers in Home Country

Q.1. What do you think about the current situation of Greek/Turkish minorities in your country?

Q.2. What are some of the policies that were designed to assist minorities?

Q.3. Which historical events do you think may have an influence or impact on the policies implemented about Greek/Turkish minorities?

Q.4. What historic events still have important impact on minority-majority relations in the host country and how do they impact these relations?

Q.5. How would you describe your interaction with the minority members? Do you have regular communication between yourself and the Greek/Turkish minority group members?

Q.6. How would you describe your interaction with the home country of the Greek/Turkish minorities regarding the status of minorities?

Notes

INTRODUCTION

1. To ensure the confidentially of my interlocutor, I use pseudonyms throughout this book.

2. Tenedos (Bozcaada) and Imbros (Gökçeada) are two Turkish islands in the northeastern Aegean Sea. The Greek Orthodox minority of the islands were exempt from the Convention concerning the Exchange of Greek and Turkish Populations (referred to hereafter as the Population Exchange).

3. For specific literature on the Pomak and Roma minorities in Western Thrace, see works that focus on the Muslim minority in the Balkans or Western Thrace (Featherstone 2011; Poulton and Taji-Farouki 1997; Aarbakke 2000) or specifically focus on Pomaks (Demetriou 2004; Papadopoulos and Petridis 2021; Adamou 2010) and Roma (Alexandridis 2001; McGarry 2010; Parthenis and Fragoulis 2016).

4. There is also literature that uses the term "Turkish Muslim minority" or "Muslim Turks" of Western Thrace to define the identity of the same group of people who are the subjects of this research (Tsitselikis 2008; Anagnostou and Triandafyllidou 2006; Onar and Özgüneş 2010; Huseyinoglu 2012).

5. Interviews were conducted mostly in Turkish, except the ones held with the Greek officials and experts. The latter ones were in English.

CHAPTER ONE

1. For an extensive literature review on the development of kin-state politics within the context of post–Cold War scholarship on ethnicity, nationalism, and conflict, please see Myra A. Waterbury, "Kin-State Politics: Causes and Consequences," *Nationalities Papers* 48, no. 5 (2020): 799–808.

2. There is an extensive literature on what a nation is, what nationalism is,

and how nations are formed through nationalist ideologies. The most important works about these concepts and processes can be found in the works of Ernest Gellner, *Nations and Nationalism* (Ithaca: Cornell University Press, 1983); Benedict Anderson, *Imagined Communities: Reflections on the Origin and Spread of Nationalism* (London: Verso, 2006); Paul R. Brass, ed., *Ethnic Groups and the State* (Totowa, NJ: Barnes & Noble Books, 1985); Paul R Brass, ed., *Riots and Incidents* (New York: New York University Press, 1996); Paul R. Brass, *Ethnicity and Nationalism: Theory and Comparison* (Newbury Park, CA: SAGE, 1991); Elie Kedourie, *Nationalism in Asia and Africa* (New York: New American Library, 1974); Edward Shils, "Primordial, Personal, Sacred and Civil Ties: Some Particular Observations on the Relationships of Sociological Research and Theory," *British Journal of Sociology* 8, no. 2 (June 1957): 130–45, https://doi.org/10.2307/587365; Clifford Geertz, *The Interpretation of Cultures: Selected Essays* (New York: Basic Books, 1977); Tom Nairn, *The Break-up of Britain: Crisis and Neonationalism*, 2nd ed. (London: NLB and Verso Editions, 1981); John Breuilly, "Bringing History Back into Nationalism?," in *Nationalism in the Troubled Triangle: Cyprus, Greece and Turkey*, ed. Ayhan Turhan Aktar, Niyazi Kızılyürek, and Umut Özkırımlı, 1–20 (Basingstoke: Palgrave Macmillan, 2010); Michael Hechter, *Containing Nationalism* (New York: Oxford University Press, 2000); Anthony D. Smith, *Nationalism* (Oxford: Polity, 2010); Eric J. Hobsbawm and Terence Ranger, *The Invention of Tradition* (Cambridge: Cambridge University Press, 1984).

3. The major international human rights conventions of particular relevance to the rights of minorities ratified by Greece and Turkey include the International Covenant on Civil and Political Rights (ICCPR), the Convention on the Rights of the Child (CRC), the International Convention on the Elimination of All Forms of Racial Discrimination (ICERD), the International Covenant on Economic, Social and Cultural Rights (ICESCR), and the Convention on the Elimination of All Forms of Discrimination Against Women (CEDAW). For further information on the treaties, see https://indicators.ohchr.org

4. In some cases, such as the apartheid regime (minority whites) in South Africa, the Assad regime (minority Alawites) in Syria, and Tutsi rule in Rwanda, we can talk about the rule of minorities. In these cases, we can talk about the minority dominating over the majority population. However, these are exceptions in terms of the rule of minorities in the world. What is more dominant is the rule of the majority over minority groups (ethnic, religious, national, linguistic groups).

5. As one of the most recent and extensive studies on the background, implementation, and impacts of the 1964 expulsion of Istanbul's Greek Orthodox community members, see İlay Örs Romain, ed., *İstanbullu Rumlar ve 1964 Sürgünleri: Türk Toplumunun Homojenleşmesinde Bir Dönüm Noktası* (Istanbul: İletişim Yayınları, 2019).

6. Article 19 of the Greek Citizenship Law that entered into effect in 1955 stated that "a citizen who is not from Greek race may be deprived of citizenship in case he/she leaves the country without the intention to come back. Deprivation of citizenship may be applied to ones that are not from Greek race, born abroad and still live out of the border of Greece. The underage children whose parents or the alive parent have been deprived of citizenship may be denaturalized as well. Ministry of Interior Affairs decided with the ratification of Citizenship Council of Greece." For more discussion on the topic, see Erdem 2024.

7. Other non-exchanged populations included Armenians and Jews that earned minority status in Turkey. The other Muslim groups in Greece that earned minority status were Pomak and Roma populations.

8. For further information on the relationship between resources and power, see Dorwin Cartwright, "A Field Theoretical Conception of Power," in *Studies in Social Power*, ed. Dorwin Cartwright (Ann Arbor: University of Michigan Press, 1959), 183–220; Morton Deutsch and Harold B. Gerard, "A Study of Normative and Informational Social Influences upon Individual Judgment," *Journal of Abnormal and Social Psychology* 51, no. 3 (1955): 629, http://dx.doi.org/10.1037/h0046408; Leon Festinger, "An Analysis of Compliant Behavior," in *Group Relations at the Crossroads*, ed. Muzafer Sherif and M. O. Wilson (Oxford: Harper, 1953), 232–56; Leon Festinger, "A Theory of Social Comparison Processes," *Human Relations* 7 (1954): 117–40; John R. P. French Jr. and Bertram Raven, "The Basis of Social Power," in *Studies in Social Power*, ed. Dorwin Cartwright. (Ann Arbor: University of Michigan, 1959), 150–67; Herbert C. Kelman, "Compliance, Identification, and Internalization: Three Processes of Attitude Change," *Journal of Conflict Resolution* 2, no. 1 (1958): 51–60.

9. For further information on alternative meanings of power as a form of domination, see Michel Foucault, "Sexuality and Solitude," in *Michel Foucault: Ethics, Subjectivity, and Truth*, ed. Paul Rabinow (New York: New Press, 1981); Max Weber, *Economy and Society: An Outline of Interpretive Sociology* (Berkeley: University of California Press, 1978); Pierre Bourdieu, "Gender and Symbolic Violence," in *Violence in War and Peace: A Reader*, ed. Nancy Scheper-Hughes and Philippe Bourgois (New York: Wiley-Blackwell, 2003), 339–42.

10. For an overview of the literature on the role of myths in nationhood, see Chiara Bottici, *A Philosophy of Political Myth* (New York: Cambridge University Press, 2007); Joanna Overing, "The Role of Myth: An Anthropological Perspective, or 'The Reality of the Really Made-Up,'" in *Myths and Nationhood*, ed. Geoffrey Hosking and George Scopflin (New York: Routledge, 1997), 1–18; Nigel Rapport and Joanna Overing, *Social and Cultural Anthropology: The Key Concepts* (London: Routledge, 2000).

11. For further information on positioning theory, see Luk Van Langenhove and Rom Harré, "Varieties of Positioning," *Journal for the Theory of Social Behaviour* 21, no. 4 (1991): 393–407, https://doi.org/10.1111/j.1468-5914.1991.tb00203.x; Luk Van Langenhove and Rom Harré, "Cultural Stereotypes and Positioning Theory," *Journal for the Theory of Social Behaviour* 24, no. 4 (1994): 359–72, https://doi.org/10.1111/j.1468-5914.1994.tb00260.x; Luk Van Langenhove and Rom Harré, "Introducing Positioning Theory," in *Positioning Theory: Moral Contexts of International Action*, ed. Luk Van Langenhove and Rom Harré (Oxford: Basil Blackwell, 1999), 14–31.

CHAPTER TWO

1. The term "negative peace" was developed by Johan Galtung, a pioneer in the field of peace studies and conflict resolution. He developed the term in the 1960s to distinguish between the mere absence of violence (negative peace) and the presence of social justice and equality, which addresses the root causes of conflict (positive peace). In the context of the interwar period, Greece and Turkey had negative peace where there was no direct violence but no sustainable peace too.

The rapprochement between the two sides came after the Lausanne Treaty (1923) in the context of international developments of the interwar years such as common threat perceptions and changing international priorities.

2. *Etabli* is a French word that can be used for "settled" or "established." The problems that emerged around etabli status were due to Greece and Turkey misinterpreting who had the right to stay in Istanbul after the Population Exchange.

3. One of the significant issues discussed at the Lausanne Peace Conference was the status of the Greek Orthodox Patriarchate in Istanbul. Ismet Pasa, the Turkish representative at that time, confessed he was under pressure from his Greek counterpart, Elefterios Venizelos, and the British representative, George Curzon, to accept their demands about the Patriarchate (Akgönül 2013, 365). As Samim Akgönül argues, it is not difficult to understand the main concern of foreign powers (as well as Greece) that motivated the debate on the people who will be exempted from the exchange. Specifically, it was "not the maintenance of a Greek population in Turkey, but rather the preservation of the Patriarchate in Phanar (the Patriarchate)" that was paramount (2008, 20).

4. Hirschon (2009) elaborates on this collective trauma due to the exchanged with respect to diminished contact, loss of shared experiences, loss of communication, and loss of familiarity, which are replaced with the sociopsychological dynamics of projecting negative stereotypes onto the other, and finally collective alienation.

5. For a detailed evaluation of the articles and their implications on minorities, see Akgönül 2008; Oran 2004; Kurban and Tsitselikis 2010.

6. Blue Homeland (Mavi Vatan) is a realist, defensive, and protectionist foreign policy and maritime doctrine initiated by Turkish admiral Cem Gurdeniz. According to Gurdeniz, the doctrine has three pillars: first, the symbol of Turkey's growing maritime claims in the twenty-first century; second, it defines Turkey's maritime jurisdiction (territorial waters), the continental shelf and the exclusive economic zone; and finally, to protect, safeguard, and develop the maritime rights and national interests of Turkey. Greece perceives this doctrine as "expansionist," as do other regional and international actors who are not comfortable with Turkey's active maritime policy and demands. The doctrine also reached its depth and breadth with the agreement signed between Turkey and Libya on maritime boundaries in the Mediterranean Sea in 2019. This was initiated by Admiral Cihat Yaycı. After this agreement, Greece and Egypt also signed a maritime delimitation agreement in 2020 (Vita 2020).

7. Volkan, 2021, personal communication.

8. For a detailed examination of Greece's perception of the Turkish Muslim minority's ethnic identity demands as a threat and policies of inclusion and exclusion against the Turkish Muslim minority in Western Thrace until 1990s, see Iliadis 2013, 2012; Papanikolaou 2007; Hasan 2023.

9. For the full interview, see "Mevlüt Çavuşoğlu Habertürk'te Soruları Yanıtlıyor" (Ersoy 2021), aired April 20, 2021, *Habertürk*. YouTube Video, 2:00:44 (uploaded April 20, 2021, accessed April 22, 2021), https://www.youtube.com/watch?v=IOETvdoG61k

10. For the full statement, see Hellenic Republic Ministry of Foreign Affairs, 2021, https://mfa.gr/en/current-affairs/top-story/statements-by-minister-of-foreign-affairs-nikos-dendias-following-his-meeting-with-the-minister-of-foreign-affairs-of-turkey-Mevlüt-Çavuşoğlu-ankara-15-april-2021.html

11. For the full speech, see Anonymous, "Bakan Çavuşoğlu'ndan Dendias'a tepki: Kabul edilemez ithamlarda bulundu!" Aired April 15, 2021, *CNNTURK*. YouTube video, 34:52 (uploaded April 15, 2021, accessed April 18, 2021), https://www.youtube.com/watch?v=-8wG8UQbCek

CHAPTER THREE

1. For a brief summary on the conflict history, see Gür 2024.

2. In 2023, more interviews were conducted with Turkish Muslim minority members in Western Thrace to learn about whether there had been significant changes in minority education. I conducted an additional five interviews. Four of these interviews were with Turkish Muslim minority members who are experts in the field of education. I conducted another interview with a college professor, Dr. Vemund Aarbakke, during which time he shared his views on minority university students. Based on this data, I have gathered additional information on how the minorities perceive two of the most significant changes announced by the Greek government: the 0.5 percent quota provided to the minorities for university admittance and the PEM project that was applied from 1997 to 2019.

3. Ex Article 19 of the Greek Nationality Code (GNC, Legislative Decree (Law) 3370/1955) (Abrogated by Law. No. 2623 of June 24, 1998) (Hellenic Republic) (Sitaropoulos 2004).

4. Vlachs, or Vlachophone Greeks, are traditionally mountain pastoralists. Most of the Vlach population lives in northern Greece, in scattered rural communities. Vlachs are more tolerated than other minority groups by the Greek state (Anonymous 2018a).

5. "Greece's Muslim Minority Hails Change to Limit Power of Sharia Law," *Guardian*, January 11, 2018, https://www.theguardian.com/world/2018/jan/10/historic-step-greek-pm-hails-change-to-limit-power-of-sharia-law

6. Depending on date and event, the newspapers focus on certain issues. At the start of the new school semester, the newspapers bring up the issue of education rights, remind readers of past injustices in the form of chosen traumas, and ask the Greek government to ease the process of approval of the new textbooks for the school year. Or, in Janaury, incidents related to the former minority parliamentarian Dr. Sadık Ahmet and peaceful protests of the minority are remembered; Sadık Ahmet's imprisonment is remembered, as are his "sacrifices" for the minority community, and nationalist feelings are raised to work toward the demands of the minority.

7. The minority appealed the decision of the Greek courts and opened a case in the European Court of Human Rights against the Greek state about the use of Turkish in the signboards. As explained in agenda item #3 of the thirty-seventh session of Human Rights Council of the UN General Assembly (February 15, 2018), there are three cases that have been brought to the European Court of Human Rights concerning dissolution and the refusal to register associations: (1) Evros Prefecture Minority Youth Association: The Case of Bekir-Ousta and others (35151/05), judgment of 11/10/2007, final on 11/01/2008; (2) Xanthi Turkish Union: The Case of Tourkiki Enosi Xanthis and others (26698/05), judgment of 27/03/2008, final on 29/09/2008; (3) The Cultural Association of Turkish Woman in the Prefecture of Rodopi: Emin and others (34144/05), judgment of 27/03/08,

final on 01/12/2008. The European Court of Human Rights decided in favor of the minorities and unanimously agreed on the violation of freedom of assembly and association (Article 11) and the right to a fair hearing within a reasonable time (Article 11 of the Convention). See http://www.mfa.gov.tr/turkish-minority-of-western-thrace.en.mfa (accessed October 1, 2015). The decisions have not yet been implemented by the Greek state.

CHAPTER FOUR

1. Yanyana-The Encounter project videos can be found at http://www.rum-vader.org/Page/2354/140/yanyana__filmi_Istanbulda.html

2. It should be noted this interview was conducted in 2020. New elections in minority foundations happened in 2022 after the Turkish government announced the Action Plan on Human Rights on March 2021 (Ministry of Justice 2021), and the new election regulation was released by the Directorate General of Foundations in June 2022 about the election of minority foundations' boards of directors (Directorate General of Foundations 2022). This decision aimed to end the stalemate about the elections due to the suspension of the election regulation by the government.

3. For further information on the legal consistencies and administrative gaps within the framework on the Greek Orthodox schools in Istanbul, see Özil 2014.

4. EOKA stands for Ethnikí Orgánosis Kipriakoú Agónos (National Organization of the Cypriot Struggle). EOKA was a paramilitary nationalist organization established in Greek Cyprus with the aim of first ending British colonial rule in Cyprus (achieved in 1960) and second achieving the eventual union (Greek *enosis)* of Cyprus with Greece (Encyclopedia Britannica 2015). This would be done through ethnically cleansing Turkish Cypriots from the island. Intercommunal clashes between the two communities ended with Turkey's intervention in the island to save the Turkish Cypriots (1974) and EOKA dissolved in 1978.

5. According to Güven (2005), the Turkish media reported 11 casualties and Helsinki Watch (1992) reported as 15 casualties.

6. The implementation of the Wealth Tax during World War II on middle class, non-Muslim minority members in Turkey is widely regarded as a "tragedy" (Ökte 1951) or as "an important measure, not only from an economic, but also from a political and cultural point of view" (Aktar 2012).

7. The September 1955 incidents, or riots, is referred to as a warning and intimidation tactics waged against the Greek Orthodox minority of Istanbul. They included systematic, violent attacks organized by mobs that were believed to be working closely with the state and in line with the homogenization of Turkish society (Güven 2005).

8. The Ankara government at the time decided not to renew the 1930 Ankara Convention, which had provided the rights of living and working to Greek citizens who were born and living in Istanbul.

9. The districts of Feriköy, Kurtuluş, and Ergenekon in Istanbul are densely populated by the Greek Orthodox minority. So, too, is the Halaskargazi district (in Istanbul's Şisli neighborhood) and the neighborhoods of Moda in Kadıköy and

Yeniköy, situated on the Bosphorus, and in the vicinity of Kuzguncuk (Kara 2009). Greek Orthodox minority foundations, churches, and schools are visible throughout these districts and neighborhoods such as Cicek Pasaji, Elhamra Hanı, Suriye Pasajı, Zografyon, Zapyon and Fener Lycees, and the churches include the Aya Triada Church in Taksim, Fener Greek Orthodox Patriarchate, and Aya Yorgi Church (Karaca 2016).

10. The integration of the Arab Orthodox community (also known as Antakyalılar) into the Istanbul Greek Orthodox community is supported by the Patriarchate, and members of this minority community are provided minor jobs in the Patriarchate or in minority institutions. From some of the interviews, it is understood that they are perceived as second-class members of the minority community because they are not as urban and educated as the Istanbul Greek Orthodox community members. However, the Greek Orthodox community approached this minority's integration pragmatically and their integration is broadly welcomed due to the demographic erosion experienced by the Greek Orthodox. Regarding the management of Vaqf (minority foundations) and their associated elections, the integration of the Arab Orthodox community into Istanbul's Greek Orthodox community allows them to participate in elections and in the foundations' management. Overall, the issue of the integration and identity of the Arab Orthodox community is an internal conflict that occupies the agenda of the minority community in Istanbul.

11. According to İlay Örs Romain, Orthodox Christians of Istanbul comprised more than a quarter of Istanbul's population at the beginning of the twentieth century. Today, they remain as a mini-minority with only 1,800 people out of the total 15 million population in Istanbul (2006, 83).

12. Minority foundations (*Azınlık Vakıfları*) are charitable and community-based organizations established by non-Muslim minority communities, such as Greek Orthodox, Armenian, and Jewish minorities. They are governed under the Foundations Law and are regulated by the General Directorate of Foundations (Vakıflar Genel Müdürlüğü). The primary role of foundations is to manage properties and assets that historically belonged to minority communities, including churches, synagogues, cemeteries, schools, and hospitals. They also play a crucial role in preserving the cultural and religious heritage of minority groups.

13. In the 2023 parliamentary elections, Seven Sivacioglu (Armenian), who was a candidate from the AKP, and George Aslan (Assyrian), who was a candidate from the Greek Left Party, became deputies in the parliament.

14. With Decree Number 651, published in the August 27, 2011 Official Gazette, the interim Article 11, which calls for the return of properties of the community foundations and third persons, was added to the Foundations Law. For further information, please see https://www.resmigazete.gov.tr/eskiler/2011/08/20110827-1.htm

15. For more examples of the reciprocal acts about the foundation issues, see the Selected Chronology of Significant Developments with respect to Community Foundations in Greece and Turkey in TESEV's report *A Tale of Reciprocity* (Kurban and Tsitselikis 2010, 28–29).

16. As the time of writing the Halki Seminary was still closed.

17. The first mosque in Athens was opened in November 2020.

CONCLUSION

1. The song “A Storm Caught Us” (Bir Fırtına Tuttu Bizi) was compiled by Yücel Paşmakçı in 1978.

2. The three Turkish writers who wrote both fiction (novels and short stories) and memoirs are Ömer Seyfettin (1884–1920), Halide Edip Adıvar (1882–1964), and Yakup Kadri Karaosmanoğlu (1889–1974).

3. Hercules Millas, October 14, 2011, available at https://www.herkulmillas.com/hm-articles/74-greek-turkish-relations/382-friendship-among-people-or-between-nations-the-case-of-greeks-and-turks-.html

References

Aarbakke, Vemund. 2000. "The Muslim Minority of Greek Thrace." PhD diss., University of Bergen, Norway. https://www.batitrakya.org/dosya/yayinlar/The-Muslim-Minority-of-Greek-Thrace.pdf

Aarbakke, Vemund. 2008. "The Concept of Reciprocity and Its Significance for the Political Organisation of the Muslim Minority in Greece." In *Reciprocity: Greek and Turkish Minorities; Law, Religion, and Politics*, edited by Samim Akgönül, 4:119–41. Istanbul: Istanbul Bilgi University Press.

Abu-Nimer, Mohammed. 1999. *Dialogue, Conflict Resolution, and Change: Arab-Jewish Encounters in Israel.* New York: State University of New York Press.

Adamou, Evangelia. 2010. "Bilingual Speech and Language Ecology in Greek Thrace: Romani and Pomak in Contact with Turkish." *Language in Society* 39 (2): 147–71.

Akçalı, Emel. 2015. "A New Vision of Good Neighbourliness." In *Resolving Cyprus: New Approaches to Conflict Resolution*, edited by James Ker-Lindsay, 16–23. London: I.B. Tauris.

Akgönül, Samim. 2007. *Türkıye Rumları: Ulus devlet çağından küreselleşme çağına bir azınlığın yok oluş süreci*. İstanbul: İletişim Yayınları.

Akgönül, Samim, ed. 2008. *Reciprocity: Greek and Turkish Minorities; Law, Religion and Politics*. Istanbul: Istanbul Bilgi University Press.

Akgönül, Samim. 2013. "Non-Muslim Minorities in the Turkish Democratization Process." In *Turkey's Democratization Process*, edited by Carmen Rodriguez, Antonio Avalos, Hakan Yilmaz, and Ana I. Planet. Oxford: Routledge.

Akhtar, Salman. 1999. *Immigration and Identity: Turmoil, Treatment, Transformation*. Northvale, NJ: Jason Aronson.

Aktar, Ayhan. 2000. *Varlık vergisi ve "Türkleştirme" politikaları*. Istanbul: İletişim Yayınları.

Aktar, Ayhan. 2009. "'Turkification' Policies in the Early Republican Era." In *Turkish Literature and Cultural Memory: "Multiculturalism" as a Literary Theme after 1980*, edited by Catharina Dufft. Wiesbaden: Otto Harrassowitz Verlag.

Aktar, Ayhan. 2012. "Tax Me to the End of My Life!" In *State-Nationalisms in the Ottoman Empire, Greece and Turkey: Orthodox and Muslims, 1830–1945*, edited by Benjamin C. Fortna, Stefanos Katsikas, Dimitris Kamouzis, and Paraskevas Konortas. London: Routledge.

Alexandridis, Theodoros. 2001. "Not Enough Action: Government Policy on Roma in Greece." *European Roma Rights Centre* (blog), August 15. Hungary. http://www.errc.org/cikk.php?cikk=1708

Alexandris, Alexis. 1992. *The Greek Minority of Istanbul and Greek–Turkish Relations 1918–1974*. Athens: Center for Asia Minor Studies.

Allport, G.W. 1958. *The Nature of Prejudice*. Garden City, NY: Doubleday Anchor.

An, Ahmet. 2015. "'Cypriotism' and the Path to Reunification." In *Resolving Cyprus: New Approaches to Conflict Resolution*, edited by James Ker-Lindsay, 24–29. London: I.B. Tauris.

Anagnostou, Dia. 2005. "Deepening Democracy or Defending the Nation? The Europeanisation of Minority Rights and Greek Citizenship." *West European Politics* 28 (2): 335–57.

Anagnostou, Dia, and Anna Triandafyllidou. 2006. *Regions, Minorities and European Integration: A Case Study on Muslims in Western Thrace*. Athens: ELIAMEP.

Anderson, Benedict. 2006. *Imagined Communities: Reflections on the Origin and Spread of Nationalism*. Rev. ed. London: Verso.

Anonymous. 2018a. "Vlachs." Minority Rights Group. September. https://minorityrights.org/minorities/vlachs/

Anonymous. 2018b. "Azınlık sorunları BM'de anlatıldı." *Gundem Gazetesi*, December 3. https://gundemgazetesi.com/detayh.php?id=5221

Anonymous. 2019. "Kanayan yara: 19. madde." *Gundem Gazetesi*, April 18. http://www.gundemgazetesi.com/haber/detay/5678 (no longer available).

Anonymous. 2020. "Vakıf seçimleri sorunu ve çözüm önerileri." *HyeTert* (blog), June 15. https://hyetert.org/2020/06/15/vakif-secimleri-sorunu-ve-cozum-onerileri/

Antoniou, Dimitris. 2005. "Western Thracian Muslims in Athens: From Economic Migration to Religious Organization." *Balkanologie: Revue d'études pluridisciplinaires* 9, nos. 1–2. https://doi.org/10.4000/balkanologie.579

Antonopoulos, Paul. 2021. "Dendias-Erdoğan Meeting Is Over—What They Discussed." *Greek City Times*, April 15, sec. Greek NEWS. https://greekcitytimes.com/2021/04/16/dendias-erdogan-meeting-over/

Askouni, Nelly, and Thalia Dragonas. 2020. "Transcending Socio-Cultural Barriers: Access to Tertiary Education of Muslim Minority Youth in Greece." In *A Better Future: The Role of Higher Education for Displaced and Marginalised People*, edited by Faraaz Mahomed, Jacqueline Bhabha, and Wenona Giles, 245–67. Cambridge: Cambridge University Press.

Asmussen, Jan. 2015. "Escaping the Tyranny of History." In *Resolving Cyprus: New Approaches to Conflict Resolution*, 31–38. London: I.B. Tauris.

Assmann, Aleida. 2006. "Memory, Individual and Collective." In *The Oxford Handbook of Contextual Political Analysis*, edited by Robert Goodin and Charles Tilly. Oxford: Oxford University Press.

Avruch, Kevin. 2012. *Context and Pretext in Conflict Resolution: Culture, Identity, Power, and Practice*. Boulder: Paradigm.

Bahcheli, Tozun, and Sid Noel. 2015. "A Bizonal Federation Is Not Viable." In *Resolving Cyprus: New Approaches to Conflict Resolution*, edited by James Ker-Lindsay, 39–47. London: I.B. Tauris.

Bell, Duncan S. A. 2003. "Mythscapes: Memory, Mythology, and National Identity." *British Journal of Sociology* 54 (1): 63–81. https://doi.org/10.1080/0007131032000045905

Billig, Michael. 1990. "Collective Memory, Ideology and the British Royal Family." In *Collective Remembering*, edited by David Middleton and Derek Edwards. London: SAGE Publications.

Bloom-Christen, Anna, and Hendrikje Grunow. 2022. "What's (in) a Vignette? History, Functions, and Development of an Elusive Ethnographic Sub-Genre." *Ethnos* (March): 1–19. https://doi.org/10.1080/00141844.2022.2052927

Bodnar, John E. 1992. *Remaking America: Public Memory, Commemoration, and Patriotism in the Twentieth Century*. Princeton: Princeton University Press.

Breuilly, John. 2010. "Bringing History Back into Nationalism?" In *Nationalism in the Troubled Triangle: Cyprus, Greece, and Turkey*, edited by Ayhan Aktar, Niyazi Kızılyürek, and Umut Özkırımlı, 1–17. London: Palgrave Macmillan. https://doi.org/10.1057/9780230297326_1

Brubaker, Rogers. 1996. *Nationalism Reframed: Nationhood and the National Question in the New Europe*. Cambridge: Cambridge University Press.

Burnet, Jennie E. 2012. *Genocide Lives in Us: Women, Memory, and Silence in Rwanda*. Madison: University of Wisconsin Press.

Çakmak, Gizem Alioğlu, and Ali Hüseyinoğlu. 2020. "Muslim Turks of Western Thrace and Turkish-Greek Relations: The Triadic Relational Nexus." In *Conflict Areas in the Balkans*, edited by Pınar Yürür and Arda Özkan, 3–24. New York: Lexington Books.

Çapan, Melike. 2019. "Asırlık okullar 280 öğrencisiyle kapanmamak için direniyor." *Independent Türkçe*, September 14. https://www.indyturk.com/node/70806/haber/as%C4%B1rl%C4%B1k-okullar-280-%C3%B6%C4%9Frencisiyle-kapanmamak-i%C3%A7in-direniyor

Chairoula, Pervin, and Sampachattin Amptourachman. 2010. "Western Thrace Turkish Minority: The Educational Rights." Vienna: OSCE Supplementary Human Dimension Meeting.

Chousein, Şule. 2009. "Unwelcome Citizens: Muslim Turks of Greece and Orthodox Greeks of Turkey." *Süleyman Demirel Üniversitesi Fen-Edebiyat Fakültesi Sosyal Bilimler Dergisi* special issue on Balkans: 69–86.

Cole, Jennifer. 1998. "The Uses of Defeat: Memory and Political Morality in East Madagascar." In *Memory and the Postcolony*, edited by Richard Werbner, 105–25. London: Zed Books.

Cole, Jennifer. 2001. *Forget Colonialism? Sacrifice and the Art of Memory*. Berkeley: University of California Press.

Colston, Stella. 2017. "Nomination Letter by Eleftherios K. Venizelos for the Conferral of the Nobel Peace Prize upon Mustafa Kemal Pasha (Atatürk)." *Greek World Media* (blog), March 19. https://greekworldmedia.com/2017/03/19/nomination-letter-by-eleftherios-k-venizelos-for-the-conferral-of-the-nobel-peace-prize-upon-mustafa-kemal-pasha-ataturk/

Confino, Alon. 1997. *The Nation as a Local Metaphor: Württemberg, Imperial Ger-*

many, and National Memory, 1871–1918. Chapel Hill: University of North Carolina Press.

Crane, Diana. 1994. *The Sociology of Culture: Emerging Theoretical Perspectives*. Oxford: Blackwell.

Cubitt, Geoffrey. 2007. *History and Memory*. Manchester: Manchester University Press.

Dayıoğlu, Ali, and İlksoy Aslım. 2015. "Reciprocity Problem between Greece and Turkey: The Case of Muslim-Turkish and Greek Minorities." *Athens Journal of History* 1 (1).

De Fina, Anna. 2012. "Discourse and Identity." In *The Encyclopedia of Applied Linguistics*. Oxford: Blackwell.

Demetriou, Olga. 2004. "Prioritizing 'Ethnicities': The Uncertainty of Pomak-Ness in the Urban Greek Rhodoppe." *Ethnic and Racial Studies* 27 (1): 95–119. https://doi.org/10.1080/0141987032000147959

Demirözü, Damla. 2008. "The Greek-Turkish Rapprochement of 1930 and the Repercussions of the Ankara Convention in Turkey." *Journal of Islamic Studies* 19 (3): 309–24.

Demirtas, Serkan. 2021. "Turkish-Greek 'Exploratory Talks' All over Again." January 25. https://www.hurriyetdailynews.com/opinion/serkan-demirtas/turkish-greek-exploratory-talks-all-over-again-161894

Denzin, Norman K. 1989. *Interpretive Biography*. Newbury Park, CA: SAGE Publications.

Directorate General of Foundations. 2022. "Election Regulation." Regulation 31870. Ankara: Republic of Turkey Directorate General of Foundations.

Döner, Berken. 2021. "Mutfak penceresinden İstanbul Rumları." October 1. https://www.gazeteduvar.com.tr/mutfak-penceresinden-istanbul-rumlari-haber-1509349

Dragonas, Thalia. 2013. "Bilingual Education in Thrace." Paper presented at the Cultural and Educational Association of Western Thrace conference, February 16.

Dragonas, Thalia, and Faruk Birtek. 2004. *Citizenship and the Nation-State in Greece and Turkey*. New York: Routledge.

Dragonas, Thalia, and Anna Frangoudaki. 2006. "Educating the Muslim Minority in Western Thrace." *Islam and Christian-Muslim Relations* 17 (1): 21–41.

Eligür, Banu. 2020. "The 1964 Expulsion of Greek Citizens from Turkey: Economic and Demographic Turkification Under Ethnocultural Nationalism." *Journal of the Middle East and Africa* 11 (4): 319–40. https://doi.org/10.1080/21520844.2020.1830606

Encyclopedia Britannica. 2015. "EOKA." August 28. https://www.britannica.com/topic/EOKA

Erdem, Ali Kemal. 2019. "Yunanistan'daki İstanbullu Rumlar, 'dönün' çağrısına rağbet göstermedi, gelenlerin yarısı gitti." *Independent Türkçe*, November 6. https://www.indyturk.com/node/89026/haber/yunanistan%E2%80%99daki-istanbullu-rumlar-d%C3%B6n%C3%BCn-%C3%A7a%C4%9Fr%C4%B1s%C4%B1na-ra%C4%9Fbet-g%C3%B6stermedi-gelenlerin

Erdem, Nilüfer. 2024. "Yunan Vatandaşlık Yasası'nın 19. Maddesi ve Batı Trakya Türkleri." In *Batı Trakya'dan Türkiye'ye Göç (1967–1995)*, edited by Nilüfer Erdem, 288–319. Ankara: YTB Yayinlari.

Erikson, Erik H. 1956. "The Problem of Ego Identity." *Journal of the American Psychoanalytic Association* 4:56–121.

Erim, Barış. 2021. "Yunan bakan Türk azınlığını inkar etti: DEB partisi sert tepki verdi." *Kırım Haber Ajansı—QHA*, April 16, 2021. https://qha.com.tr/haberler/deb-genel-baskani-asafoglu-bati-trakyada-turk-azinlik-yasiyor/316767/

Ersoy, Mehmet Akif. 2021. *Mevlüt Çavuşoğlu, Habertürk TV'de soruları yanıtlıyor.* Habertürk: Youtube Video. https://www.youtube.com/watch?v=IOETvdoG61k

Featherstone, Kevin. 2011. *The Last Ottomans: The Muslim Minority of Greece, 1940–1949.* Houndmills, Basingstoke: Palgrave Macmillan.

Foucault, Michel. 1981. "Sexuality and Solitude." In *Michel Foucault: Ethics, Subjectivity, and Truth.* New York: New Press.

Frangoudaki, Anna, and Thalia Dragonas. 2018. "'Can Turks Be Nice?' Greek Representations of the Ottomans and Turks." In *Role of Image in Greek-Turkish Relations*, edited by Zuhal Mert Uzuner, 19–40. Berlin: Peter Lang.

Galtung, Johan. 1969. "Violence, Peace and Peace Research." *Journal of Peace Research* 6 (3): 167–91.

Gavroglou, Kostas. 2012. "Istanbul Rumlari: Gelecegin Izini Surerken." In *Istanbul Rumlari-Bugun ve Yarin.* Istanbul: Istos Yayin.

Geertz, Clifford. 1973. "Thick Description: Toward an Interpretive Theory of Culture." In *The Interpretation of Cultures.* New York: Basic Books.

Gellner, Ernest. 2008. *Nations and Nationalism.* Ithaca: Cornell University Press.

Gillis, John R. 1994. *Commemorations: The Politics of National Identity.* Princeton: Princeton University Press.

Gökçe, Bayındır Goularas, and Erkan Sezgin, eds. 2017. *Rethinking Greek-Turkish Relations since 1999.* Lanham, MD: Lexington Books.

Gökçen, Salim. 2010. "Yunanistan'ın Batı Trakya politikası: Batı Trakya Türklerinin sorunları." *Atatürk Dergisi* 3 (3).

Grigoriadis, Ioannis N. 2008. "On the Europeanization of Minority Rights Protection: Comparing the Cases of Greece and Turkey." *Mediterranean Politics* 13 (1): 23–41. https://doi.org/10.1080/13629390701862574

Grigoriadis, Ioannis N. 2013. "Religion and Greek Nationalism: From Conflict to Synthesis." In *Instilling Religion in Greek and Turkish Nationalism: A "Sacred Synthesis"*, 13–49. New York: Palgrave Macmillan. https://doi.org/10.1057/9781137301208

Gülnaz Özcan, Derya. 2022. "Batı Trakya Türk azınlığı, eğitimde yaşadığı sıkıntılar için çözüm bekliyor." *Anadolu Ajansi*, July 27. https://www.aa.com.tr/tr/dunya/bati-trakya-turk-azinligi-egitimde-yasadigi-sikintilar-icin-cozum-bekliyor/2645927

Gür, Gül M. 2024. "Re-Considering Nonresolution in Cyprus: The Impact of Illiberal Conditions on Liberal Peacebuilding." *International Negotiation* 29 (1): 86–116. https://doi.org/10.1163/15718069-bja10091

Gurr, Ted R. 1970. *Why Men Rebel.* Princeton: Princeton University Press.

Güven, Dilek. 2005. *Cumhuriyet Dönemi Azınlık Politikaları ve Stratejileri Bağlamında: 6–7 Eylül Olayları.* Istanbul: Tarih Vakfı.

Habipoglu, Halit. 2021. "'Dendias Batı Trakya Türk toplumunun etnik Türk kimliğini yine inkar etti.'" *Gundem Gazetesi*, April 16. https://gundemgazetesi.com/detayh.php?id=10209

Halbwachs, Maurice. 1992. *The Social Frameworks of Memory*. Translated by L. A. Coser. Chicago: University of Chicago Press.

Hall, Edward. 1976. *Beyond Culture*. New York: Anchor.

Harré, Rom. 1986. *The Social Construction of Emotions*. London: Basil Blackwell.

Hasan, Şule Chousein. 2023. "A History of Survival: The Turkish-Muslim Minority in Rural Western Thrace." PhD diss., Atatürk Institute for Modern Turkish History, Boğaziçi University.

Helsinki Watch Report. 1992. "Denying Human Rights and Ethnic Identity: The Greeks of Turkey." New York: Human Rights Watch. https://www.hrw.org/sites/default/files/reports/TURKEY923.PDF

Heraclides, Alexis. 2010. *The Greek-Turkish Conflict in the Aegean: Imagined Enemies*. Houndmills, Basingstoke: Palgrave Macmillan.

Herz, John H. 1950. "Idealist Internationalism and the Security Dilemma." *World Politics* 2 (2): 157–80.

Hirschon, Renee. 2003. *Crossing the Aegean: An Appraisal of the 1923 Compulsory Population Exchange between Greece and Turkey*. London: Oxford University Press.

Hirschon, Renee. 2009. "History's Long Shadow: The Lausanne Treaty and Contemporary Greco-Turkish Relations." In *In the Long Shadow of Europe: Greeks and Turks in the Era of Postnationalism*, edited by Kalypso Nicolaidis Anastasakis and Kerem Oktem, 73–94. Leiden: Martinus Nijhoff.

Hobsbawm, Eric, and Terence Ranger. 1984. *The Invention of Tradition*. Cambridge: Cambridge University Press.

Horowitz, Donald L. 1985. *Ethnic Groups in Conflict*. Berkeley: University of California Press.

Human Rights Council. 2018. "Written Statement Submitted by the Federations of Western Thrace Turks in Europe, a Non-Governmental Organization in Special Consultive Status." A/HRC/37/NGO/157. United Nations General Assembly. https://digitallibrary.un.org/record/1629599?ln=en

Huseyin, Necmettin. 2021. "'Batı Trakya'da yaşayan azınlık Türk'tür, Türk kalacaktır.'" *Gundem Gazetesi*, April 16. https://gundemgazetesi.com/detayh.php?id=10200

Hüseyinoğlu, Ali. 2012. "South-Easternmost Corner of the EU: The Case of Muslim Turks in Western Thrace, Greece." Unpublished diss., University of Sussex.

Hüseyinoğlu, Ali. 2013. "Minority Education in Western Thrace under the 'Modern European Minority Policy' of Kostas Karamanlis." *Trakya Üniversitesi Balkan Araştırma Enstitüsü Dergisi* 2 (2): 51–72.

Hüseyinoğlu, Ali. 2016. "Past and Present of Islam in the Balkans: The Case of Greece." *Avrasya Etüdleri (TİKA)* 50 (2): 25–48.

Hüseyinoğlu, Ali. 2017. "Batı Trakya'da İslam ve Dini Özerklik Bağlamında '240 İmam Yasası'." *Yeni Türkiye* 97 (3): 50–59.

Hüseyinoğlu, Ali. 2018. "Muslim Turks of Western Thrace in Greece: Ethnicity, Religion, Education." In *The Forgotten Turkish Identity of the Aegean Islands: The Turkish Identity in Rhodes and Kos*, edited by Mustafa Kaymakci and Cihan Ozgun, 85–95. Konya: Egitim Yayinevi.

Hüseyinoğlu, Ali. 2022. "Soğuk Savaş Sonrası Yunanistan'ın Azınlık Politikası: Süreklilik ve Değişimler Ekseninde Batı Trakya Türklerinin Temel Meseleleri (1991–2021)." In *Tarih ve Uluslararası İlişkiler Perspektifinden Türk -Yunan İlişkileri 1821-2021*, edited by Esra Özsüer, 290–307. İstanbul: Boyut Yayınları.

Hüseyinoğlu, Ali. 2023. "Batı Trakya Türklerinin Mağduriyetleri ve Anma Günleri (29 Ocak 1988–29 Ocak 1990–24 Temmuz 1995)." In *Türklerin ve Akraba Toplulukların Acı Yıl Dönümleri: 19. Yüzyıldan Günümüze Sürgünler, Katliamlar, Etnik Temizlik Politikaları ve Soykırımlar*, edited by Mehmet Hacısalihoğlu, 502–21. Ankara: Atatürk Kültür, Dil ve Tarih Yüksek Kurumu, Atatürk Araştırma Merkezi (ATAM).

Hutchinson, John, and Anthony D. Smith. 1994. *Nationalism*. Oxford: Oxford University Press.

Iliadis, Christos. 2012. "The Turkish-Muslim Minority of Greece: 'Confidential' Discourses, Reciprocity, and Minority Subjectivity During the Emergence of the Policies of Discrimination (1945–1966)." PhD diss., University of Essex.

Iliadis, Christos. 2013. "The Emergence of Administrative Harassment Regarding Greece's Muslim Minority in a New Light: Confidential Discourses and Policies of Inclusion and Exclusion." *Nationalism and Ethnic Politics* 19 (4): 403–23. https://doi.org/10.1080/13537113.2013.847599

Itzkowitz, N. 1972. *Ottoman Empire and Islamic Tradition*. New York: Alfred A. Knopf.

Jenne, Erin K. 2007. *Ethnic Bargaining: The Paradox of Minority Empowerment*. Ithaca: Cornell University Press.

Jost, John T., and Mahzarin R. Banaji. 1994. "The Role of Stereotyping in System-Justification and the Production of False Consciousness." *British Journal of Social Psychology* 33 (1): 1–27. https://doi.org/10.1111/j.2044-8309.1994.tb01008.x

Kamouzis, Dimitris. 2020. *Greeks in Turkey: Elite Nationalism and Minority Politics in Late Ottoman and Early Republican Istanbul*. London: Routledge.

Kara, Mehmet. 2009. "The Analysis of the Distribution of the Non-Muslim Population and Their Socio-Cultural Properties in Istanbul (Greeks, Armenians and Jews), in the Frame of 'Istanbul: European Capital of Culture 2010.'" Master's thesis, Fatih University (Istanbul).

Karaca, Rustu. 2016. "Batılılaşan İstanbul'un Rum mimarları ve eserleri." *HyeTert* (blog), March 3. https://hyetert.org/2016/03/04/batililasan-istanbulun-rum-mimarlari-ve-eserleri/

Katsikas, Stefanos. 2012. "The Muslim Minority in Greek Historiography: A Distorted Story?" *European History Quarterly* 42 (3): 444–67. https://doi.org/10.1177/0265691412448044

Keohane, Robert O. 1986. "Reciprocity in International Relations." *International Organization* 40 (1): 1–27.

Korostelina, Karina V. 2007a. *Social Identity and Conflict Structures, Dynamics, and Implications*. New York: Palgrave Macmillan.

Korostelina, Karina V. 2007b. "The System of Social Identities in Tajikistan: Early Warning and Conflict Prevention." *Communist & Post-Communist Studies* 40 (2): 223–38. https://doi.org/10.1016/j.postcomstud.2007.03.001

Korostelina, Karina. V. 2014. *Constructing the Narratives of Identity and Power: Self-Imagination in a Young Ukrainian Nation*. Lanham, MD: Lexington Books.

Kurban, Dilek, and Konstantinos Tsitselikis. 2010. "A Tale of Reciprocity: Minority Foundations in Greece and Turkey." Istanbul: TESEV (Turkish Economic and Social Studies Foundation). http://tesev.org.tr/en/yayin/a-tale-of-reciprocity-minority-foundations-in-greece-and-turkey/

Kymlicka, Will. 1995. *Multicultural Citizenship: A Liberal Theory of Minority Rights*. New York: Clarendon.

Lamont, Michèle, and Virág Molnár. 2002. "The Study of Boundaries in the Social Sciences." *Annual Review of Sociology* 28 (1): 167–95. https://doi.org/10.1146/annurev.soc.28.110601.141107

Lederach, John Paul. 1997. *Building Peace: Sustainable Reconciliation in Divided Societies*. Washington, DC: United States Institute of Peace Press.

Lederach, John Paul. 2005. *The Moral Imagination: The Art and Soul of Building Peace*. New York: Oxford University Press.

Lytra, Vally. 2014. *When Greeks and Turks Meet: Interdisciplinary Perspectives on the Relationship since 1923*. Centre for Hellenic Studies, King's College London Publications 15. Farnham, Surrey: Ashgate.

Macar, Elçin. 2008. "A Victim of Reciprocity: The Greek Patriarchate of Istanbul." In *Reciprocity: Greek and Turkish Minorities; Law, Religion, and Politics*, edited by Samim Akgönül, 4:143. Istanbul: Bilgi yayınevi.

Malinowski, Bronislaw. 1954. *Magic, Science and Religion: And Other Essays*. Garden City, NY: Doubleday.

Mango, A. 1987. "Greece and Turkey: Unfriendly Allies." *World Today* 43:144–47.

Mantaş, Yeşim Nur. 2022. "Türkiye'nin en zor girilen okulu: Kuyrukta öne geçmek üçin 500 TL vermeyi gözden çıkardılar." *Gazete Oksijen*, December 21. https://www.hurriyetdailynews.com/people-queue-to-visit-fener-greek-school-179446

Mantouvalou, Katerina. 2009. "Equal Recognition, Consolidation or Familiarization? The Language Rights Debate in the Context of the Minority of Western Thrace in Greece." *Ethnicities* 9 (4): 477–506.

Markides, K. C. 1977. *The Rise and Fall of the Cyprus Republic*. New Haven: Yale University Press.

Martin, Joanne. 1986. "The Tolerance of Injustice." In *Relative Deprivation and Social Comparison: The Ontario Symposium*, edited by James M. Olson, Peter Herman, and Mark P. Zanna, 217–42. Mahwah, NJ: Lawrence Erlbaum Associates.

McGarry, Aidan. 2010. *Who Speaks for Roma? Political Representation of a Transnational Minority Community*. New York: Continuum.

Middleton, David, and Derek Edwards. 1990. *Collective Remembering*. Newbury Park, CA: SAGE Publications.

Millas, Hercules. 2002. "Non-Muslim Minorities in the Historiography of Republican Turkey: The Greek Case." In *The Ottomans and the Balkans: A Discussion of Historiography*, edited by Fikret Adanir and Suraiya Faroqhi, 155–91. Boston: Brill.

Millas, Hercules. 2004. "The Imagined 'Other' as National Identity: Greeks and Turks." Athens: Civil Society Development Program.

Millas, Hercules. 2008. "Reciprocity in National Paradigm." In *Reciprocity: Greek and Turkish Minorities; Law, Religion, and Politics*, edited by Samim Akgönül, 39–45. Istanbul: Istanbul Bilgi University Press.

Ministry of Justice. 2021. "Action Plan on Human Rights." Ministry of Justice of the Republic of Turkey. March. Available at https://inhak.adalet.gov.tr/Resimler/SayfaDokuman/1262021081047Action_Plan_On_Human_Rights.pdf

Misztal, Barbara A. 2003. *Theories of Social Remembering*. Maidenhead, Berkshire: Open University Press.

Montville, Joseph V. 2006. "Reconciliation as Realpolitik: Facing the Burdens of History in Political Conflict Resolution." In *Identity, Morality, and Threat*, edited by Daniel Rothbart and Karina Korostelina, 367–92. Lanham, MD: Lexington Books.

Mücahit, Oktay. 2022. "Türkiye'deki azınlık vakıflarının sorunlarının çözümündeki ilerlemeler Harvard'da Konuşuldu." *Anadolu Ajansi*, June 4. https://www.aa.com.tr/tr/gundem/turkiyedeki-azinlik-vakiflarinin-sorunlarinin-cozumundeki-ilerlemeler-harvardda-konusuldu/2557010#

Mummendey, Amélie, Andreas Klink, Rosemarie Mielke, Michael Wenzel, and Mathias Blanz. 1999. "Socio-Structural Characteristics of Intergroup Relations and Identity Management Strategies: Results from a Field Study in East Germany." *European Journal of Social Psychology* 29: 259–85.

Mylonas, Harris. 2012. *The Politics of Nation-Building: Making Co-Nationals, Refugees, and Minorities*. New York: Cambridge University Press.

Nora, Pierre, and Lawrence D. Kritzman, eds. 1996. *Realms of Memory: Rethinking the French Past*, vol. 1, *European Perspectives*. New York: Columbia University Press.

O'Brien, Laurie T., and Brenda Major. 2009. "Group Status and Feelings of Personal Entitlement: The Roles of Social Comparison and System-Justifying Beliefs." In *Social and Psychological Bases of Ideology and System Justification*, 427–44. New York: Oxford University Press.

Oktay, Mücahit. 2022. "Türkiye'deki Azınlık Vakıflarının Sorunlarının Çözümündeki İlerlemeler Harvard'da Konuşuldu." *Anadolu Ajansi*, June 4. https://www.aa.com.tr/tr/gundem/turkiyedeki-azinlik-vakiflarinin-sorunlarinin-cozumundeki-ilerlemeler-harvardda-konusuldu/2557010#

Ökte, Faik. 1951. *Varlık Vergisi faciasi*. Istanbul: Nebioğlu Yayınevi.

Olick, Jeffrey K., and Joyce Robbins. 1998. "Social Memory Studies: From 'Collective Memory' to the Historical Sociology of Mnemonic Practices." *Annual Review of Sociology* 24:105–40.

Olick, Jeffrey K., Vered Vinitzky-Seroussi, and Daniel Levy. 2011. *The Collective Memory Reader*. New York: Oxford University Press.

Olson, James M., and Carolyn L. Hafer. 2001. "Tolerance of Personal Deprivation." In *The Psychology of Legitimacy: Emerging Perspectives on Ideology, Justice, and Intergroup Relations*, edited by John T. Jost and Brenda Major, 157–75. New York: Cambridge University Press.

Onar, Nora Fisher, and Meriç Özgüneş. 2010. "How Deep a Transformation? Europeanization of Greek and Turkish Minority Policies." *International Journal on Minority & Group Rights* 17 (1): 111–36. https://doi.org/10.1163/157181110X12595859744240

Oran, Baskın. 1991. *Türk-Yunan iliskilerinde Batı Tarakya sorunu*. Vol. 62. Yenisehir, Ankara: Bilgi yayınevi.

Oran, Baskın. 2003. "The Story of Those Who Stayed: Lessons from Articles 1 and 2 of the 1923 Convention." In *Crossing the Aegean: An Appraisal of the 1923 Compulsory Population Exchange between Greece and Turkey*, edited by Renee Hirschon. London: Oxford University Press.

Oran, Baskın. 2004. *Türkiye'de azınlıklar: Kavramlar, teori, Lozan, iç mevzuat, içtihat, Uygulama*. Vol. 1053. Istanbul: Iletisim.

Oran, Baskın. 2008. "Reciprocity in Turco-Greek Relations: The Case of Minorities." In *Reciprocity: Greek and Turkish Minorities; Law, Religion, and Politics*, edited by Samim Akgönül. Istanbul: Istanbul Bilgi University Press.

Örs Romain, İlay. 2006. "The Last of the Cosmopolitans? Rum Polites of Istanbul in Athens: Exploring the Identity of the City." PhD diss., Harvard University.

Örs Romain, İlay. 2018. "Cosmopolitan Nostalgia: Geographies, Histories, and Memories of the Rum Polites." In *Istanbul: Living with Difference in a Global City*, edited by Nora Fischer-Onar, Fuat Keyman, and Susan Pearce, 81–96. New Brunswick, NJ: Rutgers University Press.

Örs Romain, İlay, ed. 2019. İstanbullu *Rumlar ve 1964* Sürgünleri*: Türk Toplumunun* Homojenleşmesinde *bir Dönüm Noktası*. İstanbul: İletişim.

Örs Romain, İlay. 2024. "Constantinopolitans in the Diaspora of the City." In *Routledge Handbook of Turkey's Diasporas*, edited by Ayca Arkilic and Banu Senay. New York: Routledge. https://doi.org/10.4324/9781003269021

Özil, Ayse. 2014. "Running the Greek Orthodox Schools: Law and Administration in Late Ottoman and Republican Education in Turkey." In *When Greeks and Turks Meet: Interdisciplinary Perspectives on the Relationship since 1923*, edited by Vally Lytra, 271–88. Farnham, Surrey: Ashgate.

Özkırımlı, Umut, and Spyros A. Sofos. 2008. *Tormented by History: Nationalism in Greece and Turkey*. New York: Columbia University Press.

Papadakis, Yiannis, Nicos Peristianis, and Gisela Welz. 2006. *Divided Cyprus: Modernity, History, and an Island in Conflict*. Bloomington: Indiana University Press.

Papadopoulos, Alex G., and Triantafyllos G. Petridis. 2021. "Pomaks, 'Our Forgotten Siblings': From Suspect Aliens to Fulcrum of Statecraft." In *Hellenic Statecraft and the Geopolitics of Difference*. London: Routledge.

Papanikolaou, Antigoni. 2007. "Hak Verilmez, Alınır" (Rights Are Not Granted, They Are Taken). DPhil thesis, University of Sussex.

Parthenis, Christos, and George Fragoulis. 2016. "'Otherness' as Threat: Social and Educational Exclusion of Roma People in Greece." *International Journal of Multicultural Education* 18 (2): 39–57. https://doi.org/10.18251/ijme.v18i2.1132

Pettigrew, T. F. 1998. "Intergroup Contact Theory." *Annual Review of Psychology* 49:65–85. https://doi.org/10.1146/annurev.psych.49.1.65

Pettigrew, T. F., and L. Tropp. 2011. *When Groups Meet: The Dynamics of Intergroup Contact*. New York: Psychology Press.

Poulos, Panagiotis C. 2014. "Greeks and Turks Meet the Rum: Making Sense of the Sounds of 'Old Istanbul.'" In *When Greeks and Turks Meet*, edited by Vally Lytra, 83–105. London: Routledge.

Poulton, Hugh, and Suha Taji-Farouki. 1997. *Muslim Identity and the Balkan State*. New York: New York University Press in association with the Islamic Council.

Prodromou, Elizabeth H. 2005. "Turkey between Secularism and Fundamentalism? The 'Muslimhood Model' and the Greek Orthodox Minority." *Brandywine Review of Faith & International Affairs* 3 (1): 11–22. https://doi.org/10.1080/15435725.2005.9523199

Rapport, Nigel, and Joanna Overing. 2000. *Social and Cultural Anthropology: The Key Concepts*. London: Routledge.

Ricoeur, Paul. 2004. *Memory, History, Forgetting*. Chicago: University of Chicago Press.

Ridgeway, Cecilia L. 2001. "Social Status and Group Structure." In *Blackwell Hand-*

book of Social Psychology: Group Processes, edited by Michael A. Hogg and R. S. Tindale, 352–75. Oxford: Blackwell. http://onlinelibrary.wiley.com/doi/10.1002/9780470998458.ch15/summary

Ross, Marc Howard. 2001. "Psychocultural Interpretations and Dramas: Identity Dynamics in Ethnic Conflict." *Political Psychology* 22 (1): 157–78. https://doi.org/10.1111/0162-895X.00231

Rothbart, Daniel, and Karina V. Korostelina. 2006. *Identity, Morality, and Threat: Studies in Violent Conflict*. Lanham, MD: Lexington Books.

Rouhana, Nadim N., and Daniel Bar-Tal. 1998. "Psychological Dynamics of Intractable Ethnonational Conflicts: The Israeli–Palestinian Case." *American Psychologist* 53 (7): 761.

Saideman, Stephen M., and R. William Ayres. 2008. *For Kin or Country: Xenophobia, Nationalism, and War*. New York: Columbia University Press.

Schwartz, Barry. 1982. "The Social Context of Commemoration: A Study in Collective Memory." *Social Forces* 61 (2): 374–402. https://doi.org/10.2307/2578232

Schwartz, Barry. 1990. "The Construction of Abraham Lincoln." In *Collective Remembering*, edited by David Middleton and Derek Edwards, 81–107. London: SAGE Publications.

Şeker, Nesim. 2013. "The Greek Orthodox Patriarchate of Constantinople in the Midst of Politics: The Cold War, the Cyprus Question, and the Patriarchate, 1949–1959." *Journal of Church & State* 55 (2): 264–85. https://doi.org/10.1093/jcs/css045

Sitaropoulos, Nicholas. 2004. "Freedom of Movement and the Right to a Nationality v. Ethnic Minorities: The Case of Ex Article 19 of the Greek Nationality Code." *European Journal of Migration and Law* 6 (3): 205–23. https://doi.org/10.1163/1571816043020011

Smith, Anthony D. 1986. "State-Making and Nation-Building." In *States in History*, edited by John A. Hall, 228–63. Cambridge: Basil Blackwell.

Smith, Anthony D. 1991. *National Identity*. Reno: University of Nevada Press.

Smith, Anthony D. 1997. "The 'Golden Age' and National Revival." In *Myths and Nationhood*, edited by Geoffrey Hosking and George Schöpflin, 36–59. New York: Routledge.

Smith, Anthony D. 1999. *Myths and Memories of the Nation*. New York: Oxford University Press.

Somel, Selçuk Akşin, and Nurcan Kaya. 2013. *Geçmişten günümüze azınlık okulları: Sorunlar ve çözüm önerileri*. Istanbul: Tarih Vakfı.

Somers, Margaret R. 1994. "The Narrative Constitution of Identity: A Relational and Network Approach." *Theory and Society* 23 (5): 605–49.

Suistola, J., and V. D. Volkan. 2017. *Religious Knives: Historical and Psychological Dimensions of International Terrorism*. Durham, NC: Pitchstone.

Tajfel, Henri. 1978. *Differentiations between Social Groups: Studies in the Social Psychology of Intergroup Relations*. London: Academic Press.

Tajfel, Henri. 1982. "Social Psychology of Intergroup Relations." *Annual Review of Psychology* 33 (1): 1–39.

Tajfel, Henri, and John C. Turner. 1986. "The Social Identity Theory of Intergroup Behavior." In *Psychology of Intergroup Relations*, edited by Stephen Worchel and William G. Austin, 7–24. Chicago: Nelson Hall.

Taşkın, Burcu. 2014. "Political Representation of Minorities: Comparison of Greek-Orthodox Minority of Istanbul and Muslim-Turkish Minority of Western Thrace." PhD diss., Bilgi University (Istanbul).

Taşkın, Burcu. 2017. "SYRIZA's Electoral Victory in Greek Thrace: Impact of Muslim Minority Vote in the Changing Political System." *Nationalism and Ethnic Politics* 23 (2): 155–81. https://doi.org/10.1080/13537113.2017.1311141

Taşkın, Burcu. 2019. *Political Representation of Minorities in Greece and Turkey: Nationalism, Reciprocity and Europeanization*. Istanbul: Libra Yayınları.

Tilly, Charles. 2005. *Identities, Boundaries, and Social Ties*. Boulder: Paradigm.

Toktaş, Sule, and Bülent Aras. 2009. "The EU and Minority Rights in Turkey." *Political Science Quarterly* 124 (4): 697–720. https://doi.org/10.1002/j.1538-165X.2009.tb00664.x

Triandafyllidou, Anna. 1998. "National Identity and the 'Other.'" *Ethnic and Racial Studies* 21 (4): 593–612. https://doi.org/10.1080/014198798329784

Tsitselikis, Konstantinos. 2008. "Reciprocity as a Regulatory Pattern for the Treatment of the Turkish/Muslim Minority of Greece." In *Reciprocity: Greek and Turkish Minorities; Law, Religion, and Politics*, edited by Samim Akgönül, 69–102. Istanbul: Bilgi University Press.

Tsitselikis, Konstantinos. 2012. *Old and New Islam in Greece: From Historical Minorities to Immigrant Newcomers*. Leiden, The Netherlands: Brill Nijhoff. https://brill.com/display/title/21133

Tsitselikis, Konstantinos, and Giorgos Mavrommatis. 2019. *Turkish: The Turkish Language in Education in Greece*. 2nd ed. Netherlands: Mercator European Research Centre on Multilingualism and Language Learning. https://eric.ed.gov/?id=ED599941

Turner, John C. 2005. "Explaining the Nature of Power: A Three-Process Theory." *European Journal of Social Psychology* 35 (1): 1–22. https://doi.org/10.1002/ejsp.244

Uzuner, Zuhal Mert. 2018. *Role of Image in Greek-Turkish Relations*. Berlin: Peter Lang.

Verhás, Evelin. 2019. *The Turkish Minority in Western Thrace: The Long Struggle for Rights and Recognition*. London: Minority Rights Group International.

Verkuyten, Maykel, and Kumar Yogeeswaran. 2017. "The Social Psychology of Intergroup Toleration: A Roadmap for Theory and Research." *Personality and Social Psychology Review* 21 (1): 72–96. https://doi.org/10.1177/1088868316640974

Vita, Lorenzo. 2020. "What Turkey Wants." *Inside Over*, September 8. https://www.insideover.com/politics/mediterranean-gurdeniz-turkey.html

Volkan, Vamık D. 1979. *Cyprus—War and Adaptation: A Psychoanalytic History of Two Ethnic Groups in Conflict*. Charlottesville: University Press of Virginia.

Volkan, Vamık D. 1988. *The Need to Have Enemies and Allies: From Clinical Practice to International Relationships*. Northvale, NJ: Jason Aronson.

Volkan, Vamık D. 1997. *Bloodlines: From Ethnic Pride to Ethnic Terrorism*. Boulder: Westview Press.

Volkan, Vamık D. 2001. "Transgenerational Transmissions and Chosen Traumas: An Aspect of Large-Group Identity." *Group Analysis* 34 (1): 79–97. https://doi.org/10.1177/05333160122077730

Volkan, Vamık D. 2004. "Chosen Trauma: The Political Ideology of Entitlement and Violence," 1–32. Paper presented in Berlin, Germany. In the author's possession.

Volkan, Vamık D. 2006. *Killing in the Name of Identity: A Study of Bloody Conflicts*. Charlottesville, VA: Pitchstone.

Volkan, Vamık D. 2020. *Large-Group Psychology: Racism, Societal Divisions, Narcissistic Leaders and Who We Are Now*. London: Phoenix Publishing.

Volkan, Vamık D., and N. Itzkowitz. 1994. *Turks and Greeks: Neighbors in Conflict*. Cambridgeshire: Eothen Press.

Volkan, Vamık D., and N. Itzkowitz. 1997. "Turkish and Greek Identities: A Comparison between Them." In *Proceedings of the First International Congress on Cypriot Studies*, 179–218. Famagusta, Turkish Republic of Northern Cyprus: Eastern Mediterranean University Press.

Volkan, Vamık D., and Norman Itzkowitz. 2000. "Modern Greek and Turkish Identities and the Psychodynamics of Greek-Turkish Relations." In *Cultures under Siege: Collective Violence and Trauma*, edited by Antonius C. G. M. Robben and Marcelo M. Suarez-Orozco. Cambridge: Cambridge University Press.

Weiwei, Ai. 2018. *Human Flow*. DVD. California: Participant Media. https://www.amazon.com/Human-Flow-DVD-Ai-Weiwei/dp/B079PDGK21

Werman, D. S. 1988. "Freud's 'Narcissism of Minor Differences': A Review and Reassessment." *Journal of American Academy of Psychoanalysis* 16 (4): 451–59.

Wertsch, James V. 2002. *Voices of Collective Remembering*. Cambridge: Cambridge University Press.

Yağcıoğlu, Dimostenis. 2008. "'Internalisation' of Reciprocity Among Members of the Greek-Orthodox and Turkish-Muslim Minorities: How Can It Be Explained? Some Initial Reflections." In *Reciprocity: Greek and Turkish Minorities; Law, Religion, and Politics*. Vol. 4. İstanbul Bilgi University Press.

Yeşiltaş, Murat. 2023. "Is Strategic Consensus between Türkiye and Greece Possible?" *Daily Sabah*, December 8, sec. Columns. https://www.dailysabah.com/opinion/columns/is-strategic-consensus-between-turkiye-and-greece-possible

Index